Farmhouse Cheeses of Ireland

GLYNN ANDERSON *is passionate about nature and good food and has sought out the finest cuisine in France, Spain, Italy and further afield. Early visits to France sparked his lifelong interest in cheese, and he is an aficionado of the best cheeses in the world. His first book was* Birds of Ireland: Facts, Folklore & History *(2008). He is also an experienced amateur photographer.*
glynn@irishfarmhousecheese.com

JOHN MCLAUGHLIN, *an award-winning amateur photographer, has a long-standing interest in good food. An enthusiastic cook and member of the Slow Food movement, he appreciates quality raw materials and firmly believes in supporting local producers.*
john@irishfarmhousecheese.com

www.irishfarmhousecheese.com

A lake of new milk I beheld
In the midst of a fair plain.
I saw a well-appointed house
Thatched with butter.
As I went all around it
To view its arrangement
I saw that puddings fresh-boiled
Were in thatch-rods
Its two soft door-posts of custard,
Its dais of curds and butter,
Beds of glorious lard,
Many shields of thin-pressed cheese.
Under the straps of those shields
Were men of soft sweet smooth cheese,
Men who knew not to wound a gael,
Spears of old butter had each of them.
A huge cauldron full of meat
(Methought I'd try to tackle it)
Boiled, leafy kale, browny white,
A brimming vessel full of milk
A bacon-house of two-score ribs
A wattling of trip – support of clans –
Of every food pleasant to man,
Meseemed the whole was gathered there.

From The Vision of Mac Conglinne (Aislinge Meic Con Glinne)
Anon, 11th/12th Century

FARMHOUSE CHEESES OF IRELAND
A CELEBRATION

Glynn Anderson & John McLaughlin

The Collins Press

For Aidan, forever my little treasure,
and for Camille and Amélie,
who make every day special – John

FIRST PUBLISHED IN 2011 BY
The Collins Press
West Link Park
Doughcloyne
Wilton
Cork

© Glynn Anderson & John McLaughlin 2011

Glynn Anderson & John McLaughlin have asserted their moral right to be identified as the authors of this work.

British Library Cataloguing in Publication Data

Anderson, Glynn.
Farmhouse cheeses of Ireland : a celebration.
1. Cheese--Varieties--Ireland. 2. Cheesemaking--Ireland.
3. Cheesemakers--Ireland.
I. Title II. McLaughlin, John.
641.3'73'09415-dc22
ISBN-13: 9781848891210

Design & typesetting by illuminate creative consultancy
Typeset in Scala
Printed in Italy by STIGE

Title page photos: (l–r) Cahill's Ballintubber, Cooleeney's Chulchoill and Ardrahan's Duhallow.

Contents

Acknowledgements   xiv

1 Introduction
    How to use this book   2
    Cheesemaking in Ireland today   6
        Cheesy statistics   9
    What is cheese?   10
        What is farmhouse cheese?   11
        Other dairy products and their relation to cheese   12
            Butter   12
            Cream   12
            Buttermilk   13
            Yoghurt   13
        Other farmhouse dairy producers in Ireland   13
    How cheese is made   15
        Cheese classification   20
        Variations in cheesemaking   20
            Surface-ripened cheeses   21
            Washed-rind cheeses   21
            White-mould surface-ripened cheeses   22
            Thermophilic cheeses   22
            Blue cheeses   22
            Cheddar   22
        How to make cheese in your kitchen   23
        What you need   24
            Milk   24
            Starter   25
            Rennet   25
            Salt   26
            Flavourings   26
            Sourcing supplies   26
        Making cheese on a larger scale   26

History of cheese 29

    History of cheese and cheesemaking in Ireland 30

    Folklore, myth and legends of Irish cheese 35
        and dairy products

    A few cheese proverbs and sayings 36

How to get the most from your cheese 37

    Buying cheese 37

        Supermarkets and multiples 38

        Delicatessens 39

        Farmers' markets 40

        Farm shops 41

        Sheridans Cheesemongers 41

    Cheese tips 44

Cheese administration 45

    Cheese naming in Europe 45

    CÁIS 46

    Slow Food Irish Raw Milk Presidium 47

    IOFGA (Irish Organic Farmers and 48
        Growers Association)

2 Cheesemakers and Their Cheeses

Ardagh Castle Goats Cheese 52

    Ardagh Castle Goats Cheese 53

Ardrahan Farmhouse Cheese 55

    Ardrahan 57

    Duhallow 59

Ardsallagh Cheese 61

    Ardsallagh Soft Goats Cheese 65

    Ardsallagh Hard Goats Cheese 66

Bay Lough Cheese 68

    Bay Lough Cheese 69

Béal Organic Cheese 71

    Raw Milk Handmade Mature Béal Organic Cheese 72

    Pasteurised Handmade Mature Béal Organic Cheddar 73

Bellingham Blue Cheese (Glyde Farm Produce)   74
     Bellingham Blue   75
     Boyne Valley Blue   78
Bluebell Falls Goats Cheese   79
     Cygnus   81
     Orion   82
     Pegasus   83
Boyne Pastures   84
Burren Gold (Aillwee Cave Farm Shop)   85
     Burren Gold   88
Carlow Cheese   89
     Carlow Edam   90
Carrigaline Farmhouse Cheese   93
     Carrigaline   95
Carrigbyrne Farmhouse Cheese Co.   96
     St Killian   100
     St Brendan Brie   102
     Emerald Irish Brie   103
Carrowholly Cheese Co.   104
     Carrowholly   105
     Carrowholly Old Russet   106
Cashel Blue Cheese (J & L Grubb)   107
     Cashel Blue   110
     Crozier Blue   111
Castlefarm Cheese   113
     Castlefarm Natural and Shamrock   114
Castlemary Goat Cheese   115
The Causeway Cheese Company   116
     Ballybradden, Ballyknock, Castlequarter   119
     and Coolkeeran
Cléire Goats (Gabhair Chléire)   120
     Cléire Goats Cottage Cheese   122
Clonmore Cheese   124
     Clonmore   125
     Shandrum   126

Coolattin 127
 Coolattin Cheddar 128
Coolea Farmhouse Cheese (Cáis Cúil Aodha) 130
 Coolea and Coolea Matured 132
Cooleeney 133
 Chulchoill 135
 Cooleeney 136
 Darú 138
 Dúnbarra 139
 Gleann Óir 140
 Gortnamona 141
 Maighean 142
 Tipperary Brie 143
Corleggy Cheese 144
 Corleggy 148
 Creeny 149
 Drumlin 150
Cratloe Hills Sheep's Cheese 152
 Cratloe Hills Gold 153
Derreenaclaurig Farmhouse Cheese 155
 Derreenaclaurig 156
Desmond and Gabriel Cheese 157
 Desmond 159
 Gabriel 160
Dingle Farmhouse Cheese 161
Dingle Peninsula Cheese 162
 Beenoskee 163
 Dilliskus 165
 Dingle Cream Cheese 166
 Dingle Goat Cheese 167
 Dingle Truffle Cheese 170
 Kilcummin 171
Durrus Farmhouse Cheese 172
 Durrus 174
 Durrus Óg 175

Fermoy Natural Cheese Co.   178

    St Gall   182

    St Brigid   183

    Cáis Dubh   184

    Cáis Rua   186

    Hibernia   187

    Emerald   188

    Other Fermoy cheeses   189

        Ballyhooly Blue   189

        Corkcotta   189

        St Brigid Beag   190

Fivemiletown Creamery   191

    Ballyblue   193

    Ballybrie   194

    Ballyoak   195

    Boilíe Goats Cheese and Cheese Pearls   197

    Cooneen   198

    O'Reillys   199

    Oakwood   200

Gleann Gabhra   201

    Tara Bán   202

Glebe Brethan Cheese (Tiernan Family Farm)   203

    Glebe Brethan   205

Glenilen Farm   207

    Glenilen Low-Fat Cream Cheese   208

Gubbeen Farmhouse Products   210

    Gubbeen and Smoked Gubbeen   212

Hegarty's Farmhouse Cheddar (Whitechurch Foods)   215

    Hegarty's Farmhouse Cheddar   216

Kellys' Organic Products – Moon Shine Dairy Farm   217

    Grace and Una   219

    Moon Shine Organic Emmental   220

Kilbeg Dairy Delights   221

    Kilbeg Quark and Fat-Free Quark   223

    Kilbeg Cream Cheese and Kilbeg Mascarpone   224

Killeen Farmhouse Cheese 225

    Killeen Goat Gouda 227

    Killeen Cow Gouda 229

Kilshanny Cheese 230

    Kilshanny 234

Knockalara Farmhouse Cheese 235

    Knockalara 239

    Knockalara Mature 240

    Knockalara Hard 241

    Other Knockalara cheeses 242

        Comeragh 242

        Dromana 242

        Cappagh 242

Knockanore Farmhouse Cheese 244

    Knockanore Plain White and Red 247

    Knockanore Oakwood Smoked 248

Knockatee Natural Dairy 249

    Kerry Blue 250

    Knockatee Cheddar 251

    Knockatee Gouda 252

Knockdrinna Farmhouse Cheese 253

    Knockdrinna Snow 255

    Knockdrinna Gold 256

    Knockdrinna Meadow 257

    Lavistown 258

    Original Lavistown 259

    Knockdrinna Brined Goat 259

Milleens Cheese 260

    Milleens 262

Millhouse Cheese 264

    Millhouse Sheep's Cheese 267

Mossfield Organic Farm 269

    Mossfield Organic Cheese 271

Mount Callan Farmhouse Cheese 274

    Mount Callan 275

Old MacDonnell's Farm 276
Orchard Cottage Dairy (was Magpie Cottage Dairy) 277
St Tola (Inagh Farmhouse Cheese) 278
    St Tola Log (Fresh and Mature) and St Tola Original 280
    St Tola Crottin 281
    St Tola Divine 282
    St Tola Hard 282
    St Tola Greek Style 283
Sunview Goats (Kilmichael Soft Goats' Cheese) 284
    Kilmichael Soft Goats' Cheese 285
Toonsbridge Dairy 286
Triskel Cheese 287
    Triskel Dew Drop 288
    Triskel Pyramid 289
    Triskel Gwenned 290
Tullynascreena Goats' Cheese 291
Wicklow Farmhouse Cheese 292
    Wicklow Blue 294
    Wicklow Baun 295
    Wicklow Gold 296
    Wicklow Goats Log 297
    Wicklow Goats Gouda 297
Wilma's Killorglin Farmhouse Cheese 299
Yeats Country Foods 300
    Yeats Country Organic Soft Cheese 301

3 Other Irish cheesemakers
Abbey Cheese Co. (Paddy Jack Cheese) 304
Bandon Vale Fine Cheese Co. 305
Cahill's Cheese 306
JOD – Old Irish Creamery 308
Oisín Farmhouse Cheese 309
Round Tower Farmhouse Cheese 311

4 Irish farmhouse cheese recipes

Cooking with cheese 314

Guidelines for cooking with cheese 315

Derry Clarke's carpaccio of beef with grated Gabriel
 Cheese and watercress salad, horseradish mayonnaise 317

Denis Cotter's strawberry, watercress and Knockalara Sheep's
 Cheese salad with honey-raspberry dressing and spiced
 walnut crumb 318

Darina Allen's salad of Crozier Blue Cheese with char-grilled
 pears and spiced candied nuts 319

Potato and Bellingham Blue Cheese soup 320

Roasted pepper with Ardrahan Cheese 321

Deep-fried St Killian 321

Carrigaline thatched pork chops 322

Mount Callan Cheese and leek soufflé 323

Glebe Brethan fondue 324

Durrus/Milleens tartiflette 325

Aligot (with Fermoy St Gall) 326

Darina Allen's Ardsallagh Goats Cheese croquettes with
 rocket leaves, roast pepper and tapenade oil 327

Indian potatoes topped with Castlefarm Shamrock Cheese 328

Claire Nash's Ardsallagh Goats Cheese, golden beetroot
 and roasted onion frittata 329

Denis Cotter's roast aubergine parcels of Coolea Cheese,
 black kale and hazelnuts with warm cherry tomato
 and caper salsa 330

Clodagh McKenna's baked Gubbeen Cheese with thyme
 and rosemary 331

Derry Clarke's boudin of Clonakilty black pudding with
 Cashel Blue Cheese and cider sorbet, crisp cured
 bacon and stout jus 332

Derry Clarke's Ardagh Cheese in an herb crust,
 butternut squash, honey dressing 333

Derry Clarke's Carrigbyrne Cheese pithiviers 334

Ross Lewis's Ardsallagh Goats Cheese, red pepper basquaise,
    artichoke, tomato confit, black olive oil   335
Catherine Fulvio's Ballyknocken walnut and Wicklow Blue
    Cheese bruschetta   337
Aoife Cox's Irish potato 'risotto' with Desmond Cheese   338
Aoife Cox's tricoloured Irish vegetable terrine
    (with St Gall Cheese)   339
Aoife Cox's Raclette au St Gall   340
Rachel Allen's baked eggs with creamy kale
    (with Glebe Brethan Cheese)   341
Kilbeg fruit trifle   342
Glenilen Farm lemon cheesecake   343
Murphys' Bluebell Falls Goats Cheese ice cream   344
Murphys' Wicklow Blue Cheese and caramelised
    shallot ice cream   345
Pashka (with Kilmichael Soft Goats' Cheese)   346

Appendices
    Appendix 1: Irish farmhouse cheeses   347
    Appendix 2: Farmhouse cheesemaker statistics   357
    Appendix 3: Distributors   358
        Traditional Cheese Company   358
        Horgan's Delicatessen   359
        Pallas Foods   359
        La Rousse Foods   359
        Sheridans Cheesemongers   359
    Appendix 4: Where to find Irish farmhouse cheese   360
        Irish artisanal cheese outside Ireland   361
    Appendix 5: Non-farmhouse cheesemaking in Ireland   362
Glossary   364
References   369
Useful websites   371
Bibliography   372
Index   374

Acknowledgements

Thanks to Kieran Murphy, owner of blog www.icecreamireland.com and Murphy's Ice Cream Shops in Kerry (Dingle, Kenmare and Ballyferriter) and Dublin (Wicklow Street and Temple Bar) (www.murphysicecream.ie) and co-author of *Murphy's Book of Sweet Things* (Sean Murphy and Kieran Murphy, Mercier Press, Cork, 2008), for permission to publish recipes *Bluebell Falls Goats Cheese ice cream and Wicklow Blue Cheese and caramelised shallot ice cream.*

Thanks to Darina Allen for two recipes: *Ardsallagh Goats Cheese croquettes with rocket leaves, roast pepper and tapenade oil* and *Salad of Crozier Blue Cheese with char-grilled pears and spiced candied nuts*, copyright © 2011 Ballymaloe Cookery School (www.cookingisfun.ie).

Thanks to Claire Nash of the wonderful Nash 19 Restaurant, 19 Princes Street, Cork City (www.nash19.com) for the recipe *Ardsallagh Goats Cheese, golden beetroot and roasted onion frittata*, copyright © 2011 Claire Nash.

Thanks to Clodagh McKenna for the recipe *Clodagh McKenna's baked Gubbeen Cheese with thyme and rosemary*, reproduced with her permission (www.clodaghmckenna.com). This recipe originally appeared in *The Irish Farmers' Market Cookbook* (HarperCollins, London, 2006), copyright © 2006 Clodagh McKenna.

Thanks to Derry Clarke, chef patron of L'Ecrivain, Dublin (Michelin star since 2003), for permission to reproduce four recipes (www.lecrivain.com).

Thanks to Ross Lewis, head chef and proprietor of Chapter One Restaurant, Dublin (Michelin star since 2007) (www.chapteronerestaurant.com), for permission to reproduce *Ardsallagh Goats Cheese, red pepper basquaise, artichoke, tomato confit, black olive oil.*

For permission to reproduce two of his recipes, thanks to Denis Cotter, owner/chef of the fabulous vegetarian Cafe Paradiso, Cork City (www.cafeparadiso.ie) and author of several books, including *For the Love of Food: Vegetarian Recipes from the Heart* (Collins, London, 2011).

Thanks to Catherine Fulvio, Ballyknocken House & Cookery School, Glenealy, Ashford, County Wicklow (www.ballyknocken.com), for permission to reproduce her recipe

Ballyknocken walnut and Wicklow Blue Cheese bruschetta.

Thanks to Aoife Cox, creator of the excellent Daily Spud blog (www.thedailyspud.com), for recipes *Irish potato 'risotto' with Desmond Cheese, Tri-coloured Irish vegetable terrine (with St Gall Cheese)* and *Raclette au St Gall,* copyright © 2011 Aoife Cox.

Thanks to Rachel Allen for her recipe *Baked eggs with creamy kale (with Glebe Brethan Cheese),* reproduced with permission from Rachel's book *Entertaining at Home* (Collins, London, 2010).

Thanks to our wives (one each), families, friends and work colleagues for all your help, patience and understanding and for putting up with our absences and anti-social hours.

Thanks to the staff of The Collins Press and associates for your work in bringing this book to print.

Thanks to Kevin Sheridan for permission to photograph at Sheridans' HQ in Carnaross.

Thanks to all cheesemakers for logos provided.

And last, but certainly not least, a massive thank you to all the cheesemakers featured, for your hospitality, for taking the time to talk to us on visits or on the phone and for supplying samples for tasting and photographing. Your hard work is the reason for this book's existence.

PHOTO CREDITS

The vast bulk of the photographs in this book were taken by the authors, Glynn Anderson and John McLaughlin, while researching the book. A few cheesemakers have contributed photographs, for which we are very grateful. In particular, thanks to Ardrahan for a photograph of Mary Burns; to Béal Organic Cheese for photographs of Kate Carmody and Friesian cattle grazing; to Bluebell Falls for photographs of a goat and Pegasus cheese; to Castlefarm Cheese for two photographs of Castlefarm Cheese; to Ed Harper and Lena O'Reilly for the 'Goats Rule' graphic; to Fivemiletown Creamery for a photograph of Boilíe cheese; to Glenilen Farm for a photograph of Alan and Valerie; to Kelly's Moon Shine Dairy for a photograph of an Irish Moiled bull; to Milleens for a Milleens photograph; to Wicklow Farmhouse Cheese for photographs of a Wicklow cheese selection and John Hempenstall; and to Yeats Country Foods for two Yeats photos.

1. Introduction

How to Use This Book

This book describes the cheesemakers of Ireland and their cheeses. Each cheesemaker has a section to themselves with a subsection for each of their significant cheeses. A selection of recipes using Irish farmhouse cheeses follows, many of which have been contributed by leading Irish chefs.

In each of the main cheesemaker sections an information panel gives:
- the contact information (proprietor, address, website, email, phone)
- the cheeses made
- the company size (small, medium or large, in the context of Irish farmhouse cheese[1])
- the availability of the cheese (local, national or international)
- other products that the cheesemaker may sell (usually dairy)
- (in some cases) a cross-reference to a recipe in the recipes section.

A mini-map showing the location of the cheesemaker in Ireland is also provided. In some cases, selected outlets where the cheese can be found are listed. Relevant awards for the cheese are also listed.

Within each of the cheese subsections there is a small description of the cheese and a cheese-specific information panel. The panel lists:
- the milk type (cow, goat, sheep, buffalo) depicted with the relevant icon
- the style and texture of the cheese: hard, semi-hard, semi-soft, soft, fresh
- whether the milk used to make the cheese is raw (i.e. unpasteurised) or has been pasteurised
- whether the rennet used to curdle the milk is traditional (animal) or vegetarian
- whether the cheese has been produced through certified organic principles
- other cheeses this cheese is reminiscent of, where appropriate
- the length of maturation before the cheesemaker releases the cheese
- the shape and size of the cheese

- the availability of the cheese (local, national, international)
- the fat content of the cheese, if known (including FDM (fat in dry matter) if known)
- the varieties of the cheese produced, if any
- the county in which the cheese is made (with map)

On the southern side of Bantry Bay, not far from Durrus Cheese

Cheesemaking in Ireland Today

At the beginning of the second decade of the twenty-first century, cheesemaking is a healthy industry in Ireland, with a global reputation for the high quality of its dairy products. As the Irish climate is ideally suited to dairying, it is no wonder that Ireland is full of highly productive cattle feeding off one of the world's greenest dairy pastures. By the end of the 2000s, Ireland was supporting over 1 million dairy cows.[2] As well as milk, Ireland produces large quantities of butter, yoghurt, buttermilk and, of course, cheese. Much of this is industrial produce for the export market. The industrial cheese industry in Ireland is discussed in Appendix 5. It is a highly successful and established industry, producing a very high-quality product. The Irish farmhouse cheese industry, however, is still very young.

The renaissance of Irish farmhouse cheesemaking started in the 1970s and 1980s. The reasons for this are twofold. With a higher level of prosperity, many Irish people began taking annual overseas holidays, often to western European countries with established good-food cultures. Up to this point, Irish people were established cheese eaters . . . as long as the cheese was cheddar and not too strong. Processed cheese was also well established in Ireland, and still is in the 2010s. Adventurous cheese eating meant eating strong cheddar or maybe cheese with a little added flavour. By the 1970s and 1980s, there was a smell of change on the wind. Or at least there was a smell of cheese. Irish people discovered smelly cheese on their holidays, and some of us at least could not get enough of it. Bries, camemberts and many more travelled back to Ireland, ageing with gusto on the trip. While some submitted to the smelly invaders, many of us stayed true to our cheddary upbringings. The fledgling Irish farmhouse cheeses of the period had restricted availability. Savvy restaurateurs formed an important market. For the consumer, unless you lived in Dublin, Cork or Galway and had access to long-established food meccas like Cavistons or McCambridge's, options were limited.

By the 1990s, awareness of quality Irish food was growing rapidly, due in large part to passionate and tireless campaigning by figures like Myrtle and Darina Allen of Ballymaloe.

But the holiday traffic was not all one way and here is the second reason for the Irish cheese renaissance. Europeans, our new fellow countrymen and women, were travelling to Ireland to see what the western edge of their new 'unified' continent looked like. Who could not be charmed by the easy tranquillity and sheer beauty of the west of Ireland? Many Europeans, heretofore locked in industrial suburbia, decided to stay and bought properties right along the western seaboard of Ireland. Some brought money, some brought nothing . . . and some brought cheese. Many were attracted by the relatively cheap price of land in Ireland at the time.

It is hard to find an example today of an Irish-based artisanal cheesemaker who has not been influenced in some large way by Continental European cheesemaking. Much of our cheesemaking has Dutch, English, French or German influences. We have welcomed our visitors and in many cases have set up home and family with them and we have learned, or rather relearned, cheesemaking from them. Native Irish cheesemakers were influenced by the introduction of milk quotas in 1984. With a cap on the amount of milk they could produce, they sought instead to add value to the milk they were producing. It is not yet clear how the removal of the milk quota system in 2015 will affect farmhouse cheese production.

Having learned from our Continental friends, Irish cheesemakers make washed-rind and mould-ripened cheeses in the French style. We make gouda copies and derivatives in large amounts, and while we had already been seduced by the cheddar family, albeit with an Irish slant, we now make real artisanal cheddars in a range of styles and we have copied many of the English 'territorial' cheeses. We also make natural-rind blues, blue bries and some blue gouda. Alongside that, we've had a go at Italian, Swiss and Greek-style cheeses and German quark and we make a lot of cream cheeses, to which we can perhaps allow claim to the Americans.

This might sound as if the Irish artisanal cheese industry is just a copy house, but this is far from the truth. We have all the right 'ingredients' in Ireland for cheesemaking, but perhaps what's more important is that we Irish like to deviate from instruction and experiment. This is essential to the art of cheesemaking. Many Irish cheesemakers will admit to getting it terribly wrong many times before getting it right. But when they get it right, they really get it right. Some of our best-established cheeses, the Ardrahan and Carrigaline and Cashel and Coolea and Cooleeney and Durrus and Gubbeen and Milleens and St Killian, though distinctly of one type or another, are unique cheeses in their own right.

Most Irish farmhouse cheese is made from cows' milk. An increasing amount is made from goats' milk, spurred on by the public perception of its health benefits. There are only a handful of sheep's milk cheeses, but those that are made are notable. One Cork producer is starting with water buffalo milk in 2011. Goats' milk and sheep's milk have the advantage that they are much easier for humans to digest than cows' milk and may be consumed by those allergic to cows' milk, and even to some who are lactose intolerant. Goats' milk contains a high percentage of solids and produces a high yield. Sheep's milk is also high yielding and is higher in protein than the other milks. The public are also increasingly asking for lower-fat cheese.

Most cheese is made from pasteurised milk but many artisanal producers insist on using raw milk because of tradition and the perceived better flavour. There are much more stringent regulations regarding the use of raw milk and that leads to greater overheads for producers. There is probably a roughly even split between the use of vegetarian rennet and traditional animal rennet. Some producers have had legal battles with authorities over raw milk use and the authorities have not always prevailed. Producers exporting to the US must also be aware of US regulations regarding raw milk and some produce pasteurised versions of their cheeses purely for the international market.

So now we Irish are making exceptional artisanal cheeses, but we're also buying it. Artisanal cheese is still a relatively small but growing part of the internal cheese market. For reasons of economies of scale, artisanal cheese is more expensive than block cheese and this somewhat impedes the expansion of the market here. Nonetheless, artisanal cheese can now be found in shops in every corner of Ireland where it would never have been found before. A number of food and cheese distributors are getting the cheese out there (Appendix 3), but they too take their margin, which of course pushes the price higher (See Appendix 4 for a guide to buying cheese in Ireland). The next move for Irish cheesemakers is to expand their market overseas. Tourists to Ireland are bringing Irish cheese home with them and are wondering where they can get it in their home countries. Artisanal cheesemakers, by their nature, are small operations. Many are farmers who also run the cheese dairy. Sales and marketing are often not their forte. Margins are slim, so taking on extra marketing and promotional staff is difficult. Government and local authority grants can be a help to some. Many Irish cheesemakers are husband and wife teams. Some are benefiting from adult children returning from industry with key business skills that can be used in the dairy. Some artisanal cheesemakers have grouped together, in a very loose way, to help each other with sales, marketing and distribution. Artisanal cheesemakers are also limited by an inherent glass ceiling in their industry. When does an expanding, successful artisanal cheesemaker become an industrial cheesemaker? When success does come, it can bring hard decisions with it. With Ireland heading into recession in the early 2010s, there will be more price pressure on artisanal producers. This might be mollified somewhat by a 'back-to-nature' trend and greater desire for natural, healthy, additive-free food from consumers. Many cheesemakers are going back to basics and meeting consumers face to face through the resurgence of farmers' markets around the country, thus cutting out the middlemen. Indeed, some cheesemakers are becoming food heroes; the *Sunday Independent* magazine ran an article on 7 February 2011 highlighting, amongst others, David Tiernan (Glebe Brethan Cheese) and John Hempenstall (Wicklow Farmhouse Cheese) as pioneering good-food heroes.

Cheesy statistics

In 2009, 163,000 tonnes of cheese were produced in the Republic of Ireland, of which 97.5 per cent was exported. Less than 1 per cent, in the order of 1,000 tonnes, is farmhouse cheese.[3] On top of that, 33,000 tonnes of cheese were imported. Within Ireland, 28,000 tonnes were used, with a per capita consumption of 6.4 kg.[4] Cheese production peaks every year in May and June and is at its lowest in January.

There are in the order of sixty registered farmhouse cheese producers in Ireland. Let us say that they produce perhaps three distinct cheeses on average, which gives us nearly two hundred distinct artisanal cheeses in Ireland. Some of these have a very small production indeed and can be found only locally. Of course the scene is constantly changing and many small producers appear and disappear. Nonetheless, there is a backbone of larger artisanal producers who started out in the 1970s and are still going strong. At the beginning of 2011, about 62 per cent of farmhouse cheesemakers live in Munster, 27 per cent in Leinster, 7 per cent in Connaught and a handful, 4–5 per cent, in Ulster (including Northern Ireland). Thirty per cent are in County Cork alone. Why Munster, and Cork in particular, are such havens for cheese producers is not clear, but it is probably a combination of the ideal climate for pasture and maturation coupled with scenery that has attracted Continental cheesemakers, as described previously. Cork is followed by Clare, Tipperary and Kerry as cheesemaking havens, with Meath, Waterford, Wicklow, Limerick and Louth not far behind. The Meath/Louth area is becoming a mini-centre for small-scale cheesemaking.

What Is Cheese?

To recognise good cheese:
Not at all white like Helen,
Nor weeping, like Magdalene.
Not Argus, but completely blind,
And heavy, like a buffalo.
Let it rebel against the thumb,
And have an old moth-eaten coal.
Without eyes, without tears, not at all white,
Moth-eaten, rebellious, of good weight.

Le Ménagier de Paris, 1393

At its most basic, cheese is the solid milk protein (casein) left over when most of the liquid is removed, by careful manipulation, from sour milk. Left to its own devices, milk will go sour of its own accord. However, there are two major problems; most seriously, harmful bacteria may be present and multiplying in addition to those beneficial to the process, but also there is no control over how acidic the milk will become.

The skilful cheesemaker therefore takes control of the process by first adding a starter culture to the milk. This reacts with the lactose in the milk to form lactic acid. Rennet, traditionally obtained from the stomach of a calf, is then added. The rennet assists in the coagulation or curdling of the milk. The resulting solids are called curds and the thin yellowish green liquid is whey.

Curd can therefore be considered a very unrefined form of cheese. The curd is separated from the whey and filled into moulds, which will give the cheese its shape and permit the new cheese to drain. From here, the cheese may be pressed, brine washed, exposed to bacteria to form a bloom on its rind, brushed, smear-ripened, etc. All these decisions reflect the art of the cheesemaker and give the product its individuality and character. The cheesemaking process is described in greater detail in the section on how cheese is made (pp. 15–19).

Cahill's Cheddar curd

What is farmhouse cheese?

The poets have been mysteriously silent on the subject of cheese.
G. K. Chesterton

There is no legal definition of what constitutes a farmhouse cheese. In many jurisdictions the milk must come from the producer's herd and the cheese must be made and matured entirely on the farm. A lot of what constitutes Irish farmhouse cheese fails this test and might properly be described as artisanal.

For the purposes of this book, however, we will just use the term 'farmhouse cheese' and take it loosely to imply the following:

- There is a major 'handmade' element to the product.
- Production is in general quite small. There are of course a handful of producers who produce a considerable tonnage every year and might be considered outliers, but in terms of volume they still pale into insignificance compared to the output of a typical co-op.
- Milk is from the producer's own herd or from a known source.

Other dairy products and their relation to cheese

Butter

Butter and cheese are closely related, siblings perhaps, from the same parent, milk. The word 'butter' may derive from the Greek *bou-tyron*, meaning 'cow cheese' and emphasising the link between the two. Cheese is made from milk, split into curds and whey under the action of a curdling agent. Butter is made from cream or creamy milk, split into butterfat (butter) and buttermilk through repeated agitation. The cream is not curdled, but rather is repeatedly agitated through churning, which solidifies it into butter. About 20 litres of whole milk are needed to produce 1 kg of butter, with 18 litres of skimmed milk and buttermilk as by-products. Salt is often added to extend the life of the butter. Butter is usually made from cows' milk, but can be made from any milk from which cream can be extracted. Although it is harder to extract cream from goats' and ewes' milk, butter from both animals is produced and goats' butter, in particular, can be found in Ireland.

Butter and cheese production methods are orthogonal, so it is possible to produce cheese from the casein left in buttermilk and it is possible to make a form of butter from the fat left in whey, although this is rarely done, as the yield is very low.

Cream

Cream is essentially milk with a high butterfat content. Cream is collected from milk in the traditional way, when the lighter fat rises to the top. For industrial butter production, cream is generated from milk with a centrifuge separator. Cream can be retrieved from whey and made into whey butter. Cows' milk cream is an off-white/yellow colour from the carotenoid pigments in plants consumed. Cream from goats' and ewes' milk is white. Cheese made from cream can have a much higher fat content and some cheeses have extra cream added at various stages of the process to alter the flavour and texture of the finished product. Cream is graded by its fat content and each country tends to have its own regulations regarding minimum fat content. Sour cream has been soured with a bacterial culture and is a bit like thick yoghurt. Crème fraîche is slightly soured cream. Lactic or farmhouse butter is sometimes made from sour crcam.

Buttermilk

Buttermilk is produced as a by-product of butter production. It has a sharp, tangy flavour and is used in baking and as a refreshing drink. Real buttermilk often has flecks of butter still in it, but the majority of buttermilk sold today is made by artificially souring low-fat milk with a bacterial culture. In ancient Ireland, buttermilk was sometimes used as a base for making cheese. The tartness of buttermilk is due to the presence of acid. This acid curdles some of thc buttermilk, making curd, which gives the buttermilk a somewhat thicker texture, depending on the manufacturing method.

Yoghurt

Yoghurt is produced from the bacterial fermentation of milk. Bacterial cultures, introduced either naturally or by a yoghurt maker, feed on the sugary lactose in the milk, producing acid, which gives yoghurt its characteristic tang. As with buttermilk, some of this acid goes on to curdle a portion of the milk, which gives the yoghurt a consistency thicker than milk. Yoghurt can be considered as a sort of simple, ultra-soft acidy cheese. The whey in yoghurt adds to the tang. In some Middle Eastern countries yoghurt is strained to remove the whey, producing yoghurt cheese. Greek yoghurt is a type of strained yoghurt. Goats' yoghurt is becoming popular in Ireland.

Other farmhouse dairy producers in Ireland

While outside the scope of this book, there are a number of notable artisanal dairy producers in Ireland, producing a range of milks, yoghurts, creams, butters, ice creams and even fudge. Many of the cheesemakers described in this book make other dairy products. There are many, many small producers. Here are some of the better-known ones.

- Cuinneog in County Mayo (www.cuinneog.com) make Irish fermented country butter and natural buttermilk (the by-product of the butter making).

- Glenilen Farm in County Cork (www.glenilen.com, see pp. 207–9 for their cheese) make yoghurts, mousses, clotted cream, crème fraîche, double cream, cheesecakes and slightly salted handmade country butter.
- Glenisk Organic Dairy in County Offaly (www.glenisk.com) make a range of products, including yoghurts, milk, fromage frais, cream and crème fraîche from both cows' and goats' milk.
- Barbara Harding makes Ballymassey Country Butter in her dairy in Borrisokane, County Tipperary.
- Yeats Country Foods in counties Sligo and Donegal (www.yeatscountryfoods.com, see pp. 300–1 for their cheese) make sour cream, crème fraîche, milk and buttermilk.
- Nicholas and Judith Dunne make Killowen Yoghurt, cream cheese, yoghurt desserts and smoothies at Green Valley Farms in County Wexford.

How Cheese Is Made

The talent of one cheese in mouths of ten men
Hath ten different tastes in judgement — most times when
He saith 'tis too salt'; he saith 'tis too fresh';
He saith 'tis too hard'; he saith 'tis too nesh.'
'It is too strong of the rennet,' saith he;
'It is,' he saith, 'not strong enough for me.'
'It is,' saith another, 'well as can be.'
No two of any ten in one can agree.

John Heywood, 'Of Books and Cheese' (sixteenth century)

Cheese is made from the solid protein (casein) in milk. Because the apparent presence of these solids within a liquid is not obvious, the process of creating cheese has been viewed as an alchemical, almost magical, process. The power of this process was further enhanced through the provision of food for the long winter months. Butter, made from the fat in milk, was held in similar veneration for the same reasons.

Cheese is created by curdling milk, effectively splitting it into curd(s) and whey. The curds are mostly solid and the whey is mostly liquid. Most cheese is made from the curds, although a few whey cheeses are made from the proteins remaining in the whey (Italy's ricotta is probably the best known).

The milk must be soured with an acidic souring agent like lemon or vinegar or a stronger curdling agent like rennet. Traditional animal rennet is an enzyme complex from the stomach lining of a young animal, typically a calf. The stomachs are obtained as a by-product of veal production. All infants of milk-fed animals have a rennet-like curdling agent[5] in their stomachs. When infants are fed milk by their mothers, the rennet curdles the milk, splitting it into liquidy whey and solid curds, a simple kind of cheese. The solid curds remain longer in the baby's stomach than the liquid milk, providing a slower, sustained release of nutrients. As the rennet of each species of animal is particularly tuned to the milk produced by the females of that species, it would make sense to use goat rennet when producing goats' cheese and lamb rennet when producing sheep's cheese. As these substances are often unavailable, the more ubiquitous calf rennet is used instead. Other curdling agents, derived from fungi and plants, are acceptable to vegetarians and are increasingly being used. Microbial vegetarian rennet is often used. *Rhizomucor miehei* is a mould often used in this way, but it cannot always be proved that animal products or genetically modified (GM) products were not used in production. *Bacillus subtilis*, a bacteria, is also used. Vegetarian rennet made from several species of nettle and thistle or, for example, *Galium verum*[6] or *Cynara cardunculus*[7] is also sometimes used. Acidic liquids like vinegar and lemon juice are effective souring agents and many people use them in the kitchen to make a simple cheese like paneer from India. Raw milk, left on its own, will eventually split into curds and whey. This is due to the sugar lactose present in the milk, which, under the action of bacteria present in the environment and in the milk, ferments into lactic acid which then, in turn, acts as a curdling agent.

Silke Cropp stirring the Corleggy curds and whey

In practice, in modern cheesemaking a fermentation starter or just starter is also used. This starter is a microfloral cocktail, sometimes including some element of the most recently produced cheese. It is added to the milk in the early stages, before the addition of rennet. The milk is often heated prior to the introduction of the starter and rennet to improve the action. Many artisanal producers will insist on using still-warm milk from recently milked cows in their cheesemaking. The starter bacteria consume some of the milk sugars (lactose) and produce lactic acid, which starts the curdling process. Starters are also critical in adding distinctive flavour to the cheese. Starters tend to be based on the *Lactobacillus, Lactococcus* and *Streptococcus* genera of bacteria. Industrial starters can also include yeasts, moulds and enzymes.

Most artisanal cheesemakers make batches of cheese in large vats. The vats are often food-grade stainless steel, but many cheesemakers use copper vats, as they believe this adds to the flavour of the cheese.

Not surprisingly, the quality of the cheese produced depends on the quality and type of milk. Milk can be pasteurised or raw. Raw milk contains microbes which can positively affect the taste, texture and appearance of the cheese. Most artisanal cheesemakers prefer to use raw milk, but there are stricter regulations on its use. Raw milk can be contaminated by pathogenic microbes, but these are often killed in the production process and cannot survive for any length of time in hard (dry) cheese. This is why sick people, the very young, the elderly and pregnant women are advised not to eat soft raw milk cheeses. Some cheesemakers choose to pasteurise their milk. This process kills off most pathogenic microbes in the milk, but many will argue that the good bacteria that contribute positively to the taste and character of the cheese are also killed off unnecessarily.

The breed of animal (within a species) affects the taste, cream content and fat content of the milk and the milk yield itself. Most cheese in Ireland is made from the milk of Holstein-Friesian cows. Other breeds are used because of differences in the fat content of their milk and whether they can be kept for beef. Other cattle breeds used in artisanal cheesemaking in Ireland include Dexter, Irish Moiled, Jersey, Kerry Black, Montbéliarde, Rotbunt and Shorthorn. A variety of goat and sheep breeds are also used. The goats used tend to be British Alpine, Saanen and Toggenburg and the sheep are usually Friesland.

The taste of the cheese is also affected by what the animals eat. *Terroir* is a French word describing the type of land and environment on which an animal is raised. Land varies in terms of its soil type, the minerals within the soil and the type of grass, herbs and other edible greenery present. In winter, when many animals are kept under a roof, they may be fed a mixture of grass, silage and other processed animal feeds, giving noticeably different qualities to the milk. The cheese flavour produced from such animals can differ greatly from season to season. The diurnal time of milking also affects the cheese. Morning milk tastes different from evening milk and some cheesemakers favour morning milk. Milk also varies in taste relative to the time since calving. Milk from pregnant cows or cows that have recently calved is richer in taste, minerals, protein and antibodies and lower in fat. Such milk from cows late in pregnancy or just about to give birth is called colostrum (or 'beestings' in Ireland). While constituting just a small percentage of milk produced, it is sought out for cheesemaking.

The timing of the addition of starter and rennet is carefully managed. The temperature of the milk and later the curds is also closely monitored. Some cheese needs to be constantly stirred or agitated. Some of the cheesemakers do this by hand and some have all manner of crafty mechanical assistance. Most cheese needs to be left alone, at least for a while, to separate. All these factors determine what kind of cheese will be produced. For a simple fresh cheese, like cottage cheese or quark, this can be the end of the process. For other cheeses, the manufacturing process may not be complete for many months. The cheesemaker may wish to produce a soft or a hard cheese, a washed-rind cheese, soft white-mould cheese or a blue cheese. At this point the whey can be removed or the cheese may be gently heated or 'cooked' in its own whey. Some whey is removed at every subsequent stage. When the whey is drained off, the curd may be cut. This assists with removing remaining whey from the cheese. A soft cheese will have little moisture removed while a hard cheese will have a lot of moisture removed. The smaller the pieces into which the cheese is cut, the dryer and consequently the harder the resulting cheese will be. Cheese left to drain must also be turned from time to time to ensure even drainage. The cutting and turning process can be quite quick and straightforward in the case of a soft cheese or complex and lengthy in the case of a hard cheese like cheddar. At this point, the curds are becoming young cheeses. Some may now be packaged and sent to market. Curds destined to be hard cheeses may be reheated at this stage or 'cooked'. This removes more whey.

Some cheeses may now be put into moulds. The moulds are made of food-grade plastic or metal and often have holes to allow more moisture to escape during pressing. Mould sizes reflect the sizes of the resulting cheeses; they can vary from holding a few grams to over 50 kg. Some are simple ring cylinders with neither top nor bottom. The young cheeses may now be pressed to remove more moisture. For some soft cheeses there is no pressing at all. Some semi-soft and semi-hard cheeses may be pressed under their own weight, in their moulds, by stacking several on top of each other. Hard and very hard cheeses can be deliberately pressed, with machinery, in a number of ways.

Salt is often added to the cheese to add to the flavour, to remove more moisture, to prolong the life of the cheese and to provide some control of the bacteria present and hence the rate of maturation. Soft cheeses may have their rinds washed, usually in brine, but they may also be surface-smeared with a bacterium such as *Brevibacterium linens*. For soft white cheeses like brie or camembert, a mould such as *Penicillium candidum* may be added to produce the characteristic white-mould rind. For blue cheeses, holes are usually made in the cheese at this point and a blue cheese mould such as *Penicillium roqueforti* is introduced to the cheese to start the bluing process. Such additions at this stage are called secondary cultures; the starter is referred to as the primary culture.

After pressing, the cheese can be left to mature and may be turned at frequent intervals during maturation. Some cheeses are sealed in wax or plastic wax substitute before sending to market. Others are wrapped in leaves, straw, ash or other natural protective covering.

The maturation process is often continued at the distributor's premises or in retail shops. The cheeses will be regularly turned and attention will be paid to the condition of the rind. The retail purchaser of the cheese may also continue to control the maturation of the cheese at home. Cheeses left on a shelf may mature very quickly, while maturation may be slowed by refrigeration.

See also 'How to make cheese in your kitchen' on pp. 23–6.

St Tola wooden press and moulds

A Cahill's cheese being waxed

Cheese classification

There are two types of cheese, smelly and stinky.
Anon.

Cheeses are classified in a number of different ways, including milk source (cow, goat, sheep, buffalo, yak, camel, horse, moose, reindeer, etc.), rind type (soft, hard, mouldy, natural, waxed, etc.), pate texture (soft to hard), maturity and means of manufacture (washed-rind, soft-wash, surface-smear-ripened). Classifying and assessing a cheese by the type and status of its rind are often how professionals judge a cheese.

In terms of classification based on pate texture, the most common system is based loosely on moisture content, as follows:[8]

- **Hard:** Average moisture content is <42 per cent. Typified by a long ripening, typically three months to a year, or even longer.
- **Semi-hard:** Average moisture content is in the range of 43–55 per cent. Ripening takes from two weeks to three months (or potentially longer depending on the cheese style). Sometimes cheese at the softer (i.e. with a higher moisture content) end of the semi-hard classification may be referred to as semi-soft.
- **Blue:** Typified by mould growing on the surface and/or within the cheese, otherwise generally semi-hard in texture. Ripening period varies, from around six weeks to anything up to a year. (Peter Thomas produces a fourteen-month-old vintage Bellingham Blue.)
- **Soft:** Average moisture content is >55 per cent. Short ripening time in general.

Variations in cheesemaking

If mould doesn't like your cheese, you won't like it either.
Old saying

At every stage in the cheesemaking process, a very slight change can result in a very different end product. Cheesemakers experiment with new ways to make cheese by slightly tweaking the controls. Much experimentation leads to awful cheese, but some produces exciting new products. An experimenting cheesemaker must carefully record exactly what s/he does at each stage so that when s/he gets it right, the process can be reproduced. The right temperature and acidity must be maintained for the right amount of time. The right amount of starter and rennet must be added at just the right time. The curd must be stirred with not too much and not too little force. Such differences are responsible for a range of cheeses, from soft fresh Ardsallagh goats' cheese to hard Desmond cows' cheese.

When the cheese goes into production, consistency is key. The recipe must be followed to the letter. Even with diligence, artisanal cheesemakers will tell you, no two batches of cheese are exactly the same. There are simply too many variables to manage. But this variety is part of the beauty of artisanal cheesemaking. Some of the variations in cheese production are described here.

Surface-ripened cheeses

Surface-ripened cheeses are a large group consisting of a number of sub-groups. These cheeses usually have some sort of mould or bacterium on the surface of the cheese which has appeared naturally or been applied by the cheesemonger. They include washed-rind cheeses, smear-ripened cheeses and white-mould cheeses.

Washed-rind cheeses

A washed-rind cheese is a type of surface-ripened cheese. During manufacture, washed-rind cheeses are rubbed or wiped, usually with salty water (brine) but sometimes with an alcohol like marc or brandy. This is called washing the rind. These cheeses can be washed frequently in the early maturation period, which provides the ideal environment for the growth of the desirable bacterium *Brevibacterium linens*. (When the bacterium is added deliberately, this process is called smear-ripening.) These cheeses are smelly and sticky, with a pastel pink-orange rind and soft or very soft pate. The smell and rind colour are products of the bacteria. Soft washed-rind cheeses tend to be made in small rounds, as the large ratio of surface area to volume allows the small cheese to mature from the outside inwards and because large soft cheeses will not retain their shape. Cutting a young soft cheese will often reveal a ripened pate near the edges and an unripe chalky pate in the centre. Examples of Irish washed-rind cheeses include Ardrahan, Durrus, Gubbeen and Milleens.

White-mould surface-ripened cheeses

These cheeses also tend to be thin, allowing the cheese to ripen from the outside inwards. They are characterised by the presence of a bloomy white mould on the surface. This mould is usually *Penicillium candidum* or similar, which occurs naturally or is added to the cheese by the cheesemaker. Examples include brie, camembert and Coulommiers, and in Ireland, Ballybrie, Cooleeney, St Killian and Wicklow Baun.

Thermophilic cheeses

These cheeses are made with a particular type of bacterium which is resistant to high temperatures (up to 55°C/132°F) or indeed thrives in them. This is in contrast to mesophilic bacteria (up to 30°C/102°F), which are used in most cheesemaking. The bacteria lend a particular flavour to the cheeses. They tend to be large and hard. The practice may have started in Switzerland, but there is some circumstantial evidence that Irish monks, led by St Gall, may have brought the process to Switzerland. Examples include the Jura cheeses – Comté, Gruyère, etc. – and in Ireland, Desmond, Gabriel, Glebe Brethan and St Gall.

Blue cheeses

When a blue cheese is desired, holes are usually made at the time when the young cheese is first being left to mature. A blue cheese mould, like *Penicillium roqueforti*, is introduced to the cheese to start the bluing process. Sometimes this mould is injected into the cheese. This produces blue or green veining or spotting in the finished product. The mould often takes up residence in the cheese's maturing rooms and naturally attaches itself to young cheeses. Cheesemakers must diligently separate maturing blue cheeses from non-blues, as the blue moulds will virulently attach themselves to any cheese present. Blue cheeses such as French Roquefort often have extra salt added to assist in the preservation of the cheese. Blues in Ireland include Abbey Blue, Ballyblue, Bellingham Blue, Cashel Blue, Crozier Blue, Kerry Blue, Oisín Blue and Wicklow Blue.

Blue cheeses have strong flavours and are favoured in cooking. Often used crumbled in salads or included in salad dressings, they can also be added to soups or used to give a cheesy tang to a burger.

Cheddar

Cheddar cheese originated in the village of Cheddar[9] in Somerset, England. The essential step in making cheddar cheese is the cheddaring. The cheese curd is cut into roughly 1 cm cubes for draining. It must be handled gently to prevent loss of fat and protein to the whey. Bricks of curd roughly 15 cm long are then repeatedly stacked/pressed and turned at carefully timed intervals. The curd is then milled until it's about 1 cm in size and salt is mixed through it. It is then placed in moulds and pressed. Natural cheddar is usually a pale off-white/yellow colour, but some cheesemakers add annatto[10] to make the cheese a deep orange colour. Cheddar was traditionally wrapped in larded cloth or black wax.

Examples of Irish farmhouse cheddar include Bay Lough, Béal, Cahill's, Coolattin, Hegarty's, JOD, Knockatee Cheddar, Mount Callan, Wicklow Gold; the more industrial cheddars: Bandon Vale, Fivemiletown, Round Tower, Wexford; and the numerous large-scale-production cheddars: Charleville, Coleraine (NI), Dromona (NI), Dubliner, Kerrygold (overseas), Kilmeaden, Killowen and Mitchelstown.

How to make cheese in your kitchen

Cheese — milk's leap towards immortality.
Clifton Fadiman, author

Making cheese in the kitchen is entirely feasible, and the equipment needs, above and beyond what would be found in a reasonably well-equipped kitchen, are modest. Here we present an overview of what you need to get started.

The procedure for making cheese in the kitchen is essentially similar to cheesemaking on a commercial basis, as outlined above. The details of the various stages depend on the style of cheese being produced, and an in-depth discussion is beyond the scope of this book. There are, however, many resources to be found online, including video demonstrations on YouTube and excellent books such as *Cheesemaking and Dairying*[11] by Katie Thear or *Self-Sufficiency – Cheese Making*[12] by Rita Ash.

A number of producers also offer cheesemaking courses: Judy Wotton of Ardagh Castle in County Cork and Helen Finnegan at Knockdrinna in Kilkenny are two such producers (see the respective sections for more information).

It should be said at the outset that making cheese in the kitchen solely as a money-saving exercise is probably not to be recommended unless you have your own supply of milk and have a surplus or you intend to make a fairly large quantity. In the latter case, since there is only so much of even the nicest cheese that you can eat, you will probably want to sell it. At that point you move into the realm of registration, milk quotas, regulations, health and safety, etc. and all else that that brings with it – including perhaps a section in the second edition of this book! (See below for a short guide to getting started in farmhouse cheesemaking.)

Hygiene in the cheesemaking process is essential. All equipment used must be cleaned and sterilised. Work surfaces and hands must be spotless.

The equipment required will depend on the cheese you are making. Hard and soft cheeses in particular have different requirements. In her book, Katie Thear lists the following:

- **Cheese vat** – this is used to heat the milk. In the kitchen, a bain marie or double boiler can be used, with a stainless-steel container immersed in a pot of water which can be heated. This will avoid too sudden changes in temperature.
- **Dairy thermometer** – a good thermometer is vital as even minor variations in temperature can have a big effect.
- **Knives for cutting curds** – specialist curd knives are available, but in a domestic situation a palette knife will suffice.
- **Cheese cloths** – or a fine-textured muslin. Used to drain curds and for lining moulds before the curd is added for pressing.
- **Cheese moulds** – curds can be ladled into these to drain further. The size and shape of the mould will determine the form of the cheese.
- **Mats and trays** – purpose-made cheese mats are available, as are trays for use when whey is draining from cheese.
- **Cheese press** – this is necessary if you want to make a hard cheese. Small ones suited to domestic use are available.
- **Other items** – most of these will already be to hand in a kitchen, such as measuring jugs, ladles, spoons, colanders, etc.

What you need

Milk

The first and most obvious thing you need is a milk supply. Unless you have your own supply, it will be difficult to source unpasteurised (raw) milk. While (at the time of going to press) it is not actually illegal to supply raw milk in Ireland, the Food Safety Authority of Ireland (FSAI) frowns upon it.

There are arguments for and against the use of raw milk. On one side there is the freedom of choice argument, with research suggesting that an over-emphasis on hygiene in all aspects of our lives, including the pasteurisation of milk (pasteurisation is not selective about the micro-organisms it kills), may be detrimental to the development of our immune reactions, especially in children.[13] The other side of the coin is that raw milk carries a risk, albeit a small one, of passing on pathogens such as *Escherichia coli* (*E. coli*), *Listeria, Staphylococcus* and TB.

Raw milk is not, however, a requirement to make cheese and it can be successfully made from milk bought in your local supermarket. So if in doubt, or if you or your family are in a risk group (i.e. very young, elderly, ill, pregnant), go with pasteurised milk.

Starter

The first step in cheesemaking is to effectively sour the milk. While it is possible in principle to do this with acids to hand in the kitchen such as lemon juice or vinegar, it is difficult to predict or control the acidity levels with these. It is therefore best to use a starter obtained from a specialist supplier.

While sachets suitable for adding directly to the vat are available, they are not well suited to the home producer, as they tend to be aimed at quantities of 50 litres of milk or greater.

The home cheesemaker will therefore probably find a traditional starter more suitable. It needs to be incubated by adding to scalded and cooled milk and then left in a warm place for twenty-four hours. The result should be yoghurt-like in consistency and is suitable for freezing as ice cubes. The cubes can then be used to make cheese and propagate further batches of starter.

Rennet

Rennet coagulates the milk, splitting it into solid curds and liquid whey. Like the starter, rennet will have to be sourced from a supplier, as making real rennet from an animal's stomach in your kitchen is not recommended.

Rennet can be bought in animal, vegetable or microbial form and as a tablet or liquid. The liquid form is probably best suited to the home cheesemaker as it keeps well in the fridge.

If the use of genetically modified (GM) material is of concern to you, be aware that vegetarian rennet stemming from genetically modified material has become widespread, as it can be produced much more cheaply than other forms. It is especially prevalent in the US.

Salt

Most cheeses will require salt in their production, used either as a brine wash or for dry salting hard cheeses after moulding. A brine bath can be fashioned from a large stainless-steel bowl or stockpot. Ordinary household cooking salt is fine for the job, although free-flowing table salts should be avoided, as these contain additives which may taint your cheese.

Flavourings

These are optional and the sky, and your imagination, is the limit. Herbs, berries and alcohol, among other things, can all be brought into play. No matter what is used, however, close attention, as ever, must be paid to hygiene. Herbs and fruit should be well washed to make sure that there are no mould spores and beers should be pasteurised first.

Sourcing supplies

Equipment and supplies of starter and rennet are easily found online. Some examples are www.oldmcdonald.ie (under Farmhouse Kitchen), www.brouwland.com/en/ (under Dairying) or www.cheesemaking.co.uk. Some health food shops in Ireland do stock vegetarian rennet. It can also be found in Fallon & Byrne in Dublin. Basic equipment can be found in the kitchen section of any department store.

Making cheese on a larger scale

If you have experimented with making cheese in your kitchen and you want to go further, what should you do? Many farmers are becoming interested in finding ways of adding value to their milk production. Cheese production is one answer. Others with no background at all in farming are looking to escape to the country and start a little market-gardening business, perhaps with a little cheesemaking.

An ideal place to start is with a cheesemaking course. Several of the cheesemakers in this book offer courses at different levels of formality and depth. For those seriously considering farmhouse cheesemaking as a livelihood, the courses run by Teagasc Moorepark, in Fermoy, County Cork, are perhaps the only option (www.teagasc.ie/training/courses/farmhouse_cheese_making.asp). Teagasc will also provide an advisory service before and after you set up and go into business. To become a farmhouse cheesemaker, you will need to consider:

- Where will you set up your business? You need space. The kitchen won't do.
- The source of the milk – will you keep animals yourself or buy in milk from other producers? The latter might be the best way to start.
- What sort of plant is necessary? You will need a cheese production room and some sort of refrigerated storage. You will need a vat, perhaps a pasteuriser, press and moulds, etc.
- Are you familiar with the health and hygiene regulations for cheese and indeed food production in general?
- Have you an idea of your market? What sort of cheese will you make? Who will buy it? How much will they buy?
- What are the set-up costs and what are the day-to-day running costs? Will you need other staff to help you? What government and local grants are available?

As with any new enterprise, you will need to make a business plan and decide how you will fund your business. Check out www.teagasc.ie/ruraldev/progs/business_startup and get your hands on Teagasc's farmhouse cheese factsheet: www.teagasc.ie/ruraldev/docs/factsheets/8_Farmhouse%20Cheese.pdf. Talk to your local authority. Talk to the advisers at Teagasc Moorepark. Talk to your family.

Copper vat used for cheesemaking at Dingle Peninsula Cheese

History of Cheese

We can imagine that the first man-made cheese was created by accident by travellers using sewn-up animals' stomachs as primitive bottles. Agitation of the milk, while being carried on foot or by animal, in the presence of residual rennet in the stomach created the first primitive cheese. The first butter was probably created in a similar way, when creamy milk was agitated in a sewn-up animal skin, but without rennet. Cheese is highly nutritious, being mostly protein mixed with a high percentage of fat. It was soon discovered that milk processed into cheese or butter lasted longer than the milk itself and occupied a smaller space and so was an excellent means of carrying food on long journeys or storing milk for the off-season. This must have happened in very ancient times as cheesemaking seems to have been with us throughout recorded history.

The earliest solid evidence of cheesemaking dates to Egyptian times, with some tomb murals depicting the art, side by side, with butter churning. We are also told, in the Judaeo-Christian Bible, that when King David escaped across the River Jordan, he was fed with cows' cheese (2 Samuel 17: 29) and that he presented ten cheeses to the commander of his army about to fight Saul (1 Samuel 17: 18). By the time of the Romans, the art of cheesemaking was relatively sophisticated. The Romans developed it further and, no doubt, ideas and methods travelled around the empire. Larger Roman houses often had a separate cheese kitchen called the *caseale* and rooms where cheese could be matured. There were also communal centres where cheese could be smoked. As cheese production developed in Europe, there was little in the rest of the world, with the exception of the Middle East and India.

We can't really examine the history of cheesemaking without looking at the development of the dairy industry as a whole. After animals were first domesticated, they were invariably bred and raised for their meat. A few peoples, including the Celts, kept animals for religious reasons. Where forests disappeared and rich fertile pastures took their place, the art of dairy husbandry started to develop. Animals were kept for their milk as well as their meat. Soon, certain breeds of cow, sheep and goat were being bred purely for their milk-making abilities and so we began to see separate breeds of beef cattle and milch cows. Dairying was traditionally regarded as women's work. This may be because of the obvious association of women with milk production, but dairying was also regarded as housework, the domain of women, while men worked outside. The word 'dairy' itself is probably from the Middle English *dey*, meaning a female servant. In the medieval period, far from being in a position of servitude, women's role in the dairy economy did not by any means go unrewarded. If, for example, a woman decided to divorce her husband for some offence such as spreading the secrets of the marital bed, she would be entitled to walk away from the marriage with a sizeable portion of the stored cheese as compensation.

Milk and its derivatives – butter, cheese, cream, yoghurt and milk-based drinks – became a staple food of European peoples. European countries with rich pastures, such as the Netherlands and France, developed big cheese industries. From the fall of the Roman Empire to medieval times there was very little innovation in cheesemaking. With the establishment of monasteries across Europe, the art of cheesemaking began to be explored again. Cheese popularity dropped off during the Renaissance, but with the beginning of automated dairy production in the 1800s the popularity of cheese began to rise again. In the late nineteenth century creameries and farmers' co-operatives began to appear, using milk from smallholders' stock to make cheese and butter using mass production. Farmers, because of their pooled resources, had better clout in negotiating prices and conditions. The first industrial production of cheese began in Switzerland in 1815. With the establishment of the US, many European immigrants brought their distinct dairying and cheesemaking skills with them. Dairying took place on a huge scale in the US, so it is not surprising that large-scale semi-automated production of cheese started there in the mid-nineteenth century. In the first half of the twentieth century, factory cheese production became the norm across most of Europe and the US and to this day more people eat mass-produced processed cheese than established regional artisanal cheeses.

History of cheese and cheesemaking in Ireland

We do not know when cheese was first eaten in Ireland, but we do know that people arrived here after the last Ice Age, around 8000–7000 BC, from Britain. We also know that until the introduction of the potato in the early 1600s, the Irish diet consisted of cereals, cheese, milk, meat and vegetables,[14] and cattle dominated farming. This is not surprising, since Ireland's good soil and mild climate are ideally suited to dairy production. The Roman Gaius Julius Solinus (third century AD) commented that

Hibernia 'is so rich in fodder that the cattle, if not removed from the fields from time to time, would happily gorge themselves to a dangerous point',[15] reflecting a similar comment by the earlier Roman geographer, Pomponius Mela (first century AD).[16]

There is some evidence that early Irish monks developed cheesemaking in Ireland as a means of preserving milk and having something to eat on days when the eating of meat was forbidden. Trade with the Romans may have brought some cheese to Ireland earlier and the Celts themselves may have learned the art from the Romans. The Romans regarded the northern tribes, including perhaps the Iverni (Irish), as barbarous butter eaters. The more refined Romans ate cheese. Pliny, in his *Natural History*, wrote: 'Of milk, butter was made, which is the most delicious food of barbarous nations.' The Greek historian and geographer Strabo (63 BC–AD 24) wrote: 'Some of the ancient Britons were so ignorant that, though they had abundance of milk, they did not understand the art of making cheese.'

What is certain is that cheesemaking was widespread by the early medieval period in Ireland. Many tales feature references to cheeses of all sorts, such as this from *Togail Bruidne Dá Derga* (*The Destruction of Da Derga's Hostel*) from the early medieval period. It describes a somewhat formidable character called Ingcél: 'each of his knees as big as a stripper's caldron; each of his two fists was the size of a reaping-basket: his buttocks as big as a cheese on a withe'.[17]

The importance of cattle in Ireland was reflected in the importance of milk. A lot of milk and milk products were consumed. Simple cheese and butter were widely consumed. Milk products were called white meats or white food (*bia bán, bánbíd/bán-bíd*,[18] *bánbhianna*) or summer foods, since most were produced in the summer months. The cheese was often no more than the curds (*gruth*) from soured milk. This would very much resemble modern unsalted cottage cheese. Such curds would not last and needed to be processed further into true cheese, to be kept. These cheeses were preserved by drying, pressing and salting. The leftover whey was called *meadhg*. Whey and drinks made from it were sometimes called green milk. Dependants and thralls in the lower classes of society were deprived of whole milk but given the whey, which was a rather sour, salty drink on its own. They were also given the second-rate whey butter, *gruiten*. Milk from a cow that has recently given birth is called beestings and was often used to make curds and whey, which was highly regarded.[19]

While cows were held in great esteem, goats were not. Sometimes a single goat was kept with the cows and horses for luck, but serious dairying from goats did not occur. Not so in modern Ireland, where the demand for goats' milk is seriously on the rise.

In contradiction to the Roman view, in Ireland butter was often viewed as superior to cheese and was included in rent paid to landowners. Butter stored in a cool place, for example a bog, would keep for very long periods and the old texts tell us that people saved butter in this way for a rainy day. In inter-tribal wars it was common to try to steal or else destroy the opposing community's butter store.[20] There were two types of butter produced. *Im úr* (fresh butter) was lightly salted or unsalted for immediate use and *gruiten*[21] was whey butter or heavily salted butter kept for future use; it was sometimes allowed to go rancid and stored in bogs. Butter production was always surrounded by an air of magic in Ireland and it has left behind much folklore and superstition. This reverence for the production of butter may derive from the almost alchemical transmutation of one substance, cream, into another, butter. The same perhaps can be said for the transmutation of milk into cheese. The god Goibniu was often invoked by butter makers in the ninth and tenth centuries. Words could be said on May Day to help increase your butter production at the expense of your neighbour's output.[22] By the eighteenth century, butter was a hugely important export product for Ireland and Cork was the main port of export. Founded in 1769, the Cork Butter Exchange became the largest butter market in the world. By the mid-nineteenth century, Cork was exporting around 30 million lb of butter annually, to Britain and Europe and further afield to Australia, Brazil, India, the West Indies and some American states. The butter was heavily salted for the long journey.

Milk was sometimes boiled with seaweed and allowed to set and then eaten with fruits and/or honey, as a dessert course. Yoghurt-like products and buttermilk (*bláthach*) were also drunk widely. *Tremanta/treabhandar* ('troander' in English), a no doubt chunky drink consumed in summer, was made by boiling sweet milk and adding soured buttermilk as a curdling agent. The ensuing strained buttermilk-like liquid would keep longer than the original milk. The love for natural buttermilk survives in Ireland to this day and buttermilk is used widely in baking. *Bainne clabair*, today called clabber or clabbered milk, was another type of soured milk drink. This was later brought to the US by emigrant Irish and Scots and can still be found in parts of the South and New England, where it is sometimes known as bonny clabber. It may have been similar to modern quark cheese.

The existence of cheese in ancient Ireland is indicated by the number of different names for cheese in old Irish literature. Though we have the names, we often don't know much about their production. The commonest name for cheese in pre-Norman times was *grus*.[23] *Cáise* was probably pressed cheese. *Tanach* was a hard skimmed-milk cheese. *Fáiscri grotha* were pressed curd cheeses. These were probably quite small. *Mulchán* was a firm buttermilk cheese. *Maethal* was a large, round, soft, smooth-textured cheese. *Táth* was a sour-curd cooked cheese. *Millsén* was a soft sweet-curd cheese made with rennet and flavoured with butter and honey. *Tirimcháise* was a dried cheese.

By the seventeenth century the importance of milk and milk products in the Irish diet dropped markedly as a result of the plantations and the Cattle Acts passed by Parliament. These imposed heavy tariffs in the first instance and later an all-out embargo on the export of cattle, sheep, pigs and meat from Ireland to Britain.[24] This was at about the same time as the importance of the potato increased. Farmhouse cheese production vanished from the fields of Ireland right up to the beginning of its renaissance in the 1970s. Cheese produced in Ireland in the nineteenth century was mostly at the hands of the Anglo-Irish and British visitors. The absence of cheese was marked, for example, in this dialogue from an Irish travelling guide of 1839. We reproduce it in full because of its aptness:

'Strange,' says a fellow traveller, as we passed along some beautiful pasturage lands westward of the village, 'that a soil seemingly so rich, does not produce cheese: is it the fault of your land, or is it owing to the laziness of your people, that Ireland, even from her richest soils, produces none?' 'I beg your pardon, sir,' said I, 'in my younger days I remember eating cheese made in this vicinity. To be sure, the manufacture of Kinnegad was not equal to that of Berkeley Hundred, and was, in sooth, a tough, thin, leathery sort of thing, very like, when cut into slices, so many razor strops, and I agree with you that it is very strange that our confessedly rich pastures cannot supply good cheese, though I have known great pains taken by sundry spirited landed proprietors to produce a good article, and still the attempt proved abortive, though the method of manufacture, the machinery and the makers were brought over from the most approved places in England, as Cheshire, Gloucester, or Stilton.' 'Gentlemen,' said a shrewd farming-looking fellow traveller, 'this may not be so strange as many superficial observers might be apt to suppose. The failure, instead of proving a mark of inferiority in our pasture lands, only serves as a proof of their abundant and succulent fertility. The truth is, and on this subject I am informed by a good practical chemist, that our Irish soils laid out for dairy husbandry, supply of cream instead of curd; or as my friend in learned phrase said, they enrich the cow with more of the butyraceous than the caseous matter. If unable to produce cheese in sufficient quality or quantity, we can yet supply abundantly our own and foreign markets with butter the best in the world. The bounties of Providence are various, and every country has its particular blessing. France has her wine – Italy her oil – England her cheese – Ireland her beef and her butter; and as my farm in Westmeath supplies me with my daily "mate, washing, and lodging", I do not envy the Englishman his bread, cheese and ale.'[25]

This tract reflects the belief in Ireland that both cheese and butter could not be produced from the same pasture. Though this was something of a supernatural belief, it is true that some kinds of pasture and some kinds of animal are more suited to butter production than cheese production.

Another commentary, from 1833, suggests:

It is remarkable that a country so productive of butter should utterly fail in the cognate article of cheese; yet with the exception of a small district in Antrim, chiefly in the neighbourhood of Carrickfergus, no good cheese is made in any part; the consumption of this commodity is almost wholly supplied from England.[26]

An observation in 1880 recorded that:

cheese is not generally used in Ireland as an article of food. It is regarded as a luxury rather than a necessity of life. Hence, the manufacture of cheese forms no part of Irish dairy management. A few persons, who are either Scotch or English, make cheese chiefly for their own use. [27]

A major revival came with the establishment of the Irish co-operative movement and associated creameries, initiated by Sir Horace Plunkett in 1889. Cheesemaking courses were established and cheddar and Caerphilly-style cheeses were produced, primarily for export to Britain, reaching a peak during the First World War (many modern creameries produce cheddar-style cheeses to this day). Post-war, and post-independence, the cheese price collapsed, resulting in wide-scale abandonment of cheesemaking by many creameries. Recovery would take decades.[28]

Small-scale cheesemaking was to be found in the unlikeliest of places. Mabel O'Brien, wife of the painter Dermot O'Brien, of Fitzwilliam Square, Dublin, wrote in 1931 to a Miss Langley of Castletownshend, County Cork, to thank her for her hospitality: 'I am sending you the recipe for Ardagh cheese, and I should be very proud if your mother were to try it.' She goes on to counsel about milk quality at various times of the year, and says that in addition to the Ardagh recipe, she is sending *The Practice of Soft Cheese Making,*[29] but warns: 'Don't let anything induce you to try Coulommier. I was warned against it, and rejected the warning and repented it.'

An Bord Bainne (the Milk Board) was established in 1961, and the rationalisation of the smaller co-ops and the formation of the 'super' co-ops that would become Kerry Group, Glanbia, etc. followed. Thus it was only in the mid-1960s that national cheese production began to ramp up again seriously. This was primarily led by cheddar-style cheeses, but with some examples of Continental cheeses such as Emmental, Leerdammer, etc. In 1975 this type of cheese accounted for in excess of 95 per cent of national production.[30]

Today the dairy industry is one of the biggest in Ireland and the country is renowned worldwide for the quality of its dairy produce. While exports account for a large proportion of production, huge quantities are still consumed here. As previously discussed, the vast majority of this is of the mass-produced variety, and much of this is processed cheese. While there is nothing wrong with these products and they are made from the highest-quality milk, some may find them uninteresting compared to handmade Irish farmhouse cheeses. While mass-produced cheeses are by their nature cheaper, the small premium we must pay for handmade cheeses is rewarded by a rich depth of flavour and texture and by the variety available. The primary goal of this book is to celebrate these hand-crafted cheeses and the men and women who make them.

Folklore, myth and legends of Irish cheese and dairy products

A quarrel is like buttermilk; the more you shake it, the more sour it grows.
Old Irish saying

Dairy products, forming the bulk of Irish nutrition for so long, have a rich lore attached. St Brigid (patron saint of dairy) herself was said to have been baptised in milk. Butter was big business in Ireland and was also said to be a favoured food of the little people and so was surrounded by magic. For these reasons, butter in itself was a sort of currency and was sought after. A common story across Ireland tells of a farmer who goes out one morning only to find a hare suckling at the udder of one of his cows. With the farmer in pursuit, the hare flees and nearly escapes but is wounded by the farmer's shotgun. The farmer pursues the wounded hare into an old cottage and there finds an old woman bleeding on the floor. By changing into a hare and taking the cow's milk, the woman had hoped to gain magic power to steal butter from the farmer's dairy from then until May Day.[31] When butter churning failed consistently or produced bad butter, charmed butter thieves of this type were often blamed.

One version of 'The Cattle Raid of Cooley' (*Táin Bó Cúailnge*) tells how Queen Meadhbh of Connacht was fatally wounded by a cheese fired from her nephew's sling. Another legend tells of an attack on St Patrick with a poisoned cheese.

Mulach was a hard cheese with so rounded a shape that the giant in *Togail Bruidne Dá Derga* is described as having buttocks the size of a *mulach*.[32] A derived word, *mulchán*, described above, formed part of the nickname of a twelfth-century chieftain, 'Mant na Mulchán' Ua Ruairc, translated by Fergus Kelly as 'Cheese Guzzler Ó'Ruairc'. Though one might suppose that he would have died from an excess of cholesterol, in fact he is described as dying 'from a surfeit of sex while convalescing after having been blinded'.[33] *Mulchán* was also exported in large quantities from Waterford and was described as being so hard that it had to be cut with a hatchet.

Traditionally, goats were not kept for dairying in Ireland but were kept with cattle and horses for luck. The goats were supposed to keep the cattle safe and the horses more content. Other ungulate animals seem to trust goats and some 'judas goats' were used to lead animals to slaughter. In Irish, the *bocánach* was a goat-like goblin who haunted battlefields. *Bocánachs* were present, shrieking, when Cúchulainn and Ferdia fought. The pooka often appeared in Ireland as a black goat.

A few cheese proverbs and sayings

Gruth agus meadhg.
(Curds and whey.)

Ní thig leat é a bheith ina ghruth is ina mheadhg agat.
(It can't be curds and whey – you can't have it both ways.)

Níl gruth ná meadhg aige.
(He hasn't curds nor whey – nothing is right with him.)

An gruth do Thaidhg is an meadhg do na cailíní.
(The curds for Taidhg and the whey for the girls – the son of the house gets everything, at the expense of the girls.)

How to Get the Most from Your Cheese

Buying cheese

There is never a shortage of cheese in Ireland, but most of this cheese is still the old Irish favourite, factory-made cheddar. At least our factory-made cheddar is of the highest quality. Our health standards and traceability requirements are among the best in the world and Irish milk, produced from Irish pasture, is simply of the very highest quality.

There was a time, not so long ago, when finding artisanal cheeses in Ireland needed a little detective work. Now all the convenience chains and major supermarket chains stock at least some artisanal cheeses. Some are better than others. Superquinn stocks an impressive range of Irish and other cheeses and takes its cheese seriously. SuperValu works on a franchise system, so the stock can vary from shop to shop more than with other chains. For this reason, they are always a good bet when looking for local Irish artisanal cheeses. The Celtic Tiger also brought delicatessens and other specialist shops

Irish cheeses alongside some Continental cousins at
On the Pig's Back in the English Market, Cork

to Ireland and many of those still surviving have a range of artisanal cheeses. Farmers' markets have flourished in the 2000s and they are still probably the best places to get artisanal cheeses. If all else fails, contact the cheesemakers themselves. They may be able to tell you of the nearest outlet for their cheese or indeed you may be able to buy it from them via mail order. Check the cheesemakers' and cheesemongers' websites too. Some have been setting up online shops.

Where you buy your cheese can have an important bearing on the quality of the product that ultimately reaches you, and it is worthwhile weighing up your options.

Supermarkets and multiples

In terms of choice, Irish supermarkets lag far behind what one can find in France, Spain or Italy, where one can frequently find a dedicated cheese counter with knowledgeable staff even in modest-sized supermarkets.

The problem with the supermarket model is that volume is key to profit margins and this is by no means unique to Ireland. The supermarkets are aggressive in the prices paid to suppliers, so they can afford to sell the product cheaply to the consumer. The distribution chain then typically involves producer > distributor > supermarket distribution centre > individual stores. This is the case whether the product is a bottle of shampoo, a loaf of bread or a farmhouse cheese.

This supply chain poses a number of problems for cheese. As cheese requires maturation before being ready for consumption, the producer is in the best position to determine when that is. Unfortunately, this doesn't fit in with supermarkets' requirements that products have consistency and a definite best before date. One customer may prefer a younger, milder-tasting cheese, while another may have a preference for a more mature sample. The problem is that to reach that maturity, the cheese often has to be well past its best before date and thus may end up in the bin.

Here lies the rub. In the typical supermarket supply chain, a complex product like cheese becomes a product like any other. Most supermarkets do not employ cheese experts. Cheese needs to be cared for and is particularly prone to poor storage and extremes of temperature, although at least being too cold will only slow maturation in most cases. If a customer does end up buying a cheese that is in poor condition, the chances are that s/he will lay the blame at the producer's door. Things have improved markedly over the last decade, however.

Volume is also a problem for many smaller producers. They may not have a large enough production to support the needs of a supermarket chain or they may be seasonal and have nothing to offer in the winter months or early spring.

There are some exemplary exceptions which actively seek to promote local food and/or quality produce. Ardkeen Stores in Waterford and Donnybrook Fair in Dublin are good examples.

Essentially the same applies to multiples around the country, although the selection available is likely to be more restricted. Distribution is via centralised warehousing, with trucks making deliveries to the stores.

Some supermarkets have started to sell their own-brand versions of Irish farmhouse cheeses. This is an excellent option for consumers, as farmhouse cheese can be better value in this format. Do not be put off by own-brand farmhouse cheese, since many of the chains insist that they get only the best cheese from their farmhouse providers.

Delicatessens

Though at one time confined to major population centres, today decent delis can be found in many reasonably sized towns throughout the country.

The spread of delis was fuelled by the explosion of interest in food in Ireland during the boom years. This heightened awareness came about due to factors such as more exposure to European cultures through foreign travel and the influx of immigrants, a huge increase in the number of restaurants and eating out in general and a general growing awareness of food culture courtesy of lifestyle magazines and cookery shows.

The best delicatessens strongly feature local produce and many will have a decent selection of Irish cheese.

Aldi Irish farmhouse cheese selection

Marks & Spencer Ardrahan Cheese

Farmers' markets

The last decade has seen a huge increase in the number of farmers' markets around the country. While widespread in Continental Europe, by the late twentieth century Irish markets had fallen out of favour. In fact, markets in Ireland have a long history.[34] Market rights of some sort exist for most towns in Ireland and were granted to town councils or individuals by the English Crown over the centuries. Since Irish law is based on English law, these rights were carried over post-independence. An important aspect of market rights is the public's right to trade in a certain area at a certain time and complex laws have grown around them both here and in Britain, primarily concerning the public's need for a marketplace. By this measure, market rights granted in 1611 are every bit as valid in 2011 and are constitutionally protected in Ireland. This is reflected in the fact that almost every town in the country has a Market Square, Market Street or some such where markets were traditionally held.

Despite this, in 1996 the Casual Trading Act was amended to allow for the extinguishing of market rights in the event that those rights weren't exercised for a period of ten years or more. This coincided with the beginning of a resurgence in farmers' markets nationwide. Spearheaded by influential Irish food figures such as Darina Allen (who with John Potter Cogan had been instrumental in setting up the Midleton market), Clodagh McKenna and Seamus Sheridan, a movement got under way to promote farmers' markets and the importance of local produce.

This met with considerable resistance in some quarters. Markets in modern Ireland have frequently not found favour with the relevant local authorities, many of whom have tended to see them as a nuisance at best and at worst a drain on resources requiring cleaning up behind them. Local ratepayers have also frequently viewed them as a threat to their trade – usually misplaced, as a good market will generally be a magnet attracting people to an area.

Today there are upwards of 150 markets nationwide, with varying frequency and size. These have become a vital outlet for cheese producers, since they provide local access to customers for their produce. Aside from promoting local food, the markets give the producers a chance to form a direct relationship with the customer. They can talk about their cheeses, allow customers to try them and get feedback. From the customers' perspective, first and foremost they can make their choice in the knowledge that they are buying a product in the peak of condition. They can learn about the cheeses, try unfamiliar products and appreciate that there are in fact real, passionate human beings behind the products they're buying.

Farm shops

Hand in hand with the rise in awareness of quality local food, farm shops have sprung up around the country to meet demand. In addition to their own produce, they typically sell the produce of other local producers. The Knockdrinna shop in Stoneyford, County Kilkenny, is a good example of this, and they do of course feature their own cheese range.

Sheridans Cheesemongers

A pivotal moment in the landscape of Irish farmhouse cheese came about in 1995. Kevin Sheridan, while studying in Galway, had earned money to put him through college by working in the kitchen of Galway institution Nimmos at Spanish Arch. Spurred on by his culinary experience, he and his brother Seamus spotted a gap in the market for delicatessens and opened a food shop, which was less than a roaring success. Scaling back their ambitions, they decided on the basis of a CÁIS poster that they'd had from the shop to have a go at selling cheese in the Galway market. They went about calling the producers featured on the poster and ordered cheeses of all sorts. The producers were delighted to have somebody interested in selling their cheeses properly ripened and welcomed them with open arms. With the get-up-and-go and hard work that would later build their successful company, they built their stall from wood and turned up on their first day, at 5 a.m. in the morning, to sell cheese. The stall gave them the opportunity to engage directly with their customers and from the beginning they had a policy of offering cheese to taste for all comers to the stall, a policy which continues to this day.

After a few months they tried to open another shop in a Galway city centre shopping centre, but still didn't get it right. The heat caused the cheeses to ripen too quickly and the whiff of the cheese caused complaints from their neighbours.

They were on the move again and opened their third outlet in a short space of time. This time they got it right. Having visited major UK cheese shops such as Neal's Yard and Iain Mellis, they learned by observation and installed a chiller in the ceiling of the shop rather than use large fridges. Business was soon booming and they expanded into selling British and Continental cheese, initially sourced in Dublin. In time a kitchen space above the shop would also allow them to produce a range of other food products. As time went on, the Sheridans turned to the UK to source a lot of their more exotic Continental cheeses. In the early days they made van trips to London, selling Irish cheese there and picking up English and Continental cheese for the return visit to Ireland. Their little shop in Galway was jammed with cheese.

By 1997 the Sheridans were making the round trip every Saturday to a stall in Dublin's newly established Temple Bar Food Market. This led to them opening a Dublin outlet in South Anne Street. They were joined by Fiona Corbett, who would go on to become one of the three directors of the company, alongside Kevin and Seamus.

A second Dublin shop followed, just off Upper Baggot Street (since closed), and in 2007 they opened an outlet in Waterford's Ardkeen Quality Food Store.

In between times they branched out into wholesaling. Initially, around the turn of the millennium, they rented an ex-Glanbia creamery in Athboy, County Meath, but by 2005 their business needed more space for warehousing and a definite headquarters. Already established in Meath, they bought the old station house just north of Carnaross, restoring the nineteenth-century stone buildings, creating a complex of offices, warehouses and a shop. Wholesaling to independent retailers and exporting Irish cheese to Europe now makes up about 70 per cent of their business (September 2010) and they also supply their own retail shops and market operations around the country. However, they do not, as a rule, mature cheese at their HQ or shops. Cheesemakers know how to mature their own cheeses best and often there are special local bacterial flora present in the cheesemakers' own maturing rooms.

The Sheridans still prefer to deal directly with cheesemakers. In this way they can get cheese from maker to HQ to shop in the minimum time. One of the most important roles that the Sheridans play in the Irish farmhouse cheese industry today is the feedback they give to Irish farmhouse cheesemakers. Nowadays Irish cheese makes up about 40 per cent of their cheese business and that figure has been rising and, the Sheridans hope, will continue to rise.

Sheridans Cheesemongers

Address:	Head Office & Warehouse Shop, Virginia Road Station, Carnaross, Co. Meath
Web:	www.sheridanscheesemongers.com
Facebook:	Sheridans-Cheesemongers
Email:	info@sheridanscheesemongers.com
Phone:	+353 (0)46 924 5110
Outlets:	Dublin, Carnaross, Galway, Waterford and several market stalls

Sheridans' headquarters at Carnaross

Kevin Sheridan at Carnaross

Sheridans' Chutney for Cheese

Cheese tips

- Do not buy more cheese than you intend to consume within a reasonable period of time.
- Always allow cheese to reach room temperature before eating. This maximises the natural flavour and texture of the cheese.
- Only take as much cheese out of the fridge as you intend to use. Each time cheese comes out of the fridge, it dries out a little.
- When eating from a cheese plate, try to rate the flavours of the cheeses in order of strength and begin by eating the mildest. Starting with a strong-flavoured cheese will ensure that the delicate flavours of those that follow will be overpowered.
- Use more than one knife on your cheese plate to avoid transferring strong flavours and moulds.
- Re-wrap unused cheese, preferably with cheese paper, or else aluminium foil or, if nothing else is available, clingfilm. Unwrapped cheese will dry out, even in the fridge, and will absorb other odours. Strong cheeses may need to be double or triple wrapped.
- You can speed up the maturation of a cheese by leaving it out of the fridge, in a tin box or under a bowl and you can slow down maturation by keeping the cheese in the fridge. If a cheese is too chalky in the centre, leave it out for a while (always covered) but prepare for a runny exterior.
- Fresh, soft cheese should be eaten soon after purchase. As a general rule, the harder the cheese, the longer it will keep, but it must be kept wrapped.

Cheese Administration

Cheese naming in Europe

Many cheeses (and indeed other foods) within the European Union have Protected Geographical Status or PDO (Protected Designation of Origin) to protect producers in the original production areas. This is a form of intellectual property rights protection. Only products that genuinely originate in the specified region are allowed in commerce. The EU is extending this protection through negotiation with other jurisdictions. Some of the cheeses covered include Camembert de Normandie, Feta, Gloucester, Gorgonzola, Parmigiano-Reggiano, Mozzarella di Bufala Campana, the Pecorinos, Roquefort and Stilton. These cheeses can be labelled as such only if they come from the designated region. Notably, it is also prohibited to combine the name with words such as 'style', 'type', 'imitation' or 'method' in connection with the protected names. If a proposed name is deemed to be a generic designation, the name will not be granted a PDO. 'Cheddar', for example, is regarded as a generic term but 'Feta' is not. For the traditional cheddar producers in the UK, a PDO has been granted to 'West Country farmhouse Cheddar'. Gouda is not registered, but Gouda Holland is. Edam Holland is registered similarly. Irish cheesemakers, for example, must not call a cheese 'Feta' or even 'Feta-style'. Some have referred to similar cheeses as 'Greek-style'. Irish cheesemakers should be aware of which names are protected.

Imokilly Regatto is registered for Ireland as a PDO for the Dairygold Co-operative. We believe this is the only PDO granted in Ireland as of the beginning of 2011. Other Irish cheesemakers might consider applying for a PDO/PGI/TSG or related designation to protect their names as they become more established.

A full list of protected names can be found via the DOOR database at ec.europa.eu/agriculture/quality/index_en.htm.

This description is a very brief generalised summary of the legislation for the lay reader and should not be used as a substitute for reading the full legislation.

CÁIS

CÁIS, the Association of Irish Farmhouse Cheesemakers, was founded in 1983, facilitated by the National Dairy Council, the body charged with the promotion of dairy produce in Ireland. Prior to this, the handful of pioneers had been concentrating on local markets (tourists and UK/European immigrants) or simply making cheese to their own taste.

From the outset, the primary focus of CÁIS was education – the art of cheesemaking, hygiene and the requirements in terms of premises, plant, etc. The Dairy Science Department at UCC and the Agricultural Institute (Teagasc) at Moorepark were partners in this. The Irish Export Board (An Córas Tráchtála) was also involved, organising educational trips abroad. Information exchange was also one of the key aims.

Promotion of the industry has been a key objective of CÁIS for a long time. This is exemplified by the nurturing of cheese competitions. The first important indigenous competition was the Clones Agricultural Show and this in turn led to the RDS Show actively working with CÁIS to bring in international judges to judge the ever-expanding array of cheeses being produced here.

CÁIS has also assumed the important role of presenting a united front to various arms of officialdom, liaising with the Department of Agriculture on topics such as the inspection of premises, management of milk quotas and dealing with outbreaks of animal disease such as the foot and mouth crisis of 2001. They have worked with An Bord Bia (assuming the mantle of An Córas Tráchtála) in the overseas marketing of Irish farmhouse cheese and with FÁS to create training courses.

CÁIS became the blueprint for the UK-based Specialist Cheesemakers Association (SCA), though the spark for the formation of this was the threat in February 1989 by UK Minister for Agriculture John MacGregor to ban the sale of unpasteurised cheese.[35] Although primarily a UK-focused group, the SCA is open to members from Ireland and several CÁIS members are also SCA members. An important initiative by the SCA was the inauguration of the annual British Cheese Awards, where Irish cheeses have had many successes over the years.

CÁIS has certainly been instrumental in the growth of the Irish farmhouse cheese industry. While cheese would have been sold commercially in its absence, and probably would in certain instances have been very successful, it is highly unlikely that, in the broader sense, Irish farmhouse cheese would be where it is today without it.

It remains a vital association today with over thirty members. This is evident in the fact that the majority of the founder members are still very much active – the Steele family (Milleens), Jeffa Gill (Durrus), the Willems family (Coolea), the Berridge family (Carrigbyrne), the Ferguson family (Gubbeen), the Maher family (Cooleeney) and Bill Hogan (Gabriel/Desmond). Other founders who have either stopped making cheese or handed over to someone else include Gigginstown, Lavistown, Glen O'Sheen and Boilíe (now produced by Fivemiletown Creamery, Tyrone).

Slow Food Irish Raw Milk Presidium

Slow Food was founded in Italy in the late 1980s as a reaction against the fast food culture and the ever-accelerating pace of life. Among its main aims are the promotion of local small-scale food production, environmental responsibility, the preservation of traditional food heritage, biodiversity and food sovereignty, and fair, sustainable trade.

Slow Food presidia were originally conceived in the late 1990s as the working arm of the Ark of Taste. The ark had been cataloguing hundreds of products at risk of disappearing, either from disinterest or 'progress'. Initially narrowly focused on specific local food products, as time has moved on and the presidia have spread beyond Italy, the scope has broadened to include projects such as schooling producers' children in environmental practices.

Ireland's first presidium was the Irish Smoked Wild Atlantic Salmon Presidium, but this fell victim to the precipitous decline in stocks and the 2007 ban on drift netting.

The Irish Raw Milk Cheese Presidium differs slightly from other food-focused presidia in that it covers a selection of very different cheeses, the common factor being the commitment of the producers to delivering a safe, high-quality product from raw milk from their own, or neighbouring, herds.

The first draft of the presidium production protocol appeared in 2005, covering herd management, the origin of milk and the actual cheesemaking process. Criteria specified in the protocol are that:

- the dairy herd graze on pasture for eight or nine months of the year
- each batch of milk used for cheese production should include at a maximum milk from three milkings
- the distance from milking parlour to dairy should be kept to a minimum.

The cheeses represented by the presidium are considered ambassadors for Irish raw-milk cheese. They are selected based on their taste at an annual tasting. Each producer can be represented by only one cheese at any one time. At the time of writing, the presidium members are Cooleeney (both raw and pasteurised versions of the cheese are produced), St Gall (Fermoy Natural Cheese Co.), Durrus (Jeffa Gill), Corleggy (Silke Cropp), Dingle Peninsula Cheese (Maja Binder), Bellingham Blue (Peter Thomas), Mount Callan Farmhouse Raw Milk Cheddar (Lucy Hayes), Glebe Brethan (David and Mairéad Tiernan), Béal Raw Milk Cheddar (Kate Carmody) and St Tola (Siobhán ní Ghairbhith).

The long-term goals of the presidium are to provide support and encouragement to raw-milk cheese producers throughout Ireland and to celebrate the unique characteristics of the product and the artisans who produce it. Its objectives include raising awareness of the quality of raw-milk cheese among consumers, retailers and food policy experts throughout Ireland. It is also a platform to defend the right of small producers to make raw-milk cheese.

IOFGA (Irish Organic Farmers and Growers Association)

Organic farming principles are becoming increasingly important in Ireland. Many consumers are demanding organically produced food even if, in some cases, they have to spend a little more for it. More farmers are converting to organic farming all the time, although the commitment is a big one. The basic principles of organic farming encompass (based on information found on the IOFGA website, iofga.org):

- avoiding the use of chemical fertilisers and pesticides
- ensuring the highest standards of animal welfare
- not using genetically modified organisms
- using less fossil fuel energy per calorie of food produced
- protecting biodiversity by maintaining suitable habitats for plants, animals and wildlife
- encouraging people to buy their food locally and in season.

The Irish Organic Farmers and Growers Association was established in 1982 as a voluntary organisation and Ireland's leading organic certification body, dedicated to certifying organic produce and products throughout Ireland. It has an elected board of directors and has a membership of 1,100 people (February 2011). IOFGA is approved by the Department of Agriculture, Fisheries and Food (DAFF) in the Republic of Ireland and the Department for Environment, Food and Rural Affairs (DEFRA) in the United

Kingdom to provide an inspection and certification scheme pursuant to EC Regulation 2092/91 as amended. A product which has been inspected and approved to meet the organic standards may carry the IOFGA logo.

Several Irish cheesemakers and cheesemaking farmers have converted to or adopted organic principles. Many are certified by IOFGA. As of early 2011, those cheesemakers that are certified are indicated within their relevant sections in this book.

2. Cheesemakers & Their Cheeses

Ardagh Castle Goats Cheese

Nuala, Head of Milk Production

Since 1997, Judy Wotton has been hand-making small quantities of cheese from Anglo-Nubian goats on her farm just outside Baltimore in west Cork. Judy had previously made cheese for personal use in the UK. On moving to southwest Cork she bought her 5-acre farm on hilly land, but found that all she could keep on that land were goats. At her peak she kept fifteen goats plus kids. Today she makes cheese periodically from the milk of about seven goats.

The small herd of goats are hand-milked. Judy's main production is a hard goats' cheese, but she also makes very small quantities of whey cheeses: Gjetost and goat-milk ricotta. Gjetost production was developed with a small LEADER[1] grant. Judy sells mostly from the door and at Skibbereen Farmers' Market.

Since 2009, Judy has run cheesemaking courses at her premises.

ARDAGH CASTLE GOATS CHEESE	
Proprietor:	Judy Wotton
Address:	Ardagh South, Baltimore, Co. Cork
Web:	www.ardaghcastle.com/cheese.html
Email:	jwotton@eircom.net
Phone:	+353 (0)28 20547
Cheeses made:	Ardagh Castle Goats Cheese, Ardagh Gjetost, Ardagh Ricotta
Company size:	Small
Availability:	Local

ARDAGH CASTLE GOATS CHEESE		
Milk		
Style	Hard	
Raw/pasteurised	**Raw**	
Rennet	Vegetarian	
Organic	No	
Reminiscent of	Wensleydale	
Maturation	2 months min.	
Size	2.5 kg, 3.5 kg and smaller	
Availability	Local	
Made in	Cork	

Ardagh Castle Goats Cheese

Ardagh Castle was first made in 1997 from raw milk, with non-GM vegetarian rennet, from the family's small herd of Anglo-Nubian goats and named after the ruins of a castle on a hill overlooking their land. Very small amounts are made during the summer and sold from the farm gate and also in nearby Skibbereen Farmers' Market. Somewhat resembling Wensleydale, the cheese is very mild, with a nutty aftertaste. The pale cream pate is moist, though slightly crumbly. The variable-coloured rind can be discarded.

Mary Burns

Ardrahan Farmhouse Cheese

Ardrahan is one of the stalwarts of the Irish farmhouse cheese industry. This is a truly unique cheese in its own right. Back in the early 1980s Mary Burns was one of those rare Irish people with a passion for strong-flavoured cheeses. Living on a dairy farm, it was perhaps inevitable that she would try her hand at cheesemaking. By 1983 she was making high-quality washed-rind cheeses. Despite her initial success with the cheesemaking process, her cheeses were perhaps a little exotic for the Irish palate. Tourists to Ireland were buying and seeking it out, but not the local Irish. Mary and her late husband Eugene tried their luck in Paris and soon found a regular outlet for their cheeses at the Rungis Market,[2] their enthusiasm somewhat checked by the need to constantly drive backwards and forwards from Cork to Paris. The Burns were at the forefront of the Irish cheese renaissance in the 1970s and 1980s and this renaissance was no doubt fuelled somewhat, on the demand side, by Irish holidaymakers returning from Continental Europe, and France in particular, with a new passion for 'smelly' cheese. Soon the Burns were finding a market for their cheeses in Ireland. Ardrahan cheese has now established itself not only in Ireland, but worldwide as a superior-quality cheese and one of the small group of Irish farmhouse cheeses known well to cheese aficionados the world over.

Unfortunately, Eugene Burns passed away in 2000. Mary continues to make Ardrahan cheese with her dedicated workforce and has been joined on the marketing side by her son Gerald. As well as the classic Ardrahan, the Burns now make Duhallow, a milder cheese mostly sold to the export market. They still use the pasteurised milk of their own herd of pedigree Friesian cows and all their cheese is handmade with vegetarian rennet. The herd is descended from that put together by Mary's father-in-law, Eugene Burns, Senior, in 1925. The cheese is made all year round.

The cheese is widely available throughout Ireland in delicatessens, cheese shops and several of the large supermarket chains. It is also widely available in the UK and US and can be found in France and Germany.

Ardrahan also produces Lullaby Milk, pasteurised but not homogenised morning milk with naturally high levels of melatonin, produced before daylight and purported to help with insomnia.

Ardrahan (Irish: 'the height with the ferns') is made near the village of Kanturk (Gaelic: *ceann toirc* – 'boar's head') in the north of County Cork, in the Barony of Duhallow.

Duhallow (from the Irish *dúiche Ealla*, 'district of the Ealla River') is named after the local Barony of Duhallow, itself named after the River Allow (*Abhainn Ealla*) which flows into the Blackwater, a river famous for its salmon. This is an area rich in green herby pasture which is directly responsible for the rich taste of both Duhallow and Ardrahan. This area borders the seven glens of Sliabh Luachra ('mountain of rushes'), a region famous for its musical heritage.

ARDRAHAN FARMHOUSE CHEESE	
Proprietor:	Mary Burns
Address:	Ardrahan, Kanturk, Co. Cork
Web:	www.ardrahancheese.ie
Email:	ardrahancheese@gmail.com
Phone:	+353 (0)29 78099
Cheeses made:	Ardrahan, Duhallow
Company size:	Large
Availability:	Local, national, international
Other products:	Ardrahan Lullaby Milk
Recipe:	See p. 321

Awards

2009	World Cheese Awards	Gold	Smoked Ardrahan
2009	British Cheese Awards	Bronze	Smoked Ardrahan
2008	World Cheese Awards	Silver	Smoked Ardrahan
2008	World Cheese Awards	Silver	Ardrahan
2006	Listowel Food Fair	1st Prize	Ardrahan
2006	British Cheese Awards	Silver	Ardrahan
2005	IFEX	Silver	Ardrahan

ARDRAHAN	
Milk	
Style	Semi-soft, washed-rind
Raw/pasteurised	Pasteurised
Rennet	Vegetarian
Organic	No
Reminiscent of	Swiss Appenzeller, Tomme, Livarot, Munster, Havarti
Maturation	5–8 weeks – demand
Size	1.5 kg wheels
Availability	Local, national, international
Varieties	Smoked
Fat	27.5%
Made in	Cork

Ardrahan

Ardrahan is a semi-soft washed-rind cheese made with pasteurised milk and vegetarian rennet. The cheese is cooked and pressed lightly and brushed once with *Brevibacterium linens*, which is enough to establish the rich light ochre- to terracotta-coloured rind and the distinctive rich cheesy flavour. The honey-coloured pate is firm and slightly elastic with some holes and immature cheeses can have a chalky but milder interior. The texture is buttery on the palate. While the aroma is earthy and pungent, particularly with the more mature cheese, the flavour is strong but by no means overpowering and lingers with a distinctively pleasant aftertaste. For the adventurous, the rind is natural and edible and perhaps the strongest part of the cheese. Cheese aficionados will enjoy eating it. Ardrahan goes particularly well with Irish whiskey and can be deep-fried in breadcrumbs or batter. It melts well and is excellent for the cheeseboard. Smoked Ardrahan is also available.

Ardrahan at close range

DUHALLOW		
Milk		
Style	Semi-hard	
Raw/pasteurised	Pasteurised	
Rennet	Vegetarian	
Organic	No	
Reminiscent of	Port Salut, Entrammes, St Paulin, Esrom, Havarti	
Maturation	4–8 weeks – demand	
Size	1.5 kg wheels	
Availability	Mostly international, some national	
Fat	27.5%	
Made in	Cork	

Duhallow

Duhallow is a relatively new cheese, made since 2006. Mary Burns spent three and a half years developing it. Duhallow will appeal to those who want the farmhouse cheese experience but are not yet ready for a mature Ardrahan or similar. This is a medium-hard cheese made with pasteurised milk and vegetarian rennet. Unlike Ardrahan, Duhallow has a bright orange-coated rind. The pate is an off-white colour and is somewhat reminiscent, in appearance and aroma, of Port Salut or St Paulin, though these are softer cheeses. The flavour is pleasantly mild, buttery and cheesy, with a creamy texture. It is an excellent cheese for sandwich-making and cooking.

Most Duhallow goes to the US, but from time to time it can be found in Superquinn, Tesco and SuperValu. The exported Duhallow is marketed by the Irish Dairy Board under the Kerrygold brand.

Ardsallagh soft crottin with chives

Ardsallagh Cheese

Jane Murphy's introduction to goats was a memorable one. While living in Carlow many years ago, some of her children suffered from eczema. One day an insurance salesman came to the door and Jane mentioned her children's eczema during the conversation. As people often do, the salesman recommended goats' milk to ease the eczema. He left and Jane thought no more of it. Shortly afterwards the salesman returned to the door with what he announced was the solution to Jane's problems. He went to the back of the car and brought out a nanny goat. Julia went on to be the first of many goats in Jane's life. After keeping goats for many years as a hobby, Jane and husband Gerard began serious goat farming and later moved to Youghal, relocating to Carrigtwohill only in 1996. Having built up the herd to several hundred goats, Jane eventually sold off all but a few goats to neighbouring farmers and now buys back the goats' milk. This is a true family-run business, with the whole family involved in one way or another.

The goats are milked twice a day and the milk is used to make handmade soft and hard cheese, yoghurt and pasteurised milk.

Visits can be accommodated but you must call ahead.

Selected outlets: *Dunnes Stores; Superquinn; Tesco. Distributed by Horgan's, Independent Irish Health Foods, La Rousse, Traditional Cheese Co.*

Jane Murphy

Some of the Ardsallagh range

ARDSALLAGH CHEESE	
Proprietor:	Jane Murphy
Address:	Ardsallagh Farm, Woodstock, Carrigtwohill, Co. Cork
Web:	www.ardsallaghgoats.com
Facebook:	Ardsallagh-Goat-Products
Email:	enquiries@ardsallaghgoats.com
Phone:	+353 (0)214 882336
Cheeses made:	Ardsallagh Soft Goats Cheese, Ardsallagh Hard Goats Cheese
Company size:	Large
Availability:	Local, national
Other products:	Ardsallagh Goats Milk, Ardsallagh Goats Yoghurt
Recipes:	See p. 327, p. 329 and p. 335

Awards

| 2010 | British Cheese Awards | Bronze | Ardsallagh Cranberry Roulade |
| 2010 | British Cheese Awards | Silver | Ardsallagh Smoked |

Ardsallagh soft crottins – Chives, Turmeric & Garlic, Honey-Mustard, Chilli, Pepper

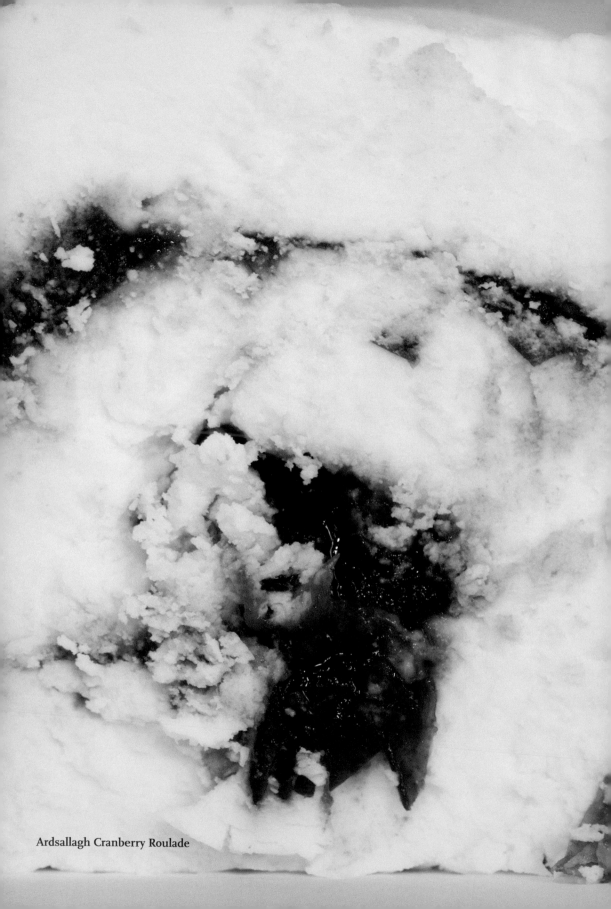

Ardsallagh Cranberry Roulade

ARDSALLAGH SOFT GOATS CHEESE		
Milk		
Style	Soft	
Raw/pasteurised	Pasteurised	
Rennet	Vegetarian	
Organic	No	
Maturation	4 days – 6 weeks	
Size	150 g crottin, 200 g tubs, 1 kg catering log	
Availability	Local, national	
Varieties	Chilli; Chives; Honey-Mustard; Pepper; Turmeric & Garlic; Cranberry Roulade	
Fat	Full	
Made in	Cork	

Ardsallagh Soft Goats Cheese

Ardsallagh is an all-year soft goats' cheese handmade with pasteurised milk from the Murphys' own and some neighbours' goats, with vegetarian rennet. Production is a deliberately slow hands-on process, *à la louche,* as the French say, following a traditional method and producing a delicate curd and particularly soft cheese, with an ultra-smooth, creamy texture. The pate is snow white and the flavour is gently goaty, so this is an ideal cheese for those starting out with goat cheese or who find goat cheese particularly strong in flavour or aroma. The cheese is ready for market after only a few days and is available across Ireland.

A number of varieties are now available from Ardsallagh. The Murphys produce a wonderful goats' Cranberry Roulade log, which can be purchased in slices. Small soft crottins are also available in a number of flavours: Chilli, Chives, Honey-Mustard, Pepper, Turmeric & Garlic, Cranberry Roulade and occasionally Oatmeal & Honey and Pecan & Maple Syrup.

The name 'Ardsallagh' is from the Irish *Ard Saileach* ('high willows'), referring to old trees on the farm.

Ardsallagh Hard Goats Cheese	
Milk	
Style	Semi-hard
Raw/pasteurised	Pasteurised
Rennet	Vegetarian
Organic	No
Reminiscent of	Pecorino, Parmesan (when hard)
Maturation	4 months – 2 years
Size	250 g, 2 kg, 3 kg, 11 kg wheel
Availability	Local, national
Varieties	Plain; Smoked
Fat	Full
Made in	Cork

Ardsallagh Hard Goats Cheese

This is a semi-hard to very hard goats' cheese, depending on maturity. Like Ardsallagh Soft, the cheese is handmade all year round, with pasteurised goats' milk and vegetarian rennet, based very broadly on a gouda recipe. The cheese is pressed under its own weight. Very mild when young, the cheese develops a distinct agreeable goaty, nutty, sweet flavour when aged. Some Ardsallagh Hard is beechwood smoked. The natural tan-coloured rind is edible. The young white pate develops an ivory tint with age, as does the smoked variety. The mature cheese can be grated in the same way as Parmesan.

Ardsallagh Hard Goats Cheese, pressed in its mould

Ardsallagh Hard Goats Cheese in the smoker

Bay Lough Cheese

In one of the greenest pastures in the world, just a walk up the hill from the village of Clogheen in southern Tipperary, on the edge of the Golden Vale and the Waterford border, Anne and Richard Keating have been hand-making Bay Lough cheese since 1984. The cheese is made from a cheddar-like recipe in the traditional way. Bay Lough is sometimes regarded as a territorial-style cheese, reminiscent of the British county/territorial cheeses. The cheese is made seasonally and is available only locally, but it is well worth tracking down. Some Bay Lough does make it to other parts of Ireland. Visitors to Bay Lough should phone before visiting.

Bay Lough (from the Irish *bealach*, 'pass') is named after a corrie lake in the local Knockmealdown Mountains and is the location of the story of the ghost of Petticoat Loose. In short, legend tells us that the ghost of a girl terrorised the district in the early 1800s. When alive, she was allegedly over-friendly with the men of the area, which explains the derivation of her name. She was drowned in the lake. A priest led a procession of locals to Bay Lough where he exorcised the ghost because it was said that the lake was bottomless. However, visitors perhaps should be aware that a presence variously described as a banshee, witch, revenant or monster is still said to haunt the lake. (Variations on this tale are widespread across the southern counties of Ireland.)

Selected outlets: *Country Choice, Nenagh; Hudson's Whole Foods, Ballydehob, West Cork; McCambridge's, Galway; On the Pig's Back, English Market, Cork; SuperValu, Poppyfield, Clonmel; several farmers' markets and delis.*

Bay Lough Cheese	
Proprietors:	Anne and Richard Keating
Address:	Bay Lough Cheese, Clogheen, Co. Tipperary
Phone:	+353 (0)52 746 5275
Cheeses made:	Bay Lough and varieties
Company size:	Medium
Availability:	Local, some national

BAY LOUGH CHEESE

Milk	
Style	Hard
Raw/pasteurised	Raw (some pasteurised)
Rennet	Vegetarian
Organic	No
Reminiscent of	Old-style cheddar
Maturation	A few months
Size	300 g round, 1.5 kg wheel
Availability	Local, some national
Varieties	Plain; Smoked, Garlic & Herb; Smoked G&H
Fat	32%
Made in	Tipperary

Bay Lough Cheese

This is a full-fat cheddar-like cheese made with raw milk from the Friesian cows of neighbouring farmers and vegetarian rennet. A little pasteurised cheese is available. The pate is ivory coloured and the plain cheese is wrapped in colourful yellow natural wax, which should be discarded. The young cheese has a mild cheddary flavour while the extra mature has the rich taste of an old-style traditional cheddar, with a nutty, slightly sweet fudgy richness. Smoked (brown wax) and Garlic & Herb (black wax) varieties are also produced. The cheese is cooked and pressed and then cloth-wrapped and matured in the traditional way. While made seasonally, it is available all year. Bay Lough is named after a lake on the scenic tourist drive over the nearby Knockmealdown Mountains.

69

Friesian cattle busy making milk for Béal cheese

Béal Organic Cheese

Kate Carmody came to the attention of the Irish public in early 2010 when she appeared on the popular TV show *Dragons' Den*, where she successfully convinced two of Ireland's top businessmen, Bobby Kerr and Niall O'Farrell, to invest in her artisanal cheesemaking business.

Long before the fame of 2010, since 1987, in fact, Kate had been making her handmade organic cheese on her farm near Listowel in north Kerry. She began her working life as a biochemist before marrying a dairy farmer. The idea of cheesemaking was sparked by a gift from her mother of a cheese press and a book on the subject and the knowledge that her great-aunt had made Wensleydale cheese in Yorkshire. Kate began making her cheese in the kitchen before converting an outhouse to a dairy. By 1997 Kate had started to convert the farm to organic principles, and the process was completed by 2000. Kate's qualification as a biochemist has no doubt contributed to the success of the cheese and she still finds some time in the week to work in her original discipline.

Kate hand-makes two cows' milk cheeses, one with raw milk and the other with pasteurised milk. Both are made on GM-free organic principles, in which Kate believes passionately. A mild block cheddar has recently been added to the range. The *Dragons' Den* publicity has been good for Kate's business and her cheeses can be found right across Ireland.

The cheese is named after the village of Béal, or Beal, depending on which local you speak to. Béal means 'mouth' in the Irish language, as the village lies on the mouth of the Shannon estuary, close to the homelands of the writers Brendan Kennelly and John B. Keane.

Kate can accommodate tourist visits and there is a video you can watch, but you must phone ahead before calling as, luckily for Kate, some days are just too busy for visitors.

Awards

| 2010 | Irish National Organic Awards | Highly Commended | Béal Organic Mature Cheddar |
| 2009 | World Cheese Awards | Silver | Béal Organic Cheese Unpasteurised |

BÉAL ORGANIC CHEESE	
Proprietor:	Kate Carmody
Address:	Béal Lodge, Asdee, Listowel, Co. Kerry
Web:	www.bealorganiccheese.com
Facebook:	Bealcheese
Twitter:	Bealcheese
Email:	info@bealorganiccheese.com, info@beal.ie
Phone:	+353 (0)68 41137
Cheeses made:	Raw Milk Handmade Mature Béal Organic Cheese, Pasteurised Handmade Mature Béal Organic Cheddar, Pasteurised Mild Béal Organic Cheddar
Company size:	Medium to large
Availability:	National

RAW MILK HANDMADE MATURE BÉAL ORGANIC CHEESE	
Milk	
Style	Hard
Raw/pasteurised	Raw
Rennet	Vegetarian
Organic	Organic
Reminiscent of	Old-style cheddar
Maturation	6 months – 2½ years
Size	8–10 kg rounds
Availability	National
Made in	Kerry

Raw Milk Handmade Mature Béal Organic Cheese

This is a hard cheddar-style farmhouse cheese handmade on organic principles, with raw Holstein/Friesian cows' milk and vegetarian rennet. This cooked and pressed cheese is made only during the summer months. It is old-fashioned crumbly cheddar with an almost Parmesan-like aroma and tang. The flavour is piquant and fiery with a rich aftertaste. The dark brown natural rind is edible. The mature cheese ages for nine months.

PASTEURISED HANDMADE MATURE BÉAL ORGANIC CHEDDAR		
Milk		
Style	Hard	
Raw/pasteurised	Pasteurised	
Rennet	Vegetarian	
Organic	Organic	
Reminiscent of	Mature cheddar	
Maturation	3 months (mild), 6 months – 2 years (mature)	
Size	8–10 kg rounds, 12–15 kg blocks	
Availability	National	
Made in	Kerry	

Pasteurised Handmade Mature Béal Organic Cheddar

This traditional cheddar has been made since 2007. The pasteurisation gives a distinctly different taste to the raw-milk cheese. The production principles and standards are organic and the rennet used is vegetarian. Like the raw-milk Béal, the cheese is cooked and pressed. The texture is crumbly and pleasantly crystalline. Like the raw-milk cheddar, the mature cheese ages for nine months. A mild block cheese with a buttery flavour and pliable texture is released after three months' maturation and can be found in many health food shops around the country.

Bellingham Blue Cheese (Glyde Farm Produce)

Peter and Anita Thomas make Bellingham Blue cheese on their farm just off junction 15 of the M1 in County Louth. The cheese is one of only a handful of blue cheeses produced in Ireland. Despite the small numbers, we are blessed with blue cheeses of exceptional quality, the others being Abbey Blue, Ballyblue, Cashel Blue, Crozier Blue, Kerry Blue, Oisín Blue and Wicklow Blue. Bellingham Blue distinguishes itself by being a raw cows' milk cheese; if you get your hands on a mature one, it will blow your head off with flavour, in the best possible way. If you do not like your cheese so feisty, try the younger Bellingham.

Peter was a printer by trade and came to Ireland from Glasgow in 1977. He ran a printing business in Donegal until 1993. His wife Anita comes from a history of dairy farming in County Louth and has degrees in food science and marketing. They saw an opportunity to leverage the milk produced from Anita's family farm and thus create alternative income. Peter took a number of courses in cheese production and together they set up Glyde Farm Produce in Louth in 1996. By May 2000 they were producing Bellingham Blue Cheese. Production has increased greatly in the intervening years and the cheese has won a number of awards and international acclaim.

In 2011 Peter started making a new cheese, Boyne Valley Blue, made in association with Michael Finnegan. This is made with unpasteurised goats' milk with vegetarian rennet to the same recipe as Bellingham Blue. Peter's next move, if he can get enough milk to make it viable, might be an unpasteurised sheep's blue.

Peter Thomas in his dairy

GLYDE FARM PRODUCE (BELLINGHAM BLUE CHEESE)

Proprietor:	Peter Thomas
Address:	Mansfieldstown, Castlebellingham, Co. Louth
Web:	www.irishcheese.ie/members/glydefarm.html
Email:	glydefarm@eircom.net
Phone:	+353 (0)42 937 2343
Cheeses made:	Bellingham Blue, Boyne Valley Blue
Company size:	Medium
Availability:	National
Recipe:	See p. 320

BELLINGHAM BLUE

Milk	
Style	Semi-hard
Raw/pasteurised	Raw
Rennet	Vegetarian
Organic	No
Reminiscent of	Stilton
Maturation	8 weeks min. Best between 5 and 6 months
Size	200 g, 500–800 g, 1–2 kg, 3–4 kg rounds
Availability	National
Made in	Louth

A Bellingham Blue ready to eat

Bellingham Blue

This wonderful cows' raw-milk cheese is one of Ireland's handful of blue cheeses. The semi-hard Bellingham has a fresh, creamy, slightly salty taste. It has a crumbly, melt-in-the-mouth texture, somewhat reminiscent of Stilton. If you like a little more bite and you can get your hands on one, try a Bellingham that has matured for a number of years. The taste can be intense and exciting. If you dare to eat the aged natural rind, it can add a not unpleasant crystalline texture. The rind is thin and slightly bloomy and the pate shows a creamy yellow hue, of course with blue-green veins. The cheese is uncooked and is pressed under its own weight. Bellingham Blue is excellent in the company of sweet fruit.

The cheese is named after the local townland in County Louth, Castlebellingham.
Selected outlets: *Cavistons, Dublin; Sheridans; Superquinn; On the Pig's Back, English Market, Cork.*

BOYNE VALLEY BLUE		
Milk		
Style	Semi-hard	
Raw/pasteurised	Raw	
Rennet	Vegetarian	
Organic	No	
Reminiscent of	Goat Stilton	
Maturation	As Bellingham	
Size	As Bellingham	
Availability	Local, some national	
Made in	Louth	

Boyne Valley Blue

Boyne Valley Blue is a rare breed indeed – an Irish blue made from goats' milk. This is a new cheese, made in association with Michael Finnegan, to the recipe of Bellingham Blue and is quite reminiscent of Bellingham. The outside of the cheese (there's no rind as such) is a dark greyish-yellow, the pate being lighter grey-yellow, with veins of blue running through it. There is a strong classic blue nose, and in the mouth it has a strong attack, a quite dry, crumbly texture, with some crystalline elements. Fiercely piquant, there's a strong yeasty tingle on the finish.
Selected outlet: *Sheridans.*

Bluebell Falls Goats Cheese

Traditionally a cattle and sheep farm, Bluebell Falls Farm, overlooking the River Shannon estuary, is owned by Paul Keane and his family. In 1995 the Keanes diversified into goat farming and by 1998 had well over 100 Saanen and Toggenburg goats. By 2000 the farm specialised in goats' milk and cheese production. Today there are over 200 goats. The range of cheese is handmade entirely from the milk of their own goats. The cheeses are named after astronomical objects: Cygnus, Orion, Pegasus and sometimes Delphinus. Cygnus is the main cheese produced. The cheeses are not pasteurised in the strict sense of the word but are heated to 60°C for thirty minutes and then cooled quickly. This kills pathogens while retaining more flavour than pasteurisation, where the temperature is raised to 72°C for a few seconds.

The name of the company derives from the small waterfall across the road from the farm, on the Owenslieve River (*Abhainn Sleibhe* – 'mountain river'), decorated as it is with natural bluebells every spring.

Cheeses can be ordered from the website. At present, tourist visits are not possible.

Selected outlets: *Donnybrook Fair, Dublin; Fallon & Byrne, Dublin; Gourmet Store, Ennis; McCormick's, Westport; Mange Tout, Kinsale; Morton's, Galway; Open Sesame, Ennis; On the Pig's Back, English Market, Cork.*

BLUEBELL FALLS GOATS CHEESE	
Proprietors:	Paul Keane and the Keane family
Address:	Ballynacally, Ennis, Co. Clare
Web:	www.bluebellfalls.ie
Email:	bluebellfalls@gmail.com
Phone:	+353 (0)65 683 8024/+353 (0)86 813 4600
Cheeses made:	Cygnus and varieties, Orion, Pegasus
Company size:	Medium
Availability:	Local, national
Recipe:	See p. 344

One of Bluebell's workers

CYGNUS	
Milk	
Style	Soft
Raw/pasteurised	Heat-treated
Rennet	Vegetarian
Organic	No
Reminiscent of	Goaty cream cheese
Maturation	None
Size	150 g portion, 500 g log
Availability	Local, national
Varieties	Plain; Honey; Pepper
Made in	Clare

Cygnus

Cygnus is a fresh soft goats' milk cheese made all year round from the milk of Saanen goats and vegetarian rennet. The pate colour is snow white, the flavour is very mildly goaty and the texture is smooth and creamy. While not pasteurised, the cheese is heat-treated. As well as the plain variety, Cygnus Honey is made with added honey, garlic and thyme. Cygnus Pepper has added garlic, herbs and black pepper. The sweetness of

Cygnus Honey predominates, while the garlic taste of Cygnus Pepper predominates.

Available in 500 g paper-wrapped logs and 150 g sections, the cheese can be found locally and nationally.

The cheese is named after the eponymous constellation Cygnus, the swan, in the northern skies.

Orion		
Milk		
Style	Semi-hard	
Raw/Pasteurised	Heat-treated	
Rennet	Vegetarian	
Organic	No	
Reminiscent of	Goat Parmesan	
Maturation	6–12 months	
Size	By the kg	
Availability	Local, national	
Made in	Clare	

Orion

Orion is a semi-hard goats' cheese made with the milk of Saanen goats and vegetarian rennet. While the milk is not pasteurised, it is heat-treated. The curd is pressed but not cooked. The rind is lightly orange-coloured and is edible. The pate is an off-white creamy colour and the texture is firm. The flavour is nutty and slightly sweet and, with age, becomes somewhat reminiscent of a goaty Parmesan. The cheese is made all year round and is sold by the kilogram. It can be found both locally and nationally.

The cheese is named after the eponymous constellation Orion, the hunter.

PEGASUS		
Milk		
Style	Soft, white-mould	
Raw/pasteurised	Heat-treated	
Rennet	Vegetarian	
Organic	No	
Reminiscent of	Goat Reblochon	
Maturation	2 weeks	
Size	170/180 g portion	
Availability	Local, national	
Made in	Clare	

Pegasus

Pegasus is a white-mould soft cheese made with heat-treated Saanen goats' milk and vegetarian rennet. The texture is soft and the flavour fresh, strong, grassy and a little sulphurous, somewhat reminiscent of French Reblochon. The white-mould rind is edible and the pate is white. The aroma is strong and a little sulphurous.

The cheese is named after the eponymous constellation Pegasus, the winged horse.

Boyne Pastures

Des Crinion has a passion for food. Having worked in the hotel business for many years, he finally gave in to his passion for farming and began to work a bit of land left to him by his uncle. Des has grown most things, including mushrooms and strawberries. Now he sells his organic eggs and vegetables at local markets and will soon be selling them in his new farm shop. Des also keeps about fifty-five East Friesland sheep, from which he makes a little ice cream and cheese. He has been doing this since about 2006. The cheese is made with his own pasteurised sheep's milk and vegetarian rennet. The main cheese, Toto, is from a gouda-style recipe. It is semi-hard and somewhat reminiscent of an Italian Pecorino and named after a beloved, respected and somewhat eccentric late cousin whom Des wanted to commemorate. The pate is full of holes. A blue version of Toto has a little goats' milk added, which comes from a neighbour's herd. In summertime, Des also makes a Feta-style cheese.

Des's passion for food has led him to set up a local Slane Food Circle, which encourages the production of local, fresh, high-quality food at affordable prices. Several local growers, producers, restaurateurs and, indeed, customers are on board and Des hopes the idea will spread to other local communities.

Boyne Pastures	
Proprietor:	Des Crinion
Address:	Boyne Pastures, Cruicetown, Stackallen, Slane, Co. Meath
Web:	+353 (0)41 982 4588/+353 (0)85 715 1277
Cheeses made:	Toto, Toto Blue
Company size:	Small
Availability:	Local

Burren Gold (Aillwee Cave Farm Shop)

A visit to north Clare is not complete without a visit to the Aillwee Cave system. As part of that experience, you may get to visit the Aillwee Cave shop and the Burren Gold cheese production facility. Ben Johnson has made Burren Gold cheese here, near Ballyvaughan, since 1984. Ben arrived in Ireland at the age of two from Scotland with his Scottish mother and English father. His father had been a mining engineer in Africa and put that experience to use developing the Liscannor Stone Company and the Aillwee Cave system and visitor centre.

On leaving school in 1984, Ben needed a career. His mother had often made cream cheese at home and Ben took a decision to learn the art of cheesemaking and develop an existing building as a cheese dairy. He needed to produce a non-exotic cheese that would appeal to the Irish public who were, at that time, very much cheddar eaters. Ben settled on gouda cheese. He took the admirable step of contacting the Dutch Dairy Bureau. They placed him on a farm near Amstelveen in the Netherlands for a year and a half as a trainee cheesemaker. At the end of that period Ben returned to Ireland with a lot of expensive cheesemaking equipment. With no grant, this was a big risk. As is often the case, a lot of trial and error was required before he got his cheese right. Now this high-quality cheese continues to be sold, albeit locally. Several flavours are available. Ben has experimented successfully with a Stilton-like blue in the past and we can only hope that he might make some more in the future.

The cheese dairy is now an established part of the Aillwee Cave visitor attraction. Burren Gold can also be found in Ballyvaughan Farmers' Market.

Bird enthusiasts may like the Burren Bird of Prey Centre, which is run by Ben. Honey is also produced and sold on site in the Aillwee Cave Farm Shop.

Tourist visits are welcomed, with cheese tours daily. Call or check the website for details.

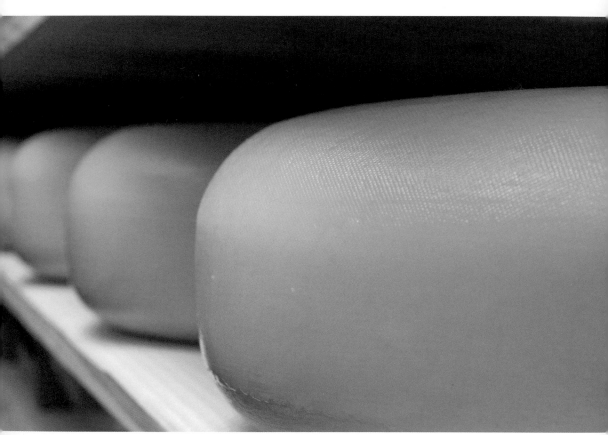

Curling stone-like wheels of Burren Gold maturing near the Aillwee Cave

BURREN GOLD (AILLWEE CAVE FARM SHOP)	
Proprietor:	Ben Johnson
Address:	Aillwee Cave, Ballyvaughan, Co. Clare
Web:	www.aillweecave.ie/aillwee_cave_farmshop.htm
Email:	bensboats@gmail.com
Phone:	+353 (0)65 707 7036
Cheeses made:	Burren Gold
Company size:	Medium
Availability:	Local
Other products:	Cave tours, fudge, jams, honey and more

Awards

2009   British Cheese Awards   Gold/Silver/Bronze
2006   British Cheese Awards   Silver/Bronze

Smoked Burren Gold maturing

Burren Gold	
Milk	
Style	Hard
Raw/pasteurised	Raw and pasteurised
Rennet	Traditional
Organic	No
Reminiscent of	Gouda
Maturation	8 weeks – 18 months
Size	0.5, 4, 8 kg round
Availability	Local
Varieties	Plain; Smoked; Black Pepper; Cumin; Nettle & Garlic; Fenugreek Seed; Piri Piri
Made in	Clare

Burren Gold

Reminiscent of gouda, Burren Gold is available in a number of varieties. Both raw and pasteurised cows' milk varieties are made. Traditional animal rennet is used and the cheese is produced only in the summer months from local grass-fed Friesian cows. The cheese is cooked, pressed and double washed, producing a very creamy texture, almost buttery when young. The rind is yellow and the pate shows a creamy yellow hue. The aroma is reminiscent of yoghurt and mushrooms and the taste is rich and buttery, lingering with a slightly acidic finish. The rind of the smoked cheese is deep red. A number of varieties are available, including Smoked, Black Pepper, Cumin, Nettle & Garlic, Fenugreek Seed and Piri Piri.[3]

The cheese is named after the local Burren region of County Clare and for its colour. It is available in the Aillwee Cave Farm Shop and in the Ballyvaughan Farmers' Market.

Carlow Cheese

In 2007, Elizabeth Bradley began making cheese on her farm in Carlow as a means of generating a little extra cash. Benefiting from assistance from the European LEADER project to get established, her Carlow Cheese, in its bright yellow wax, is somewhat reminiscent of both gouda and edam. She makes her cheese all year round from the raw cows' milk of neighbour Sven Harrenberg's all-Friesian herd. Elizabeth is looking at getting into sheep, so we may see a sheep's cheese from her at some point in the future. As well as selling it herself at the Carlow town market, Carlow Cheese is available in Ireland in other local farmers' markets in the southeast and some local retail shops.

CARLOW CHEESE	
Proprietor:	Elizabeth Bradley
Address:	Ballybrommell, Fenagh, Co. Carlow
Web:	www.irishcheese.ie/members/carlowcheese.html
Email:	e.bradley@o2.ie
Phone:	+353 (0)59 972 7382
Cheese made:	Carlow Edam
Company size:	Small
Availability:	Local

Elizabeth Bradley

89

CARLOW EDAM		
Milk		
Style	Semi-hard	
Raw/pasteurised	Raw	
Rennet	Traditional	
Organic	No	
Reminiscent of	Edam, gouda	
Maturation	6 weeks – 8 months max.	
Size	4–4.5 kg round	
Availability	Local	
Varieties	Sun-dried Tomato with Basil and a Hint of Garlic; Nettle & Dried Onion; Black Pepper; Chilli; Cumin; Green Peppers; Garlic & Herb; Mature (7–8 months)	
Made in	Clare	

Carlow Edam

Carlow Cheese is in the edam style but is also somewhat reminiscent of gouda. The cheese is made with traditional rennet from raw cows' milk from the Friesian herd of a local farmer. It is sold in rounds of 4–4.5 kg. The curds are heated and pressed for six hours, washed in brine and matured for between six weeks to six or seven months. Attractive yellow wax is used to seal the cheese. The yellow-ivory tint in the pate probably comes from carotene in the cows' diet. The aroma is mild and the flavour is mellow yet complex. The texture is smooth with some small holes. Typically, cheeses are sold at three months. The cheese is available in a number of varieties including plain, Chilli, Black Pepper, Cumin and Garlic & Herb. Aged cheeses are also available. This is a great general purpose cheese, which grills and melts well and can be used in a salad or as a snack with crackers. It is available in farmers' markets across the southeast of Ireland and in local retail outlets.

Carlow Edam

Carrigaline cheeses

Carrigaline Farmhouse Cheese

Since 1982, Ann and Pat O'Farrell have been hand-making Carrigaline Farmhouse Cheese in their dairy near the village of Carrigaline, just south of Cork City. Pat took over his father's 40-acre Friesian cattle dairy farm in 1987. The farm has been passed down from generation to generation, since Pat's grandmother inherited it from her father. When the local Carrigaline Pottery Company closed down, Pat needed to generate more income to support his family, so he took a cheesemaking course in UCC,[4] supported by AnCO.[5] At the time the O'Farrells used their own milk to make their cheese. Around 2000 they sold their cattle and leased their land and now buy in milk from a neighbour. The cows still graze on the grass of rich limestone soil.

The O'Farrells also sell handmade savoury cheese biscuits made with Carrigaline Cheese by Seymours of Cork under the Carrigaline label. There are three flavours: Natural, Garlic & Herb and Chilli.

The name 'Carrigaline' is taken from the name of the local village. It comes from the Irish *Carraig uí Leighin,* meaning 'rock of the Lynes', the Lynes being an old Irish family who built a stone castle on a limestone rock cliff in AD 1170. The cheese is still made under the watchful eye of the castle ruins.

Ann and Pat do cater for tourist visits, but you must call in advance to arrange a date and time.

Ann O'Farrell in the Carrigaline dairy

Carrigaline Cheese Biscuits

Carrigaline Farmhouse Cheese	
Proprietors:	Ann and Pat O'Farrell
Address:	The Rock, Carrigaline, Co. Cork
Web:	www.carrigalinecheese.com
Email:	pat@carrigalinecheese.com
Phone:	+353 (0)21 437 2856
Cheeses made:	Carrigaline and varieties
Company size:	Medium
Availability:	National, international (US)
Recipe:	See p. 322

Awards

2010	British Cheese Awards	Gold	Smoked Carrigaline
	World Cheese Awards	Bronze	Smoked Carrigaline
2008	British Cheese Awards	Silver	Low Fat Cheese
	British Cheese Awards	Gold	Smoked Cheese
	World Cheese Awards	Gold	Smoked Cheese

CARRIGALINE	
Milk	
Style	Semi-hard
Raw/pasteurised	Pasteurised
Rennet	Vegetarian
Organic	No
Reminiscent of	Havarti
Maturation	3–6 months
Size	150 g, 200 g, 400 g, 1.8 kg wheels
Availability	National, international
Varieties	Natural; Smoked; Garlic & Herb
Fat	26%
Made in	Cork

Carrigaline

Somewhat reminiscent of Danish Havarti, Carrigaline has a firm but supple texture with some Swiss-like holes. The cooked and pressed cheese is made all year round from pasteurised Friesian cows' milk and vegetarian rennet. The delicate flavour is mild and buttery, becoming more piquant with age, but at all ages has a distinctive Havarti-like tang. The cheese is enveloped in colourful wax, the colour denoting the variety: yellow for the natural cheese, brown for smoked and yellow-green for Garlic & Herb. The local Coolmore estate provides beechwood for the smoked variety. The cheese is suitable for use in cooking, in sandwiches and on the cheeseboard after dinner with a glass of port. Discard the natural-wax rind.

Carrigbyrne Farmhouse Cheese Co.

One of the stalwarts of Irish farmhouse cheese, largely due to the extremely popular St Killian, with its distinctive hexagonal shape, Carrigbyrne Farmhouse has been making cheese since 1982.

Patrick Berridge and his wife Juliet, having spent a period in New Zealand in the early 1970s, returned to run the family farm near Adamstown, County Wexford. Patrick's interest in cheese was sparked by a French cheesemaker who was living in Wexford at the time. On foot of a bit of experimentation, he came up with a good attempt at a cheddar-style cheese. While in the larder, however, the cheese became infiltrated with blue mould and by Christmas it had turned into a good Stilton-type cheese.

By the early 1980s Patrick was running the farm, which was, and remains, a relatively large dairy concern. It was a period of upheaval in the dairy industry – quotas were being introduced and prices were stagnating. Patrick considered his options for maximising the return from his raw materials and, discounting beef farming, decided to see what he could do with his milk supply. Given his dabbling some years earlier, cheese seemed a good possibility.

Contemporary cheesemaking in Wexford has a relatively long history. Wexford Creamery had been making cheese since the end of the Second Word War. In common with most other creameries, they produced mostly cheddar-style cheeses. In the late 1950s/early 1960s a small creamery called Edelweiss Dairy Products, based at

Patrick Berridge

Rocklands, Wexford Town, had been producing camembert- and brie-style cheeses. Their acquisition in the early 1960s by Wexford Creamery called a halt to this, however. Following a change of ownership, Wexford Creamery briefly revived the camembert style in the mid-1970s, but this too was short-lived. Patrick decided to have a go at this style, and the first St Killian left the dairy in March 1982.

The modern Carrigbyrne cheese plant is streamlined in its operation. Milk, all of which comes from their own 180-strong herd, is pumped underground across the yard from the milking parlour directly into a 3,000-litre stainless-steel tank. Starter is added and the lactic acid content carefully monitored and plotted on a graph until it reaches an ideal level. The plot of how the milk gets to this level will influence the rest of the process and the form follows the batch through the process, being updated as it progresses (e.g. with time of moulding, brining, for how long, etc.). This ensures a high degree of traceability.

The milk is transferred to small, 200-litre French-style vats before the rennet is added. The curds are then transferred to moulds, drained, washed in brine for about one hour and transferred to the drying room. While there, the cheese is blown with spores to start the formation of the mould on the rind. The cheese is transferred to the ripening room, where it remains for about nine days – much more and the rind becomes too thick. Finally, the cheese is wrapped and packed by hand, ready for distribution.

For now, they have plenty of room for expansion, as only a fraction of the milk production is used in cheese production. Patrick did attempt to diversify into the

St Killian cheeses maturing

production of yoghurt, to the extent that he actually invested in some plant. He found that the yoghurt market was very different from the cheese market; it was much more homogenised and more difficult to create an identity, so this was parked.

Recent developments have included Patrick encouraging his son Charlie to make a Vacherin-style cheese. Vacherin is traditionally enclosed in a belt (sangle) of birch bark and, in the case of the smaller cheeses, packed in a wooden box. To have the right properties, the bark has to be stripped from the tree the day after felling (the workers who do the stripping are known as *sangliers* – 'belt makers'). For this reason, they imported the authentic bark from France. Despite being happy with the outcome, the cheese has been put on hold for the time being due to Charlie's professional commitments. It may be revived in the future should the resident cheesemaker have the capacity to do so alongside the current range.

Patrick has taken a couple of initiatives with regard to taking more control of the distribution of his products over the past five years. In 2005, in the company of a number of other producers (non-cheese), he established a farm shop in New Ross on a co-operative basis whereby each partner would take it in turn to staff the shop. Originally the idea had been to open the shop in Wexford Town, but this had to be abandoned, as an important retail chain threatened to delist the products of any of the participants, several of whom had existing national distribution, were it to go ahead. Indeed, the venture probably ultimately failed due to time pressures on the participants. It was also arguably just ahead of its time, as two of the original participants subsequently proceeded to set up a venture essentially along the same lines, which, having learned from past mistakes, is currently thriving.

The other initiative has been to take charge of their own distribution. This has led to an arrangement between Patrick and several other prominent farmhouse cheesemakers to take control of their own distribution to the multiples. Today there are daily deliveries to the distribution depots of Musgrave and Dunnes and negotiations are continuing with other prominent national retailers. The upshot is a much larger slice of the retail price for the producers. In addition to a more attractive profit margin, this gives them the financial scope to stage the promotions required by large retail concerns.

Aside from cheese, Patrick has a couple of other interesting initiatives. In common with many of our Western neighbours, Ireland's prosperity has unfortunately led to a lot of food waste. This waste comes from many sources. The most obvious from a consumer perspective is simply food going off in the fridge, but the main culprit is probably large supermarkets. A 2010 British TV documentary challenged several top chefs to create a banquet from waste food. The level of waste they discovered was truly shocking, from perfectly good produce being consigned to the bin as a result of conservative best before dates to entire fields of lettuces being ploughed straight back into the ground because they didn't fit the description of what a supermarket thought a lettuce should look like.

Patrick's initiative is to collect this waste food and convert it to biogas, which he readily admits is not the most desirable outcome, but is at least preferable to consigning it to landfill, which is what would otherwise happen.

The other initiative is to introduce primary school students to green energy. He constructed a trailer, roughly three cubic metres in size, with a number of energy demonstrations inside, powered entirely by renewable sources. It has a small wind turbine and photovoltaic panels for solar energy. The trailer travels from school to school, typically spending a week at each one.

Patrick is happy to welcome visitors, but strictly by appointment only.

CARRIGBYRNE FARMHOUSE CHEESE CO. LTD	
Proprietor:	Patrick Berridge
Address:	Adamstown, Enniscorthy, Co. Wexford
Web:	www.carrigbyrne.ie
Email:	info@carrigbyrne.ie
Phone:	+353 (0)53 924 0560
Cheeses made:	St Killian, St Brendan Brie, Emerald Irish Brie
Company size:	Large
Availability:	Nationwide distribution, supermarkets and multiples, UK, Germany
Recipe:	See p. 321 and p. 334

ST KILLIAN	
Milk	
Style	Soft, white-mould
Raw/pasteurised	Pasteurised
Rennet	Vegetarian
Organic	No
Reminiscent of	Camembert/brie
Maturation	2–3 weeks
Size	250 g, 150 g (Mini)
Availability	National, international (UK, Germany)
Varieties	Mini
Made in	Wexford

St Killian

One of the iconic Irish cheeses, St Killian can be found throughout the country in its distinctive hexagonal packaging.

Named after the seventh-century Irish missionary, St Killian is a soft mould-ripened cheese, though its taste lies somewhere between that of brie and camembert. The drained and brined cheese is coated with spores of *Penicillium candidum*, which, over the course of several days, leads to the development of a brilliant white coating, or bloom. The bloom provides the ideal conditions for the ripening of the cheese. The thickening of the bloom is halted when the cheese is wrapped, which usually takes place after eight to ten days.

Wrapping the cheese does not stall the ripening, however, which continues to take place. The images on p. 101 show St Killian at varying levels of maturity. The cheese ripens from the rind towards the centre; thus, in the young cheese, the rind will be snowy white and the pate creamy white with a ripe exterior and a firm core with a crumbly, almost Feta-like texture. On the nose there is a slight hint of mushrooms, which is carried through on the palate. There is also a hint of damp cellars, with a slight saltiness, but overall it is quite mild.

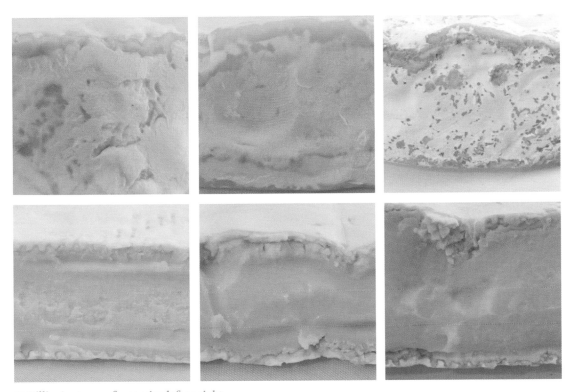

St Killian's stages of maturity, left to right

• **Three weeks** (St Kilian Mini) – *heart of cheese retains slightly chalky dryness*

• **One month** – *pate has a silky sheen throughout*

• **Four months** – *rind is taking on reddish spots; pate is drying out slightly and has darkened*

The cheese reaches optimum ripeness at around one month. At this point the ripeness should have extended throughout the cheese and a slice shows a silky sheen throughout the pate, which by now has a buttery texture and which can become quite runny. The rind retains its white bloom coating, but from this point onwards it will start to develop reddish patches. The mushroom nose persists and is slightly more marked on the palate. There are also notes of warm butter and green grass. The saltiness is also still evident at this point and the cheese is just beginning to develop barnyard notes.

With age, the cheese can become quite strong. By four months, the rind is liberally flecked with red patches and the cheese is physically somewhat smaller due to having dried out slightly. The pate is firmer and has darkened to a light mocha colour. The nose is of cellars and barnyard aromas, and on the palate the cheese has strong fungal and cellar notes – much more intense than its younger siblings. There is a slight ammonia kick after a few seconds and there is a very long finish, with lingering mushroom aftertaste.

The cheese is also available in a smaller 'Mini' portion. Interestingly, this does not mature at a noticeably different rate from the larger cheese, but it does develop a slightly different taste profile. Patrick is interested in experimenting with some of the specific cultures used in the production of French camembert such as Le Rustique, which gives interesting cabbage-like notes to the cheese. He is conscious, however, of people's familiarity with St Killian, so may ultimately try this on the Mini or another cheese entirely.

St Killian is widely available and can be found in supermarkets and delis throughout the country. It is distributed in the UK by Waitrose and in Germany by the Metro chain. Germany is currently a strong growth market and at the moment is taking one or two pallets per week (a pallet contains approximately 300 kg). It is hoped to expand this considerably in the near future.

St Brendan Brie	
Milk	
Style	Soft, white-mould
Raw/pasteurised	Pasteurised
Rennet	Vegetarian
Organic	No
Reminiscent of	Brie
Maturation	2–3 weeks
Size	1.5 kg round
Availability	National
Made in	Wexford

St Brendan Brie

What is the difference between a brie and a camembert? On the face of it, there is little difference between these two cheeses in terms of the manufacturing process. Both are made in different parts of France, hence the names, but this might not necessarily result in radically different cheeses. Also, while the primary spore responsible for the bloom on both is *Penicillium candidum*, some bries additionally use *Brevibacterium linens*, though nowadays this is frequently not the case.

The main distinguishing factor is probably size. Bries are much larger cheeses than camemberts and since both are mould-ripened and thus ripen from the outside in, they will develop differently.

Mirroring St Killian somewhat, St Brendan is made as a distinctive octagonal (as opposed to hexagonal) round, weighing about 1.5 kg. The label is attached in a segmented fashion with a view to the cheese being easily divided into eight segments at the point of sale.

EMERALD IRISH BRIE		
Milk		
Style	Soft, white-mould	
Raw/pasteurised	Pasteurised	
Rennet	Vegetarian	
Organic	No	
Reminiscent of	Brie	
Maturation	3+ weeks	
Size	3 kg round	
Availability	National	
Made in	Wexford	

Emerald Irish Brie

Emerald is a much larger cheese than St Brendan, weighing in at around 3 kg. It is also distinguished from its siblings in that it is the only one which is round in shape, as opposed to some form of polygon.

From the point of view of the cheese connoisseur, however, the difference is in the taste. Being a larger, thicker cheese, maturation takes longer – a minimum of three weeks before distribution. As a result, the cheese develops an extremely creamy texture, with notes of mushroom and lemon on the palate.

Carrowholly Cheese Co.

Andrew Pelham-Burn has been producing cheese on the shores of Clew Bay near Westport since 1999. In that year he took over the production of Carrowholly, having worked there for the previous year. A one-man operation, he produces small quantities of high-quality gouda-style cheese, which see mostly local distribution. The cheese is handmade from raw milk from local farmers' cows.

Selected outlets: *Christy's Harvest, Westport; Clarkes, Ballina (www.clarkes.ie); The Connemara Hamper, Clifden; McCormack's Butchers, Westport; St Georges Market, Belfast*

Awards

2008	World Cheese Awards	Gold	Carrowholly Nettle
	World Cheese Awards	Silver	Carrowholly

CARROWHOLLY CHEESE CO.	
Proprietor:	Andrew Pelham-Burn
Address:	Carrowholly, Westport, Co. Mayo
Facebook:	Carrowholly-Cheese
Email:	carrowhollycheese@gmail.com
Phone:	+353 (0)87 237 3536
Cheeses made:	Carrowholly, Carrowholly Old Russet
Company size:	Small
Availability:	Local

CARROWHOLLY	
Milk	
Style	Hard
Raw/Pasteurised	Raw
Rennet	Vegetarian
Organic	No
Reminiscent of	Gouda
Maturation	10 weeks
Size	500 g, 1 kg and 5 kg wheels
Availability	Local
Varieties	Plain; Garlic & Chive; Nettle; Cumin; Pepper
Fat	50% fat in dry matter
Made in	Mayo

Carrowholly

First produced in 1999 from raw milk locally sourced from Friesian cattle and vegetarian rennet, Andrew hand-makes this gouda-style cheese year round. The cheese is pressed but not cooked. This is a full-fat cheese with 50 per cent fat in dry matter. The edible rind is pale yellow and at ten weeks the cheese has a creamy yellow pate. On the palate the flavour is fresh and full, with a slightly nutty undertone. The texture is firm, smooth and slightly moist. Varieties made include plain, Garlic & Chive, Nettle, Cumin and Pepper.

The cheese takes its name from the Mayo townland where Andrew makes it (in Irish, *Ceathrú Chalaidh*, 'quarter of the landing place').

CARROWHOLLY OLD RUSSET	
Milk	
Style	Hard
Raw/pasteurised	Raw
Rennet	Vegetarian
Organic	No
Reminiscent of	Gouda, Parmesan, Old Amsterdam
Maturation	9 months
Size	5 kg wheels
Availability	Local
Varieties	Plain; Garlic & Chive; Nettle; Cumin; Pepper
Fat	50% fat in dry matter
Made in	Mayo

Carrowholly Old Russet

In 2001 Andrew decided to make a more mature cheese. Using the same production techniques, Carrowholly Old Russet is matured for nine months, during which time it develops a hard, crumbly, Parmesan-like texture. On the nose there is a strong aroma, with a strong, acidic yet fruity taste that lingers on the palate. The inedible rind is red and the pate is a dark yellow. The cheese is pressed but not cooked with full fat (50 per cent in dry matter). Varieties are the same as for Carrowholly.

Cashel Blue Cheese (J & L Grubb)

The Grubb family has had a long history of producing dairy products on their farm in the gently rolling landscape of Beechmount near Fethard, County Tipperary. After a period working as an agricultural researcher, Louis Grubb returned to the farm in 1978 accompanied by wife Jane and young daughter Sarah. Initially they developed the farm as a commercial dairy entity, selling milk to the local creamery, but the depressed agricultural economy of the late 1970s/early 1980s, coupled with boredom with the daily routine of producing milk to sell for ever-decreasing rewards, led them to look at ways of diversifying from straightforward farming.

Having previously worked as a chef on a floating restaurant in the southeast, Jane had developed a love of fine food. Among the avenues they explored was cheese production, researching various styles and learning how to make them. Blue cheese, primarily Danish Blue, was quite popular at the time, and they noted a market opportunity for a high-quality native Irish blue cheese.

From an initial modest production of eight cheeses per day when first launched in 1984, Cashel Blue has gone on to become hugely successful and has garnered numerous national and international awards. It was joined in 1993 by Crozier Blue, produced from sheep's milk, utilising the same artisanal production methods. Both cheeses are handmade under the guidance of head cheesemaker Geurt Van den Dikkenberg.

In 2001, following a period working in the wine trade, daughter Sarah returned to the family business accompanied by husband Sergio Furno, himself skilled in cheese production, having worked for a French cheese producer, thus ensuring continuity into the next generation. Nephew Louis Clifton Brown has also joined the small but dedicated team.

Beechmount Farm

CASHEL BLUE CHEESE (J & L GRUBB LTD)	
Proprietor:	Louis Grubb
Address:	Beechmount, Fethard, Co. Tipperary
Web:	www.cashelblue.com
Facebook:	CashelBlue
Twitter:	CashelBlue
Email:	sergio@cashelblue.com
Phone:	+353 (0)52 613 1151
Cheeses made:	Cashel Blue, Crozier Blue
Company size:	Large
Availability:	Local, national, international (US)
Recipe:	See p. 319 and p. 332

Awards

2010	World Cheese Awards	Gold	Cashel Blue
	Great Taste Awards	3 stars	Cashel Blue
	SHOP Awards	Bronze	Cashel Blue
2009	World Cheese Awards	Gold, Best Irish Cheese	Cashel Blue
	World Cheese Awards	Bronze	Crozier Blue
	International Cheese Awards	Gold	Cashel Blue
	Great Taste Awards	3 stars	Cashel Blue[6]
	Great Taste Awards	2 stars	Crozier Blue
	SHOP Awards	Gold	Cashel Blue
2007	Prima Roma	Supreme Champion	Crozier Blue

Henry Clifton Brown's Friesland sheep

CASHEL BLUE		
Milk		
Style	Semi-soft, blue	
Raw/pasteurised	Pasteurised	
Rennet	Vegetarian	
Organic	No	
Reminiscent of	Bleu de Bresse, Bleu d'Auvergne	
Maturation	3–4 weeks, then up to 12 weeks	
Size	1.5 kg wheel, 350 g and 175 g wedges	
Availability	Local, national, international	
Fat	50% fat in dry matter	
Made in	Tipperary	

Cashel Blue

One of the best-known Irish cheeses, Cashel Blue was first produced in 1984. Deriving its name from a local landmark, the Rock of Cashel, it was the first native Irish blue cheese and was also notable for being the first semi-soft blue cheese produced in the British Isles.

The first Cashel Blue was produced on a small scale in an old 90-litre brewer's vat and initially was sold locally at markets and a handful of shops in Dublin and Galway. Its quality was soon recognised, and it won the Supreme Champion prize at the Clones Agricultural Show in its first year. Today the Grubbs produce 240 tonnes of Cashel Blue annually, with widespread availability in Ireland. Other important markets are the UK, the US and Continental Europe, with customers as far afield as Japan, South Africa and Australia. Most of the milk still comes from their own pedigree herd of Holstein-Friesian cows, the remainder being sourced from local suppliers.

The cheese is made and matured on the premises for three to four weeks before being dispatched to market. It is available in a variety of formats, from full 1.5 kg wheels to smaller 350 g and 175 g wedges.

When young, the cheese is firm and crumbly, and at around six weeks has a tangy flavour. As the cheese ages it becomes creamier, developing a fuller flavour up to about twelve weeks. Beyond this, the flavour will become too strong for many, though some may relish it! The blue is from the artificially introduced mould *Penicillium roqueforti*, the same mould as is used in French Roquefort.

CROZIER BLUE	
Milk	
Style	Semi-soft, blue
Raw/pasteurised	Pasteurised
Rennet	Vegetarian
Organic	No
Reminiscent of	Roquefort
Maturation	12–30 weeks
Size	1.5 kg wheel
Availability	Local, national, international
Fat	50% fat in dry matter
Made in	Tipperary

Crozier Blue

In 1993 Louis Grubb's nephew, Henry Clifton Brown, began making a blue cheese from sheep's milk. He experimented with the recipe over the next few years, and by 1999 was producing the cheese in commercial quantities. For logistical reasons it was decided that the cheese should be made on the Grubb premises, with the milk supplied by Henry from his flock of 200–300 (depending on the season) pedigree Friesland sheep. The new cheese was named Crozier Blue, retaining a brand link to Cashel Blue (the Rock of Cashel was an ancient bishop's seat and croziers are used by both bishops and shepherds).

Producing around 1 tonne annually at the turn of the millennium, current production levels are about 12 tonnes per year – about 5 per cent of the volume of Cashel Blue. It is available through farmers' markets in the region, speciality shops nationwide and is exported to the UK and Europe in small quantities.

Crozier is slower to mature than Cashel, becoming ready for market at around the twelve-week stage. The flavour profile progresses in a similar manner to Cashel up to about thirty weeks, with the texture progressing from crumbly to a creamier consistency.

Maturing cheese

Castlefarm Cheese

Peter is the third generation of Youngs to farm Castlefarm at Narraghmore, south of Kilcullen in north Kildare. This is primarily a dairy farm, with some seventy head of cattle in the winter herd alongside some tillage, beef, eggs and organic vegetables. After taking over the farm, Peter and wife Jenny set up a farm shop selling their produce. They found the easiest way to sell their milk was to turn it into cheese. Jenny took a cheesemaking course at Teagasc Moorepark, Fermoy, County Cork. Now she makes the brilliant-green-waxed gouda-like cheese on the premises of cheesemaker Elizabeth Bradley (see pp. 89–90), but with the milk of the Youngs' own Friesian/Jersey herd. Two versions are made: Natural and Shamrock, which has added fenugreek.

As perhaps Kildare's only farmhouse cheese, Castlefarm was fittingly launched at Taste Kildare at the K Club in August 2008. The farm was later awarded Bridgestone plaques for three years running and is one of *FOOD&WINE* magazine's top 100 Irish food destinations. Castlefarm is also a Teagasc/Department of Agriculture demonstration farm. The Youngs not only produce good food, but also educate people about good food, offering group tours of the farm and educational courses as well as cookery demonstrations and producer talks.

CASTLEFARM CHEESE	
Proprietors:	Jenny and Peter Young
Address:	Castlefarm Shop, Narraghmore, Athy, Co. Kildare
Web:	www.castlefarmshop.ie/castlefarm-food.asp
Email:	jenny@castlefarmshop.ie
Phone:	+353 (0)59 863 6948/+353 (0)87 678 5269
Cheeses made:	Castlefarm Natural and Shamrock
Company size:	Small
Availability:	Local
Other products:	Organic vegetables, eggs, other local foods
Recipe:	See p.328

Castlefarm Natural and Shamrock		
Milk		
Style	Hard	
Raw/pasteurised	Raw	
Rennet	Traditional	
Organic	No	
Reminiscent of	Gouda	
Maturation	6 weeks	
Size	5 kg wheel	
Availability	Local	
Varieties	Natural; Shamrock (fenugreek)	
Fat	4.2%	
Made in	Kildare	

Castlefarm Cheese

This is a gouda-like cheese with distinctive green wax, made since 2008. The raw cows' milk comes from the Youngs' own herd of Friesian/Jersey cows. The rennet is traditional. The cheese is cooked, pressed and matured for six weeks. Two varieties are available: Natural and Shamrock (with fenugreek), in 5 kg wheels. The plastic-wax rind is not edible. The flavour is fresh and milky and the texture is firm.

The cheese is available only directly from the Castlefarm shop and Athy and Carlow farmers' markets.

Castlemary Goat Cheese

John and Olive Hallahan, faced with a change in their farming circumstances, had to carefully evaluate the best way forward for them in order to make a living. They decided on goat farming and have been making cheese since 2009.

With a herd of around sixty goats, they produce goats' milk, cheese and yoghurt, which they sell from their farm shop situated near Cloyne, County Cork (open Saturdays 10 a.m. – 4 p.m.). Local response has been favourable and word about their cheese is spreading. The cheese can be sourced also from Midleton Farmers' Market.

CASTLEMARY GOAT CHEESE	
Proprietors:	John and Olive Hallahan
Address:	Castlemary Farm, Cloyne, Co. Cork
Email:	fionahallahan@hotmail.com
Phone:	+353 (0)87 797 7203/+353 (0)87 264 7728
Cheeses made:	Goat Cheddar, Goat Gouda, various soft goat cheeses
Company size:	Small
Availability:	Local
Other products:	Yoghurt

The Causeway Cheese Company

While a majority of Irish artisanal cheesemakers are concentrated in the southwest of the island, a few are dotted about the rest of the land. You can't really get much further away from the Golden Vale, on the island of Ireland at least, than Loughgiel, County Antrim, in the far northeast, the home of the Causeway Cheese Company. Since 2001, Damian and Sue McCloskey have been hand-making their traditional cheddar cheese here just on the edge of the startlingly beautiful Glens of Antrim and a stone's throw from the unique Giant's Causeway.[7] Four artisanal cheddars are made from neighbours' pasteurised milk with vegetarian rennet: mature Castlequarter, Ballyknock (with black pepper), Ballybradden (with herbs and garlic) and Coolkeeran, made with dulse[8] seaweed. All the cheeses are named after townlands or place names near the village of Loughgiel.

Damian started his working life as a cheese technologist, grading cheddar cheeses at Unigate Dairies in Britain, where he met his future wife, Sue. When he returned to Northern Ireland he worked for a while for DARD[9] and later on the family farm. Soon he was looking for a way to diversify his dairy farming. By 1999 Damian was taking a course in cheesemaking at Loughry College,[10] County Tyrone. As part of the course they visited some established cheesemakers in the Republic of Ireland and set up their fledgling outfit with the knowledge they had gained.

Since those early days, Causeway Cheese has prevailed, with only minimal funding from Invest NI and a handful of other government grants. In their first year of cheesemaking they made about 120 small cheeses. By 2010 they were making about 12,000 cheeses per year. They now supply locally in Northern Ireland to shops, restaurants and markets, but their main market is the hamper industry. While the McCloskeys have experimented with other cheeses, experience tells them that high-quality cheddar cheese is what their customers are looking for in Northern Ireland. Causeway has a very distinctive brand linked to the local Giant's Causeway, with the hexagonal-shaped cheeses, made using purpose-designed moulds, reflecting the Causeway itself. The first Northern Irish cheese in the Irish cheese renaissance (and one of very few), Causeway Cheese is worth seeking out.

Causeway Ballybradden hexagons starting the maturing process

THE CAUSEWAY CHEESE COMPANY	
Proprietors:	Damian and Sue McCloskey
Address:	Unit 1, Millennium Centre, Lough Road, Loughgiel, Ballymena, Co. Antrim BT44 9JN
Web:	www.causewaycheese.com
Email:	info@causewaycheese.com
Phone:	+44 (0)28 2764 1241
Cheeses made:	Ballybradden, Ballyknock, Castlequarter, Coolkeeran
Company size:	Medium
Availability:	Local

BALLYBRADDEN, BALLYKNOCK, CASTLEQUARTER AND COOLKEERAN

Milk	
Style	Hard
Raw/pasteurised	Pasteurised
Rennet	Vegetarian
Organic	No
Reminiscent of	Cheddar
Maturation	2–12 months
Size	175 g, 200 g waxed hexagons, 175 g wedges, 700 g half-moon, 2.8 kg wheel
Availability	Local
Varieties	Plain; Black Pepper; Herbs & Garlic; Dulse
Fat	35%
Made in	Antrim

Ballybradden, Ballyknock, Castlequarter and Coolkeeran

These are fine traditional cheddars with a range of additives. Castlequarter is a plain, mature cheddar (blue wax), Ballyknock (orange wax) has black pepper added, Ballybradden (green wax) has herbs and garlic added and Coolkeeran (purple wax) has dulse seaweed added. All are made for a full ten months of the year from local pasteurised Holstein cows' milk and vegetarian rennet. The cheddar is full fat and is cooked and pressed in the traditional manner. The wax rind should be removed before eating. The cheese, especially the mature, has an open texture with a strong traditional cheddary cheese bite.

Cléire Goats (Gabhair Chléire)

By any standards, Ed Harper has had an extraordinary life. Born in Lancashire, England, he got his first goat at age seven, enabling him to have a glass of goats' milk each day. At the age of sixteen, while at boarding school, he met a lady who kept goats. He arranged to go there at the weekends to look after the animals and so his lifelong partnership with goats began. Later he attended the University of York, where he kept a billy goat. He completed his Certificate of Education and began to teach. Later, while in Cork for his honeymoon, he travelled to Clear Island, off Baltimore, arguably one of the remotest places in Ireland. When the boat's engine broke down he ended up spending ten days on the island. Later, in nearby Skibbereen, he saw an advertisement for a house on the island, with 27 acres. With no kids and no mortgage, he bought the house in the winter of 1976. It wasn't long before Ed was keeping British Alpine goats and making cheese. For many years he made a rich goats' cheese, somewhat resembling Coulommiers and called Cáis Chléire (Clear Island Cheese). Today, with the help of WWOOFers,[11] Ed continues to make cheese, but he no longer makes Cáis Chléire and now makes very limited quantities of goats' garlic cottage cheese, which he sells to tourists and which can be frozen. If you are lucky, in summertime Ed might sell you some goat ice cream. Ed is also an accomplished singer of English and Irish folk songs, so you might pick up one of his CDs[12] while in the area.

Ed also runs goat husbandry courses and can tailor a course to your needs. A trip to Clear Island is a journey that will never be forgotten. If you are in the west Cork area, make the trip, weather permitting, and maybe call ahead if you intend to visit Ed and his fifteen goats.[13]

Running a goat farm and cheesemaking dairy on 27 acres of rocky land on the side of a hill sweeping down to the sea on a remote island off the coast of Ireland would be a challenge for anyone. Ed's achievements are so much more impressive considering that he is totally blind.

CLEIRE
GOATS
FARM SHOP

Ed Harper and Izzy

Cléire Goats (Gabhair Chléire)	
Proprietor:	Ed Harper
Address:	Cape Clear Island, Skibbereen, Co. Cork
Web:	www.emara.com/goats www.oilean-chleire.ie/english/goats.htm
Email:	goat@iol.ie
Phone:	+353 (0)28 39126
Cheese made:	Cléire Goats Cottage Cheese
Company size:	Small
Availability:	Local
Other products:	Goats' ice cream

Cléire Goats Cottage Cheese		
Milk		
Style	Fresh, soft	
Raw/pasteurised	Raw	
Rennet	Vegetarian	
Organic	No	
Reminiscent of	Cottage cheese	
Maturation	None	
Size	100 g tubs	
Availability	Local	
Made in	Cork	

Cléire Goats Cottage Cheese

This is a soft white rindless cottage cheese made from unpasteurised British Alpine goats' milk, with vinegar as coagulant. The cheese is cooked and pressed somewhat through hanging. Made by Ed Harper in small quantities in spring and summer, it is available all year, as it can be frozen. The only additives to the goats' milk are vinegar, salt and plenty of garlic. The rind is natural and the pate is white. The cheese is available only from Ed.

Ed Harper's goats on Clear Island

Clonmore Cheese

The Golden Vale is arguably Ireland's, and perhaps the world's, richest dairy land. This rich pasture blankets portions of three counties – south Limerick, south Tipperary and north Cork – and stretches to Tom and Lena Biggane's dairy farm near Charleville in north Cork. Tom has been farming here all his life. A long-time dairy cattle farmer, he diversified into goats in 1994 and started supplying goats' milk to other cheesemakers. When a local Dutch cheesemaking client closed his business, Tom bought his equipment. He took a number of courses in cheesemaking, attending the Teagasc Dairy Products Research Centre in Moorepark, Fermoy, County Cork, and received support from the LEADER programme and Ballyhoura Development.

Tom embarked on cheesemaking as a means of generating more income, producing the first Clonmore Cheese in 2001 from the pasteurised milk of his own herd of 100 free-range goats. In 2009, joined by their son William, the Bigganes began making Shandrum, a cows' cheese made from their own herd.

A Clonmore cheese at Sheridans' HQ

CLONMORE CHEESE	
Proprietors:	Tom and Lena Biggane
Address:	Newtown, Charleville, Co. Cork
Phone:	+353 (0)63 70490
Cheeses made:	Clonmore, Shandrum
Company size:	Medium
Availability:	Local, national

CLONMORE	
Milk	
Style	Hard
Raw/pasteurised	Pasteurised and raw
Rennet	Vegetarian
Organic	No
Reminiscent of	Goat gouda
Maturation	2–12 months
Size	2 kg round
Availability	Local, national
Made in	Cork

Clonmore

Clonmore is a hard gouda-like goats' cheese made with pasteurised milk. The pate is an off-white colour with small holes and the rind is beige. The flavour is mild, milky, smooth and slightly nutty with a sweet goat aftertaste. With age, the flavour becomes more intense and robust. Some raw-milk Clonmore is available. The cheese is made seasonally, when the goats are out grazing. Clonmore, from the Irish *cluain mór* ('big field'), is named after the locality in which it is made.

SHANDRUM	
Milk	
Style	Semi-hard
Raw/pasteurised	Pasteurised
Rennet	Vegetarian
Organic	No
Reminiscent of	Gouda
Maturation	4–5 months
Size	2–2.5 kg round
Availability	Local, national
Made in	Cork

Shandrum

Shandrum is a delicately flavoured cows' milk cheese made, since 2009, by Tom Biggane from the milk of his own cattle. Like Clonmore, it is produced seasonally. The pate is an ivory colour. The distinctive black plastic-wax rind can be discarded. The flavour is pleasantly intense, with a unique but not disagreeable tang. With age, the flavour gets even richer. The texture is quite soft, as most of the cheese is released at a young age. There are some holes. The name is from the local region and from the Irish *seandrom* ('the old hill ridge').

Coolattin

Since 2004, Tom Burgess has been making Coolattin Cheddar by hand on his farm on the Carlow/Wicklow border, forming part of the old Coolattin estate. The cheese is made from raw morning milk from Tom's own 100-strong herd of Friesian and Jersey cows, and only in the summer months. Despite this seasonality, the fact that cheddars can be aged for long periods permits Tom to have stock to sell all year round.

The cows feed on clover-rich grass. Like many Irish cheesemakers, Tom got into cheesemaking as a means of adding value to a portion of his high-quality milk. He benefited from funding under the European LEADER project and has received advice from an English cheddar expert. The result is a full-flavoured sweet cheddar.

Tom had known Elizabeth Bradley of nearby Carlow Cheese since their college days, when Tom had studied for a B.Ag. degree. Both embarked on their cheesemaking journey at about the same time, sharing knowledge and information and providing mutual support.

Coolattin Cheddar is available locally in south Wicklow and Carlow at a number of farmers' markets – in Carlow, Kildavin and in Farmleigh estate in Dublin's Phoenix Park. It is also available in a number of retail outlets, including the Avoca chain, and can be found on the cheese platter of a number of local restaurants.

COOLATTIN	
Proprietor:	Tom Burgess
Address:	Knockeen House, Knockeen, Coolkenno, Shillelagh, Co. Wicklow
Web:	www.coolattincheddar.com
Email:	tofiburgess@eircom.net
Phone:	+353 (0)86 389 4482
Cheese made:	Coolattin Cheddar
Company size:	Small
Availability:	Local, some national

Awards

| 2010 | British Cheese Awards | Bronze | Coolattin Cheddar |

COOLATTIN

Milk	
Style	Hard
Raw/pasteurised	Raw
Rennet	Traditional
Organic	No
Reminiscent of	Sweet cheddar
Maturation	1–3 years
Size	12–15 kg truckle
Availability	Local, some national
Made in	Wicklow

Coolattin Cheddar

Coolattin is a full-flavoured sweet cheddar sealed in a distinctive bright red plastic wax. The cheese is made during the summer using raw milk from Tom Burgess's own herd of Friesian and Jersey cows.

The still-warm raw morning milk is pumped immediately from the milking parlour to the cheese dairy. Cheddar cheese making is a complex, labour-intensive process. With starter and traditional rennet added, the curd is cut, scalded, drained and pitched. Then it must be cut and re-cut into tiny pellets, then milled, salted and mixed by hand. The curd is packed into 40-lb moulds and pressed for two days in a pneumatic press under its own weight. It then matures for over a year at 10°C. The taste is of sweet cheddar; it is somewhat nutty, with an aroma of fruit.

As a cheddar, Coolattin is a good multipurpose cheese. It melts and grills well, can be grated onto pasta and is great in sandwiches with chutney.

Coolattin is named after the old Fitzwilliam Coolattin estate (from the Irish *cúil aiteann*, 'the corner of the furze'), an apt description of the beautiful countryside.

Red Waxed Coolatin Cheddar truckles maturing

Coolea Farmhouse Cheese (Cáis Cúil Aodha)

Dicky Willems inherited his cheesemaking business from his parents, Dick and Helene. They had started to make cheese in 1979, initially as something of a hobby, but the quality of the cheese shone through and soon they had a small business going. Dicky joined the crew in 1991 and by 1993 was the main cheesemaker. When Dick and Helene retired in 1999, Dicky's wife Sinéad joined him and they continue to make their highly successful gouda-like cheese. Though they started out using raw milk from their own cows, they now pasteurise the milk sourced from neighbours' Holstein/Friesian cattle. Made with traditional rennet from a very old Dutch gouda recipe, Coolea is a full-cream pasteurised cheese. Recently the Willems added Coolea Matured cheese to the range. The cheese is covered with a distinctive yellow plastic wax. Production is seasonal, but the cheese is available all year. Visits are possible, but strictly by prior appointment.

Coolea, pronounced 'coo-lay', is named after the local village (*Cúil Aodha*, 'Aodh's Corner') in the beautiful Gaeltacht region of Muskerry in County Cork, high in the Derrynasaggart Mountains.

COOLEA FARMHOUSE CHEESE	
Proprietors:	Dicky and Sinéad Willems
Address:	Milleens, Coolea, Macroom, Co. Cork
Web:	www.cooleacheese.com
Email:	info@cooleacheese.com
Phone:	+353 (0)26 45204
Cheeses made:	Coolea, Coolea Matured
Company size:	Large
Availability:	Local, national, international
Recipe:	See p. 330

Dicky Willems amidst maturing Cooleas

Awards

2010	British Cheese Awards	Best Irish Cheese	Vintage Coolea
2010	British Cheese Awards	Best Modern British Cheese	Vintage Coolea

COOLEA AND COOLEA MATURED		
Milk		
Style	Semi-hard to hard	
Raw/pasteurised	Pasteurised	
Rennet	Traditional	
Organic	No	
Reminiscent of	Gouda	
Maturation	2–18 months Matured 12–24+ months	Coolea
Size	9.2 kg wheel	
Availability	Local, national, international	
Fat	38%, 50–55% fat in dry matter	Mature Coolea
Varieties	Matured Coolea	
Made in	Cork	

Coolea and Coolea Matured

These are gouda-like cheeses made from full-cream pasteurised cows' milk with traditional rennet. Coolea Matured is produced in the same way but is matured from between twelve to twenty-four months and can age for up to thirty-six months to order. The cheese is cooked and pressed. The texture is pliable when young, crumbly when older and showing a few holes.

The young cheese has a mild yet distinctive pleasant flavour, which matures with age. Matured cheeses take on a somewhat sweet and savoury flavour, the sweet tasting somewhat of toffee, caramel and butterscotch. Very mature Coolea begins to take on a

Cooleeney

Parmesan-like flavour and texture. The aroma is milky when young and sweet when older. Breda and Jim Maher, now with the help of their son Pat, have been making and selling artisanal cheese on their farm near Thurles, County Tipperary, since 1986. The rich, peaty Tipperary pasture is among the best in the world and ideal for producing artisanal cheeses. The purpose-built dairy sits beside the impressive farmhouse, built in 1760, where Jim grew up and which, together with the farm, he inherited from his father Patrick in 1978. Patrick Senior had been master of the house and dairy farm since 1930, having in turn inherited the house from his uncle Richard Maher, who had bought the farm in 1893. Cooleeney thus has a rich history of dairying, gaining its first award for top-quality milk in 1905. The line continues, as Jim has now passed the farm on to Pat Junior.

As with many Irish cheesemakers, the introduction of European milk quotas in 1984 left the Maher family looking to add value to their milk and maximise the income from it. Breda, who already had a degree in hotel management, took a course in cheesemaking in University College, Cork. She also took instruction from Ryefield Farm in Cavan, which at that time was making Boilíe cheese (now made by Fivemiletown). The first stage of the cheese plant was completed in 1989. In 1999 the Dublin-based Dúnbarra cheese company was purchased, which added sales channels to Cooleeney. Goats' cheeses were introduced in 2000, initially with imported goats' milk. Nowadays the goats' milk is sourced locally.

Since September 1986, when Cooleeney was first produced, the Mahers have extended their range and now offer eight handmade artisanal cheeses: Chulchoill, Cooleeney, Darú, Dúnbarra range, Gleann Óir, Gortnamona, Maighean and Tipperary

Breda Maher

Brie. The cheeses are made year round from the milk of their own closed herd of pedigree British Friesian cows and locally sourced goats' milk.

With Ireland's modern road system, Tipperary is not such a long way away any more and Breda is successfully exporting her cheese to the UK, Europe and the US. In Ireland, most of the cheeses are available nationwide and can be found in many of the main grocery and convenience chains. Breda is also using her sales channels to provide a wholesale export service for other Irish farmhouse cheeses.

COOLEENEY FARMHOUSE CHEESE	
Proprietors:	Breda and Pat Maher
Address:	Cooleeney, Moyne, Thurles, Co. Tipperary
Web:	www.cooleeney.com
Facebook:	Cooleeney-Cheeses
Email:	info@cooleeney.com
Phone:	+353 (0)504 45112
Cheeses made:	Chulchoill, Cooleeney, Darú, Dúnbarra, Gleann Óir, Gortnamona, Maighean Tipperary Brie
Company size:	Large
Availability:	Local, national, international

Awards

2010	World Cheese Awards	Silver (under Traditional Cheese Co. label) Cooleeney		
	World Cheese Awards	Silver	Gortnamona	
	Great Taste Awards	2 stars	Gleann Óir	
	Great Taste Awards	3 stars	Tipperary Brie	
	Great Taste Awards	1 star	(Traditional Cheese Co. label)	Cooleeney
	Great Taste Awards	2 stars	(Traditional Cheese Co. label)	Gortnamona
2009	Great Taste Awards	1 star	(Traditional Cheese Co. label)	Cooleeney
	Great Taste Awards	2 stars	(Traditional Cheese Co. label)	Gortnamona
2008	Great Taste Awards	1 star	Cooleeney Unpasteurised	

CHULCHOILL	
Milk	
Style	Soft
Raw/pasteurised	Pasteurised
Rennet	Vegetarian
Organic	No
Reminiscent of	Chèvre
Maturation	Shelf life 12 weeks
Size	1 kg log
Availability	Local, national, international
Made in	Tipperary

Chulchoill

Chulchoill is a handmade soft goats' milk cheese in the form of a log. The milk is pasteurised and the rennet is vegetarian. The flavour is fresh and goaty, with a hint of almond. The texture is creamy round the edge, somewhat chalky in the centre in the young cheese and creamier with age. The pate is a creamy white colour and the rind is natural and very edible. The strong-flavoured mature Chulchoill yellows somewhat with age and is worth seeking out. The cheese is excellent on a cheeseboard or as the starring role in a warm goats' cheese salad. The name is derived from the local village of Chulchoill (Cullahill in English, meaning 'the back of the wood').

COOLEENEY		
Milk		
Style	Soft-ripened, white-mould	
Raw/pasteurised	Raw, pasteurised	
Rennet	Vegetarian	
Organic	No	
Reminiscent of	Camembert	
Maturation	8–12 weeks shelf life	
Size	200 g, 1.7 kg wheel	
Availability	Local, national, international	
Made in	Tipperary	

Cooleeney

Cooleeney is a soft-ripened white-mould cows' milk cheese in a camembert style from the milk of the Mahers' own Friesian herd. Both pasteurised and unpasteurised versions are available, made with vegetarian rennet.

The flavour is rich with hints of oak and mushroom and increases in intensity with age, as the texture becomes less chalky and more liquid. The pate adopts more of an ivory colour with age. The cheese matures for a minimum of eight weeks. A new product, Baking Cooleeney, has been introduced for the Christmas market.

Cooleeney ready to be eaten

Darú	
Milk	
Style	Semi-hard
Raw/pasteurised	Pasteurised
Rennet	Vegetarian
Organic	No
Reminiscent of	Wensleydale, cheddar
Maturation	6–9 months
Size	350 g, 2.85 kg wheel
Availability	Local, national, international
Fat	23–25%
Made in	Tipperary

Darú

Darú is semi-hard cows' milk cheese with a cheddar-like flavour and hints of lemon, earth, flowers and herbs. The mottled rind is natural. The pate has a distinct cream colour. Made with microbial vegetarian rennet, the crumbly texture is somewhat reminiscent of Wensleydale. *Darú* is the Irish name for the local village of Durrow, County Tipperary.

DÚNBARRA

Milk	
Style	Soft, white-mould
Raw/pasteurised	Pasteurised
Rennet	Vegetarian
Organic	No
Reminiscent of	Flavoured brie
Maturation	8–12 weeks shelf life
Size	180 g, 1.7 kg wheel
Availability	Local, national, international
Varieties	Plain; Pepper & Poppy Seed; Garlic & Dill
Made in	Tipperary

Dúnbarra

Originally a cheese made in Dublin and regarded as Dublin's only artisanal cheese, Dúnbarra is now part of the Cooleeney range. This is a soft-ripened white-mould cows' milk cheese, available in wheels, with a distinctive Celtic swirl pattern. The milk is pasteurised and the rennet is vegetarian. A range of flavours are available, including plain, Pepper & Poppy Seed and Garlic & Dill.

GLEANN ÓIR	
Milk	
Style	Semi-hard
Raw/pasteurised	Pasteurised
Rennet	Vegetarian
Organic	No
Reminiscent of	Goat Wensleydale
Maturation	Shelf life 6–9 months
Size	350 g, 2.85 kg wheel
Availability	Local, national, international
Fat	23–25%
Made in	Tipperary

Gleann Óir

Gleann Óir is a semi-hard goats' milk cheese with a nutty yet slightly sweet flavour and natural rind. The texture is somewhat crumbly and the cheese is handmade in a similar fashion to Darú but with goats' milk. *Gleann Óir* is the Irish for 'golden glen' or 'golden vale', referring to the Golden Vale region of Tipperary and Munster, one of the greenest dairy pastures in the world.

GORTNAMONA		
Milk		
Style	Soft-ripened, white-mould	
Raw/pasteurised	Pasteurised	
Rennet	Vegetarian	
Organic	No	
Reminiscent of	Goat brie	
Maturation	8–12 weeks shelf life	
Size	190 g, 1.7 kg wheel	
Availability	Local, national, international	
Made in	Tipperary	

Gortnamona

As a soft-ripened white-mould cheese, Gortnamona is made in a similar style to Cooleeney but with pasteurised goats' milk and vegetarian rennet. The goats' milk is sourced locally to Cooleeney farm. The taste is distinctively 'goaty' yet remains delicate and buttery. The texture is soft and creamy. When young, the centre can be chalky with a mild taste, reminiscent of a goaty brie. The mature variety is rich and creamy with a stronger taste.

MAIGHEAN	
Milk	
Style	Soft, white-mould
Raw/pasteurised	Raw
Rennet	Vegetarian
Organic	No
Reminiscent of	Camembert
Maturation	Best at 10 weeks
Size	200 g, 1.7 kg wheel
Availability	Local, some national, international
Made in	Tipperary

Maighean

Maighean is a soft artisanal cheese made from raw cows' milk and vegetarian rennet. The pate is particularly creamy and the taste is strong when mature. The raw milk from the grass-fed Friesian cows on the edge of the Golden Vale brings a depth of flavour to the cheese. Maighean is great as a snack, alone or with a biscuit or bread. Maighean (pronounced 'moyne') takes its name from the Irish name of the local village of Moyne, County Tipperary.

TIPPERARY BRIE

Milk	
Style	Soft-ripened, white-mould
Raw/pasteurised	Pasteurised
Rennet	Vegetarian
Organic	No
Reminiscent of	Brie
Maturation	12 weeks shelf life
Size	200 g, 1.7 kg, 3 kg
Availability	Local, national, international
Fat	52% fat in dry matter
Made in	Tipperary

Tipperary Brie

Tipperary Brie is a pasteurised cows' milk brie with a rich buttery flavour and creamy texture, made with vegetarian rennet. The pate is a rich ivory-cream colour and the rind shows a classic, bloomy, edible white mould.

Corleggy Cheese

The Cavan village of Belturbet abuts the border between Northern Ireland and the Republic of Ireland and on the nearby tranquil waters of the River Erne, tourists cruise in bucolic bliss between north and south and back.

A teacher by training, Silke Cropp came to Ireland in 1980. Today she lives in a quaint but remote cottage just outside Belturbet, where she makes her cheese. Soon after arriving, Silke found herself teaching in a secondary school in County Cavan, where she remained for eighteen years. Silke had a goat that provided daily milk for her children. The goat was a good producer and, finding that she had surplus milk, Silke experimented with making cheese. Soon, with the help of some books, she was making a small amount of goats' cheese every day for her own use. When some French tourists bought all the cheese she had, she began to think about making a business. Silke expanded to five goats and sold some cheese locally. With the financial support of a friend, she built a dairy and shed for the goats. Soon she was milking 120 goats, selling cheese in Dublin and establishing her reputation. Later she decided to sell her goats to a friend and buy back the milk. The goats are of mixed breed: Saanen, British Alpine and some Toggenburg and Nubian. Silke also started buying in cows' milk and started making Drumlin cheese to complement the Corleggy goats' cheese. By 1994 she had given up teaching and was producing cheese full time. By 2005 she was taking sheep's milk from a farmer near Enniskillen, from which she makes Creeny sheep's cheese.

Silke Cropp

Occasionally, in the summer months, Silke also makes Quivvy soft cheese from raw goats' milk, preserved in oil, with edible flowers, fresh herbs and peppercorns.

Silke makes all her cheeses by hand from raw milk. The cow, goat and sheep herds are all within ten to twenty minutes of her dairy. When the animals are milked in the morning, Silke immediately starts making cheese from the still-warm raw milk. Raw-milk cheese production is subject to more regulation than that of pasteurised milk, but Silke believes the end product is of a higher quality.

The cheese can be found at farmers' markets around Ireland and some speciality food shops. Corleggy cheeses can also be found in restaurants in Dublin and locally in Cavan. Occasionally the cheeses can be found in markets in France and Germany.

Silke also runs an annual summer cheesemaking school. Contact her for details.

Idyllic cheesemaking in rural Cavan

CORLEGGY CHEESE	
Proprietor:	Silke Cropp
Address:	Corleggy, Belturbet, Co. Cavan
Web:	http://corleggycheeses.bigcartel.com
Facebook:	Corleggy-Cheese
Email:	corleggy@eircom.net
Phone:	+353 (0) 49 952 2930
Cheeses made:	Corleggy, Creeny, Drumlin, Quivvy (sometimes)
Company size:	Medium
Availability:	Local, national

Awards

2010	World Cheese Awards	Silver	Creeny
2009	World Cheese Awards	Silver	Creeny
	World Cheese Awards	Silver	Corleggy
	World Cheese Awards	Gold	Drumlin
	Great Taste Awards	2 stars	Creeny

Corleggy, wrapped and ready for eating

CORLEGGY	
Milk	
Style	Hard
Raw/pasteurised	Raw
Rennet	Vegetarian
Organic	No
Maturation	3–6 months
Size	450 g, 1 kg
Availability	Local, national
Varieties	Smoked
Made in	Cavan

Corleggy

Corleggy is a hard goats' cheese in the shape of a small truckle. It is handmade with raw morning milk and vegetarian rennet. The light brown-yellow natural rind contrasts with the very white pate. The rind is edible and something of a delicacy. Corleggy's flavour is smooth and clean and definitely goaty. The mature cheese is decidedly nutty with a firm but not quite crumbly texture. The cheese is produced all year, with reduced production in winter. The cheese is named after the local Cavan townland, Corleggy, possibly from the Irish *cor lagach*, 'hill of hollows'.

CREENY	
Milk	
Style	Hard
Raw/pasteurised	Raw
Rennet	Vegetarian
Organic	No
Reminiscent of	Manchego, Pecorino
Maturation	3–18 month
Size	450 g, 1 kg
Availability	Local, national
Varieties	Smoked
Made in	Cavan

Creeny

Creeny is a hard ewes' cheese, handmade from raw morning milk with vegetarian rennet. The curd is cooked and pressed, resulting in a somewhat elastic texture. The mature cheeses are drier and very hard, with a rich flavour. The aroma is clean and faintly sheepy. The flavour is mild when young, getting sharper with age, with a distinctive sheep's cheese bite. The pate is ivory coloured and the edible full-flavoured rind is a natural yellow-brown. The little that is smoked is worth seeking out. Creeny is named after the hill beside the Corleggy dairy.

DRUMLIN		
Milk		
Style	Hard	
Raw/pasteurised	Raw	
Rennet	Vegetarian	
Organic	No	
Maturation	2–12 months	
Size	450 g, 1 kg	
Availability	Local, some national	
Varieties	Plain; Green Peppercorn; Garlic; Cumin; Beechwood Smoked	
Made in	Cavan	

Drumlin

Drumlin is a hard cows' milk cheese, handmade from raw morning milk and vegetarian rennet. The curd is cooked and pressed and the resulting texture is hard but elastic. The beige-yellow rind is natural and edible and full of flavour. The cheese is produced all year, with reduced production in winter. Varieties include plain, Green Peppercorn, Garlic, Cumin and Smoked. Lovers of smoked cheese should seek out the smoked variety. This is a real smoked cheese, beechwood-smoked by Frank Hederman at Belvelly Smoke House in Cork (www.frankhederman.com). The smoked cheese looks and indeed tastes somewhat like a piece of roast meat. Vegetarians looking for a meat substitute snack, take note. This is a delicacy to be sought out. The cheese is named after the drumlins that dot the north Cavan countryside.

Beechwood-smoked Drumlin

Cratloe Hills Sheep's Cheese

Seán and Deirdre Fitzgerald have been making sheep's cheese on their farm in the townland of Cratloe, near Shannon in County Clare, since 1988. Seán inherited the farm in the 1970s. He saw a niche in the Irish market and carried out a feasibility study in 1986. The positive results led to the production of the first commercial sheep's cheese in Ireland. Friesland sheep were imported in 1987 and development of the cheese started in 1988 as part of the Shannon Development initiative. Seán built his own cheese dairy with financial assistance from the LEADER fund. The cheese has been through a number of evolutionary steps, as Seán believes in listening to feedback from his customers. The result of this wealth of experience is a specialised cheese crafted to the tastes of his customers.

The cheese is available in a number of local regional outlets and in other outlets throughout Ireland, through Horgan's distributors. Some can be found in the UK. Tourist visits to the working farm are not accommodated.

CRATLOE HILLS SHEEP'S CHEESE	
Proprietors:	Seán and Deirdre Fitzgerald
Address:	Brickhill House, Cratloe, Co. Clare
Email:	cratloehillscheese@eircom.net
Phone:	+353 (0)61 357185
Cheeses made:	Cratloe Hills Gold Mild, Cratloe Hills Gold Mature
Company size:	Medium
Availability:	Local, national, international

CRATLOE HILLS GOLD	
Milk	
Style	Semi-hard
Raw/pasteurised	Pasteurised
Rennet	Vegetarian
Organic	No
Reminiscent of	Manchego
Maturation	Mild 3 months, Mature 8–9 months
Size	100 g, 125 g, 150 g, 175 g, 200 g, 220 g, 450 g, 2.5 kg
Availability	Local, national, international
Varieties	Mature
Made in	Clare

Cratloe Hills Gold

Cratloe Hills is a handmade sheep's cheese available in mild and mature varieties. Made only in the summer months and using traditional methods, this is a speciality cheese made with pasteurised milk and vegetarian rennet. The curd is cooked and pressed and the cheese is then brined and covered in yellow plastic wax (discard before eating). The pate is ivory-white and the texture is semi-hard and dense. The mild cheese has a unique yet subtle flavour. The mature cheese has a distinctive yet not overpowering sheep's milk taste, with an enjoyable aftertaste.

The cheese is named after the local townland of Cratloe in County Clare, from the Irish *An Chreatlach*, meaning either 'the place of willow trees' or perhaps *Croit-shliabh*, meaning 'hump-backed hill', referring to the nearby Woodcock Hill.

Looking like freshly baked buns, some of these Cratloe Hills cheeses are just starting the maturation process

Derreenaclaurig Farmhouse Cheese

Harry van der Zanden has been making his gouda-like cheese from raw milk since 1991. All the cheese is made from Harry's own herd of Jersey cows in this remote corner of the Iveragh Peninsula at Derreenaclaurig, just east of Sneem. Harry also sells a range of vegetables.

Outlets: *The van der Zanden farm; shops in Sneem; markets in south Kerry.*

DERREENACLAURIG FARMHOUSE CHEESE	
Proprietor:	Harry van der Zanden
Address:	Derreenaclaurig, Sneem, Co. Kerry
Web:	www.irishcheese.ie/members/ derreenaclaurig.html
Phone:	+353 (0)64 664 5330
Cheeses made:	Derreenaclaurig
Company size:	Small
Availability:	Local

Derreenaclaurig	
Milk	
Style	Hard
Raw/pasteurised	Raw
Rennet	Traditional
Organic	No
Reminiscent of	Gouda
Maturation	At least 6 weeks (mature 10 months)
Size	2.5–3 kg wheels
Availability	Local
Varieties	Plain; Mature; Garlic; Cumin
Made in	Kerry

Derreenaclaurig

This is a gouda-like cheese, made from the raw milk of the van der Zandens' own herd of Jersey cows, using traditional rennet. The cheese is pressed and not cooked and has a natural yellow rind, washed in vinegar. As well as plain, the cheese is available matured or with garlic or cumin.

The cheese is named after the local townland, Derreenaclaurig (from the Irish *Doirín an Chláraigh,* 'little oak wood of De Clare') .

Desmond and Gabriel Cheese

For many years Bill Hogan and Seán Ferry have been making their famous Desmond and Gabriel cheeses in the little village of Schull, on the Mizen peninsula, in farthest west Cork. As of early 2011, the cheesemaking has been halted due to circumstances including Bill's poor health, but Bill is hoping to restart, albeit on a small scale, within a year or two with local farmers in the Schull area.

Desmond and Gabriel are hard cheeses, made from raw cows' milk, in the Swiss thermophilic style. To you and me, this means that the bacterial starters used are not initially killed by the high temperatures used in the cheesemaking. However, not even the thermophilic starter culture can survive the later high scald temperature. Appenzeller, Emmental, Gruyère and Parmesan are other thermophilic cheeses. The cheeses are made only from summer milk, in large copper vats, and are matured for at least ten months, but often for several years. Some customers prefer cheese that has matured for two to three years. Both can be used in a similar way to Parmesan and are favoured by Irish restaurateurs 'in the know'. They can be eaten as table cheeses, but Gabriel is extra hard.

Bill Hogan started life in New York. When he came to Ireland in the late 1970s he already had a wealth of life experience behind him, having worked with Dr Martin Luther

Bill Hogan with his cheeses

King in the civil rights movement in the 1960s and later moving to Costa Rica, where he met a Swiss cheesemaker, Josef Dubach. He was inspired to make cheese by a childhood visit to a Canadian cheddar factory and by a book written by Gandhi, which was given to him by King. Bill learned the craft of thermophilic cheesemaking from Josef Dubach and later, while spending some time in Switzerland, from Josef Enz. Thermophilic cheesemaking dates back to at least the Bronze Age and may have developed in the eastern Mediterranean or indeed Ireland. Ironically, there is some evidence that Irish monks helped revive thermophilic cheesemaking in what is now Switzerland, after the Dark Ages, under the guidance of St Gall (c. 550 – c. 646).

With the help of Dubach, Bill started his first cheese operation in County Donegal. Seán, a builder's son from Donegal, had been making cheese since the age of seventeen. When they returned from Switzerland, they set up their cheese manufacturing business in west Cork.

Bill and Seán had a legal dispute with the Irish Department of Agriculture and the Food Safety Authority about the safety of their raw-milk cheeses, which culminated in 2005. Their cheesemaking was halted and their 2002 cheese production put under several detention orders, without compensation, due to a bovine TB scare. Bill, along with other cheese experts, believed that mature thermophilic cheeses, whether made from pasteurised or raw milk, do not support bacteria, including pathogens. After five court cases, where detention orders were appealed, Bill and Seán won their appeal. With their position vindicated, they returned to cheesemaking with a clean bill of health.

DESMOND AND GABRIEL CHEESE	
Proprietors:	Bill Hogan and Seán Ferry
Address:	Dereenatra, Schull, Co. Cork
Phone:	+353 (0)28 28593
Cheeses made:	Desmond, Gabriel
Company size:	Medium
Availability:	Local, national
Recipe:	See p. 317 and p. 338

DESMOND	
Milk	
Style	Hard, thermophilic
Raw/pasteurised	Raw
Rennet	Vegetarian
Organic	No
Reminiscent of	Parmesan, Pecorino
Maturation	10 months – 4 years
Size	6–36 kg wheel
Availability	Local, national
Fat	30%
Made in	Cork

Desmond

Desmond is a hard cheese made in the thermophilic style. The cheese is made from raw cows' milk with vegetarian rennet during the summer months. The milk is scalded in processing and the cheese is pressed. The rind is thick, hard and bacterial-smeared. The dense pate shows a golden-yellow colour. The taste is piquant and somewhat spicy, with a rich, lingering, floral aftertaste. Desmond is somewhat reminiscent of Parmesan cheese, with a complex flavour profile, being handmade with care. It is used in cooking and fondues and is favoured by many fine dining restaurants across Ireland. The cheese is aged for at least ten months, but cheeses aged for a specific period can be ordered on request. Desmond is named after the ancient eponymous Munster region. Desmond can be found in the best cheese shops and restaurants in Ireland.

Gabriel	
Milk	🐄
Style	Very hard, thermophilic
Raw/pasteurised	Raw
Rennet	Vegetarian
Organic	No
Reminiscent of	Parmesan, hard Gruyère
Maturation	10 months – 4 years
Size	6–36 kg wheel
Availability	Local, national
Fat	30%
Made in	Cork

Gabriel

Gabriel is a very hard raw cows' milk cheese, named after Mount Gabriel, which overlooks the village of Schull in west Cork. Like Desmond, it is handmade in the Swiss thermophilic style with summer milk. The milk is scalded and the cheese is pressed. The rind is natural and bacterial-smeared and the pate shows an ivory to light gold/honey colour. The aroma is fresh and mild. The texture is pleasantly granular and crystalline and somewhat reminiscent of Parmesan. The flavour is slightly fruity, nutty and salty, with a smooth aftertaste and is milder and sweeter than that of Desmond. Gabriel is used in cooking, for pasta sauces and in fondues. Like Desmond, the cheeses are made only in summer and in huge rounds, perhaps the second largest in Ireland, behind David Tiernan's Glebe Brethan.

Dingle Farmhouse Cheese

Mai and Tomás O'Bruic started making cheese on the Dingle Peninsula in the early 2000s but started to take it seriously only in the last few years of the decade. They make a semi-hard cows' and goats' cheese in the summer months and will be starting with a soft goats' cheese in 2011. The herds of Friesian cows and Saanen goats are their own. They pasteurise the milk and curdle it with vegetarian rennet. Like many Irish goats' cheese makers, the O'Bruics got started with goats when one of their children had asthma and goats' milk was recommended as a remedy. Now they have about fifteen goats and thirty cows. The cheese can be found locally in shops and restaurants and perhaps shortly at the market in Dingle.

DINGLE FARMHOUSE CHEESE	
Proprietors:	Mai & Tomás O'Bruic
Address:	Baile Ghainín Beag, Ballydavid, Tralee, Co. Kerry
Email:	dinglefarmhouse@eircom.net
Phone:	+353 (0)87 648 3018
Cheese made:	Dingle Farmhouse Cheese
Company size:	Small
Availability:	Local

Dingle Peninsula Cheese

Maja Binder has been making cheese on the north coast of the Dingle Peninsula since 1997. Though German by birth, Maja began her enduring interest in cheese in Italy at the age of seventeen, working as a WWOOFer[14] on a goat farm, followed by a couple of years with cows on an organic farm in the German Black Forest. She completed this thorough apprenticeship working as a cheesemaker in the Swiss Alps, where she also completed a cheesemaking course. During this period her mother lived in Ireland and Maja came to visit her every summer. Her lifelong desire for a dairy farm of her own was fulfilled when she settled in Ireland in 1997. She started to make cheese, using neighbours' milk, in an 8-litre pot in her kitchen. She began with a strong Munster-like cheese that she no longer makes and the same semi-hard seaweed cheese she makes today. All her equipment, including her wonderful copper vat, was bought in Switzerland.

Today she makes a number of cheeses: the aforementioned seaweed cheese Dilliskus, the plain and flavoured Kilcummin and Beenoskee, a stone-pressed Swiss-style hard cheese. She also has a new goats' cheese, an Italian mozzarella-style cheese, a cream cheese and a small soft rind-washed cows' cheese called Dingle Truffle Cheese. Her cows' milk is bought in from neighbours and she makes cheese through spring, summer and autumn. Her goats' milk comes from the local hamlet of Camp.

Maja lives with her three children and partner Olivier. Olivier smokes mackerel and other fish in his own oak smoker. In addition to making five different fish dips (or tartars) using Maja's cream cheese, he also finds time to make six different meat pâtés (venison, pork, rabbit, chicken, pigeon and duck liver) and cooks and pickles seaweed.

Maja's cheeses can be found in local markets in north Cork, Kerry and Dublin and a in a number of fine food shops around the country. It can also be found in the La Fromagerie (www.lafromagerie.co.uk) cheese shop in London. If you are in the area and you have time, it is well worth seeking out Maja's dairy and buying a little cheese on site and maybe some of Olivier's artisanal meat products. If you can, it might be nice to phone before visiting. Maja has recently opened her own shop: The Little Cheese Shop, Grey's Lane, Dingle, County Kerry.

DINGLE PENINSULA CHEESE	
Proprietor:	Maja Binder
Address:	Kilcummin Beg, Castlegregory, Tralee, Co. Kerry
Web:	www.irishcheese.ie/members/dingle.html
Email:	majabinder@hotmail.com
Phone:	+353 (0)66 713 9028
Cheeses made:	Beenoskee, Dilliskus, Dingle Cream Cheese, Dingle Goat Cheese, Dingle Truffle Cheese, Kilcummin, Mozzarella
Company size:	Medium
Availability:	Local, national, international

BEENOSKEE	
Milk	
Style	Hard, washed-rind
Raw/pasteurised	Raw
Rennet	Vegetarian
Organic	No
Maturation	6 months
Size	4–6 kg rounds
Availability	Local, some national
Fat	45%
Made in	Kerry

Maja Binder

Beenoskee

Beenoskee has been made since 1997 and is named after the mountain behind the dairy. It is a hard washed-rind cheese made from the raw milk of local Friesian cows with vegetarian rennet. The rind is coppery brown and the pate ivory-yellow. The texture is both creamy and crumbly and there is a sweet and sour and somewhat nutty tang to the flavour. The rind is edible.

Beenoskee (pronounced Bean-osh-kee) is from the Irish *Binn os Gaoith* ('Peak above the Wind'), the largest mountain in the central Dingle range.

DILLISKUS		
Milk		
Style	Semi-hard, washed-rind	
Raw/pasteurised	Raw	
Rennet	Vegetarian	
Organic	No	
Reminiscent of	Tomme de Savoie	
Maturation	4 months	
Size	700 g – 1 kg rounds	
Availability	Local, some national, international	
Fat	45%	
Made in	Kerry	

Dilliskus

This is a semi-hard, washed-rind, raw cows' milk cheese, with dillisk[15] seaweed added. The curd is heated but not pressed. The pate has a pale yellow hue speckled with burgundy-purple dillisk flecks. The flavour is of farmyard animals and vegetables and is pleasantly salty, perhaps thanks to the seaweed. The texture is creamy and the aroma is of white wine, sand and sea. The orange-brown rind is edible and pleasantly textured. The name is a portmanteau of the name of the seaweed used, dillisk, and the discus, because of the shape.

Dingle Cream Cheese	
Milk	
Style	Fresh, soft
Raw/pasteurised	Raw
Rennet	Vegetarian
Organic	No
Reminiscent of	Cream cheese
Maturation	None
Size	Up to 5 kg
Availability	Local, some national
Varieties	Plain; Garlic & Fenugreek; Salt & Pepper
Fat	45%
Made in	Kerry

Dingle Cream Cheese

This rich cream cheese has been made since 1997. It is made from the raw milk of local Friesian cows with vegetarian rennet. The aroma is of sweet cream, the texture is creamy and the flavour is sweet and buttery. Plain, Garlic & Fenugreek and Salt & Pepper varieties are available. The cheese is made from April to October and is sometimes available in Sheridans.

DINGLE GOAT CHEESE	
Milk	
Style	Semi-hard
Raw/pasteurised	Raw
Rennet	Traditional
Organic	No
Reminiscent of	Goats' Munster
Maturation	6 weeks
Size	Round
Availability	Local
Made in	Kerry

Dingle Goat Cheese

This is a new cheese with what can only be described as an aggressive aroma. Like many smelly cheeses, the flavour is more refined than the aroma. Nonetheless, this is strong cheese, tasting of the earth, the goat and the farmyard. The cheese is made from raw goats' milk sourced from the local village of Camp. The pate is an off-white colour and the natural washed rind is a mottled orange-pink-brown colour. The rind is only for the very brave.

Dingle Cream Cheese

DINGLE TRUFFLE CHEESE (PEPPER & GARLIC BALLS)		
Milk		
Style	Hard	
Raw/pasteurised	Raw	
Rennet	Traditional	
Organic	No	
Maturation	2 months	
Size	30 g balls	
Availability	Local	
Fat	45%	
Made in	Kerry	

Dingle Truffle Cheese

Maja Binder commenced production of this cheese in 2010. It is made only during the months of May to September. This is a hard cheese made from the raw milk of local Friesian cows with animal rennet. It starts life as cream cheese. After hardening with age, it is flavoured with garlic, rolled in cracked black pepper and then slightly smoked. It then matures for two months. The result is a little bit of cheesy fire, about the size of a golf ball and looking something like a truffle. It can be eaten as a snack or grated over food. The pate colour is a light creamy brown and the edible peppery 'rind' is brown-black. The outside is hard but gets a little softer and creamier towards the centre. If it is not strong enough for you as it is, you can always let it mature longer! It can be found only locally in north Kerry but is worth seeking out.

KILCUMMIN	
Milk	
Style	Semi-hard
Raw/pasteurised	Raw
Rennet	Vegetarian
Organic	No
Reminiscent of	Tomme de Savoie
Maturation	4 months
Size	700 g – 1 kg, 2.5 kg rounds
Availability	Local, some national, international
Varieties	Plain; Peppercorn; Fenugreek
Fat	45%
Made in	Kerry

Kilcummin

This is a semi-hard raw cows' milk cheese made with vegetarian rennet. The curd is heated but not pressed. The edible washed rind has a sandy-brown colour and the cheese pate itself is ivory to yellow in colour. The texture is creamy and the flavour is gentle, with hints of rich pasture and the aroma of the earth. Kilcummin is also available flavoured with peppercorns or fenugreek.[16] The cheese is named after the townland in which it is made (Irish *Cill Chuimín*, 'Church of St Cummian').

Durrus Farmhouse Cheese

Jeffa Gill has been making cheese since 1979, having left behind a city career in fashion. Now you can get directions at the little post office in Durrus, County Cork, to Jeffa's cheese dairy on the Sheep's Head peninsula. Though not so far away, it does seem to take an age to ascend the little narrowing boreen up the mountain to Jeffa's house and modern dairy. Along with Milleens and Coolea, Durrus led the Irish farmhouse cheese renaissance in the 1970s and quickly established itself as one of the premier modern Irish farmhouse cheeses.

In the early 1980s, Jeffa took some courses and bought some equipment with money from a grant. Production soon outstripped the capacity of her eight Friesian cows and she began to buy in milk from a local producer for year-round cheese production.

The market for Durrus expanded from Ireland to the UK, Europe, Japan and, to a small extent, the US. Jeffa is now producing a young variety, appropriately christened Durrus Óg ('Young Durrus').

Tourist visits are catered for, but you must call ahead. You can taste the cheeses and watch the manufacturing process through a window. You might even pick up a few free-range eggs while you're there.

Jeffa Gill (and Tess)

DURRUS FARMHOUSE CHEESE	
Proprietor:	Jeffa Gill
Address:	Coomkeen, Durrus, West Cork
Web:	www.durruscheese.com
Email:	durruscheese@eircom.net
Phone:	+353 (0)27 61100
Cheeses made:	Durrus, Durrus Mini, Durrus Óg, Dunmanus
Company size:	Medium
Availability:	Local, national, international
Recipe:	See p. 325

Awards

Many awards prior to 2008 are not listed.

2010	British Cheese Awards	Gold	Durrus
2009	SHOP Awards	Gold	Durrus
2008	World Cheese Awards	Silver	Durrus Óg
	World Cheese Awards	Bronze	Durrus

The Durrus range

DURRUS	
Milk	🐄
Style	Semi-soft, surface-ripened, washed-rind
Raw/pasteurised	Raw
Rennet	Traditional
Organic	No
Reminiscent of	Tomme de Savoie Toma, Munster, Reblochon
Maturation	3–5 weeks good for 5 months
Size	360 g, 1.4 kg
Availability	Local, national, international
Varieties	Dunmanus, Durrus Mini
Fat	26% (57% fat in dry matter)
Made in	Cork

Durrus

Durrus is handmade from raw Friesian cows' milk sourced from a single local herd. This hay-coloured cheese has a smooth, creamy texture, a rich, earthy, lingering flavour and an inviting cheesy aroma. The flavour strengthens with age.

The cheeses are made in a copper vat, cooked and pressed under their own weight and matured in curing rooms with carefully controlled temperature and humidity. Durrus is ripened with *Brevibacterium linens* bacteria over a three- to five-week period.

It is an excellent accompaniment to fruit and melts well in cooking. It is not recommended to eat the rind. A normal-sized Durrus weighs in at about 1.4 kg. Durrus Mini cheeses weighing 360 g are now available through many retail outlets. For the adventurous, a new matured Durrus, the Dunmanus, weighing about 3 kg, will come into production in 2011. Durrus is named after the local village.

Durrus Óg	
Milk	
Style	Semi-soft, surface-ripened, washed-rind
Raw/pasteurised	Raw
Rennet	Traditional
Organic	No
Reminiscent of	Tomme de Savoie Toma, Munster, Reblochon
Maturation	2+ weeks
Size	250 g round
Availability	Local, national, international
Fat	26% (57% fat in dry matter)
Made in	Cork

Durrus Óg

Made since 2008, Durrus Óg is an immature version of Durrus, óg being Irish for 'young'. The difference in manufacturing is the shortened length of maturation and the time in the vat. This leads to a creamy, milder-tasting cheese than its older brother, which some people prefer. Like the more mature Durrus, only animal rennet, starter cultures and salt are added. Durrus Óg is surface-salted and ideally eaten between two and three weeks of manufacture.

Durrus cheeses, in various sizes, maturing

Fermoy Natural Cheese Co.

Frank Shinnick, from a farming background near Fermoy, County Cork, met his wife-to-be, Gudrun, in the late 1980s. Gudrun, a chemistry graduate from the University of Kiel on Germany's Baltic coast, had spent time working on an organic farm in Germany and the young couple had it in mind from an early point to make cheese. First, though, they had to learn how to do it, and this came through a six-month stint working for a cheese producer in the Swiss Alps.

Having married and moved to Ireland in the 1990s, they built up a dairy herd. In a climate of falling milk prices, they decided they had to try to extract more value from their milk production. Cheese production was the logical next step.

Copper vats are widely used in the production of great Continental cheeses such as Parmesan, Grana Padano, Gruyère and Comté, and it was one of these that Frank set his sights on. He tracked down a 1,500-litre example in Switzerland and set about importing it. Official scepticism on the use of copper was faced down when they presented research showing that dangerous strains of *E. coli* survived a mere four hours on copper, compared to anything up to thirty-six days on stainless steel.

They commenced their experiments in 1997, resulting in their first cheese, St Gall. Frank estimates that it took about two years of tweaking to perfect the cheese. From the outset, the cheese was sold through local outlets and farmers' markets around the region, with the company launching as a going concern in 2002.

Frank and Gudrun Shinnick

Clockwise from top: St Gall Label, stirring curds in a copper vat, Ballyhooley Blue maturing

All production uses raw milk from their own herd, though cheese production does not account for the entirety of their milk production at present. Frank stresses the overlooked benefit of energy saving arising from the use of raw milk. Pasteurisation requires rapid heating to 71°C and equally rapid cooling of the milk, both of which consume large amounts of energy (milk from the previous night will typically be at a temperature of 10°C). At one point, they investigated the possibility of looking for organic certification, but decided that it would not be cost effective. Having experimented with vegetarian rennets, Frank has fallen back on traditional rennet in the production of his cheeses. He found that the vegetarian rennets lent a metallic note to his hard cheeses.

Ever dynamic and inventive, the Shinnicks have pursued their path and produced a wide range of cheeses – St Brigid, Cáis Dubh, Cáis Rua and, more recently, Hibernia and Emerald. This dynamism attracts young enthusiastic cheesemakers, a succession of whom have worked with them over the years. New cheeses will be tweaked and refined, with careful notes made of each iteration until they are satisfied with it. One thing has not changed since the beginning – Frank estimates that it still takes around two years from inception to perfect a cheese.

Their latest cheeses are a blue to be called Ballyhooly Blue (named for the village near Fermoy where Frank's father grew up); Corkcotta, inspired by ricotta and as a way to avoid the whey from the production of the other cheeses going to waste; and, most recently, a low-fat 'grey cheese' inspired by the very strong Tyrolean Graukäse.

FERMOY NATURAL CHEESE CO.	
Proprietors:	Frank and Gudrun Shinnick
Address:	Strawhall, Fermoy, Co. Cork
Email:	gudrun1@eircom.net
Phone:	+353 (0)25 31310/+353 (0)87 253 3108
Cheeses made:	St Gall, St Brigid, Cáis Dubh, Cáis Rua, Hibernia, Emerald, Ballyhooly Blue, Corkcotta
Company size:	Medium
Availability:	Through farmers' markets; nationally in speciality shops. Some exports to UK, Germany and US
Recipe:	See p. 326, p. 339 and p. 340

St Gall

ST GALL		
Milk		
Style	Semi-hard, thermophilic	
Raw/pasteurised	Raw	
Rennet	Traditional	
Organic	No	
Reminiscent of	Comté	
Maturation	9–12 months	
Size	5 kg wheel	
Availability	Local, national, international (UK)	
Made in	Cork	

St Gall

In the early seventh century the Irish missionary St Gall, accompanied by Columbanus, set out to bring Christianity back to the remains of the recently Hun- and Visigoth-overrun Roman Empire. He founded his monastery near what would become the modern Swiss city of St Gallen. It was also near here, almost fourteen centuries later, that Frank and Gudrun learned their trade and it seemed fitting to borrow the name, though Frank had wanted to call it Hibernia, as the nine- to twelve-month maturation time seemed like a long period of hibernation.

St Gall is a semi-hard Swiss-style thermophilic cheese produced at a temperature of 48°C. The cheese is pressed into 5 kg wheels of about 6 cm thickness and matured for nine to twelve months.

The cheese has a brownish rind with a creamy yellow pate, darkening slightly towards the rind and pocked with small to medium-sized air holes.

On the nose there is a distinct buttery note and on the palate it is deliciously creamy, with an intense nuttiness kicking in as the cheese is moved around the mouth.

It melts very well and is well suited to cooking.

ST BRIGID	
Milk	
Style	Semi-hard, brine-washed
Raw/pasteurised	Raw
Rennet	Traditional
Organic	No
Reminiscent of	Tilsiter
Maturation	6–8 weeks
Size	3 kg square loaf
Availability	Local, national, international (UK)
Varieties	Cumin; Italian Herbs
Made in	Cork

St Brigid

Having probably started out as the important Celtic goddess Brigid, whose feast Imbolc at the start of February heralds the coming of spring, St Brigid in her Christian guise is the patron saint of Irish dairy.

St Brigid the cheese has a very distinctive square loaf shape resembling German Tilsiter. During its maturation period, the cheese is turned daily and brushed with a brine solution that encourages the development of beneficial bacteria on the rind, giving it its orange-red colour. The pate is semi-hard and quite elastic in texture, a buttery yellow in colour and liberally specked with air holes.

In its youth, the cheese is quite mild and as such finds favour with those who are not fond of stronger cheese. Mild it may be, but bland it is not. Mildly creamy, with a slight barnyard note on the nose, the flavour profile is buttery and creamy, and has a subtle complexity, with decent length and a slight saltiness on the palate.

As it ages, the flavour becomes more pronounced, developing vegetal notes without becoming aggressive.

A substantial quantity of the cheese is exported to Scotland, where it is popular.

Selection of St Brigid Cheeses

CÁIS DUBH

Milk	![horse icon]
Style	Semi-hard
Raw/pasteurised	Raw
Rennet	Traditional
Organic	No
Reminiscent of	Gruyère, Comté
Maturation	4 months min.
Size	5 kg wheels
Availability	National
Varieties	Fenugreek; Italian Herbs
Made in	Cork

Cáis Dubh

Cáis Dubh ('Black Cheese') takes its name from the distinctive black wax coating protecting the cheese. Frank tells the story that when the cheese was being developed, he had a conversation with a Japanese food expert. He told him that in Japan, certain types of clear coating, sometimes used on gouda-style cheeses, had question marks over them from a health point of view. Not wanting to risk excluding a potential market, Frank looked for an alternative coating. Killing two birds with one stone, he chose a black coating on the basis that nobody would ever ask, 'Can you eat the rind?'

Some time later he received an enquiry about the new cheese from a potential customer. The customer referred in particular to the 'black-coloured one' and asked what the name was. Put somewhat on the spot, as it had not occurred to him to give the cheese a name until that point, Frank said, 'Oh, that's Cáis Dubh,' and so the name was born.

Under the rind, the pate is a creamy yellow, darkening slightly towards the edge and pocked liberally with small to medium-sized gas holes. There is a slightly gamey nose and the palate has well-balanced acidity, with a salty/sweet taste and a delicate finish.

Cáis Dubh cheeses

Cáis Rua	
Milk	
Style	Soft, washed-rind
Raw/pasteurised	Raw
Rennet	Traditional
Organic	No
Reminiscent of	Reblochon
Maturation	6 weeks – 2 months
Size	2.5 kg wheel, 500 g round
Availability	Local farmers' markets and speciality shops, but very limited
Varieties	Smoked
Made in	Cork

Cáis Rua

Cáis Rua ('Red Cheese'), in homage to Cáis Dubh, takes its name from the colour of the rind. It was developed in 2006 for the Christmas market. In fact, the primary reason it is made only in winter is purely practical rather than technical. It falls into that category of cheese adored by flies, so to make it in the height of summer would effectively involve a hermetically sealed ripening room with airlocks.

The cheeses are made in large flat rounds. The primary size is about 45 cm in diameter and 5 cm thick. In some cases smaller rounds are made by punching a smaller cheese out of the large young round, leaving a ring-shaped cheese. Frank is currently assessing whether the ring-shaped cheese ripens differently to the normal cheese. They are washed-rind cheeses. The rind is red in colour and the pate of the fully mature cheese is soft, becoming runnier the more mature the cheese becomes.

Unfortunately, due to time constraints and the limited availability of the cheese, none was available for tasting.

HIBERNIA		
Milk		
Style	Semi-hard	
Raw/pasteurised	Raw	
Rennet	Traditional	
Organic	No	
Reminiscent of	Mature Gruyère, Laguiole	
Maturation	12 months	
Size	12 kg wheels	
Availability	National, some exports to Germany	
Made in	Cork	

Hibernia

Frank Shinnick finally got to use his Hibernia name on this cheese, which he began developing in 2008. Hibernia is the classical Latin name for the island of Ireland.

Hibernia is a mature cheese, aged for at least twelve months, in the style of the classic French and Swiss alpine cheeses. It is coated in the same black wax as Cáis Dubh (the sample shown in the photos had not been waxed). Beneath the wax, the rind is an orange-brown colour. The pate is creamy yellow, darkening towards the rind, and liberally flecked with air holes.

There is a nuttiness on the nose and on the palate the cheese has an intense attack, with the nuttiness coming through. The aftertaste is long and there is a yeasty bite to it that tingles the palate on the finish.

The cheese is made in quite small quantities at present, so availability is restricted.

EMERALD	
Milk	
Style	Semi-hard
Raw/pasteurised	Raw
Rennet	Traditional
Organic	No
Reminiscent of	Emmental
Maturation	12 months
Size	12 kg wheels
Availability	Local, international – limited regional availability, some to US
Made in	Cork

Emerald

An American client told Frank Shinnick that there was a demand for Emmental, or Swiss-style cheeses with larger holes, so Frank set about developing just that.

The name comes from the distinctive emerald green wax covering the cheese, which is made in large wheels. Under the wax, the rind is an orange-yellow colour. The pate is firm and elastic, creamy yellow in colour, with plenty of large holes distributed throughout.

On the nose the cheese has a nutty aroma. The palate is sweet with an intense nuttiness. The finish shows well-balanced acidity and leaves a slight yeasty tingle on the tongue.

Other Fermoy cheeses

In addition to the main production cheeses already discussed, Frank and Gudrun make several other cheeses and are continually experimenting with other types of cheese. Not all were available to taste or are not yet made in production quantities, but they merit a mention.

Ballyhooly Blue

Ballyhooly Blue is Frank and Gudrun's first foray into making blue cheese. Made from raw cows' milk, it is a creamy blue, and though his first batch was not blue enough, Frank estimated that it would be sufficiently developed to bring to market at about the time this book went to press. Ever the perfectionist, he estimated that it would be about another year before it would be perfect. It is produced in large form similar in size to a Stilton, weighing around 6 kg, but also in a smaller 600 g form. They also intend to offer a smoked version.

Corkcotta

Probably the most significant by-product of cheesemaking, certainly in terms of volume, is whey. When the rennet is added at the start of the process, the milk separates into solid curds and watery whey. The curds are used to make the cheese, leaving a large amount of whey for disposal.

Methods of disposal range from slurry tanks to feeding pigs and research is ongoing to find new uses for it (whey retains around 50 per cent of the nutrients of the original milk).

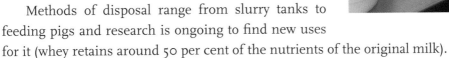

One use, which has been around for millennia, is whey cheese. Ricotta is the best-known example and was referred to by Cato the Elder (234–149 BC). The yield is quite low, considering the amount of whey required to produce it, and involves heating the whey to 90°C to curdle out the remaining protein. This is then put into moulds to drain. The result is a fresh white cheese with a slightly grainy texture and a sweetish taste.

Frank has named this cheese Corkcotta and its intended market is the catering industry (baking, desserts, etc.) rather than consumers.

St Brigid Beag

On visiting, one of the experimental cheeses being developed was a small, square-shaped cheese based on the St Brigid recipe and flavoured with green peppercorns. The rind is reddish and wrinkled and the pate soft in texture and a rich cream in colour, with the peppercorns flecked throughout.

It is somewhat similar to Pont-l'Évêque in appearance and taste (except for the peppercorns). The pate is creamy and sweet on the palate when eaten without the rind and the whole combines to give a pleasantly pungent experience.

While it may never see market, it is worth noting here both as a very fine cheese in its own right and as an indication of the tireless innovation of the Shinnicks.

Fivemiletown Creamery

Fivemiletown Creamery is pushing the boundaries of Northern Irish cheesemaking with a range of high-quality distinctive speciality cheeses. This farmers' co-operative was formed in 1898 and began getting awards for its butter in the early twentieth century. After delivering milk through the rest of the twentieth century, the creamery began making cheddar cheese in 1972. They later expanded into Red Leicester, Double Gloucester and one of the first successful reduced-fat cheddars in Ireland.

Today, Fivemiletown continues to make its successful cheddar range, but now also boasts a range of handmade speciality cheeses: Ballyblue (blue brie), Ballybrie (brie), Ballyoak (smoked brie), Boilíe (cow and goat cream cheese), Cooneen (goats' brie), O'Reillys (goat) and Oakwood (oak-smoked cheddar). The cheese is made all year round. The cows' milk comes from the farmers' own herds of cows grazing the green dairy land of Northern Ireland's Clogher Valley. The goats' milk is sourced from local herds. Boilíe cheese became a product and brand of Fivemiletown after the acquisition of the assets of Ryefield Farm (County Cavan) in 2007. The cream cheese came from a similar earlier acquisition of a Ballycastle-based company. The company also provides curd products to other cheesemakers on the island of Ireland and markets primarily in the Republic of Ireland. The market is expanding in Northern Ireland and the UK and some cheese is exported to the US, France, Denmark and Hong Kong.

In addition to their artisanal cheese range, Fivemiletown makes a range of cheddar cheeses for the retail and wholesale industry. The cheddars are made from pasteurised cows' milk with vegetarian rennet. A number of aged varieties are available: mild, mature, extra mature and low fat. The pate is beige-yellow and the cheddar is usually supplied rindless.

The name 'Fivemiletown' derives from the fact that town is about five Irish miles from each of its nearest neighbouring towns.

FIVEMILETOWN CREAMERY	
Proprietors:	Farmer-owned co-operative
Address:	14 Ballylurgan Rd, Fivemiletown, Co. Tyrone BT75 0RX
Web:	www.fivemiletown.com
Facebook:	Fivemiletown Creamery
Email:	welovecheese@fivemiletown.com
Phone:	+44 (0)28 8952 1209
Cheeses made:	Ballyblue (blue brie), Ballybrie (brie), Ballyoak (smoked brie), Boilíe (cow and goat cream cheese), Cooneen (goats' brie), O'Reilly's (goat) and Oakwood (oak-smoked cheddar)
Company size:	Large
Availability:	Northern Ireland, Republic of Ireland, UK, US, France, Denmark, Sweden, Norway, Hong Kong
Other products:	Block cheddar

Awards

2010	British Cheese Awards	Bronze	O'Reillys Original
	British Cheese Awards	Gold	Goats Boilíe
	World Cheese Awards	Bronze	Ballyoak
	Great Taste Awards	2 stars	Goats Boilíe
	Great Taste Awards	2 stars	Natural Goats Log
	Great Taste Awards	2 stars	Mature & Extra Mature Cheddar
	Great Taste Awards	1 star	Ballybrie Wedge
2009	World Cheese Awards	Silver	O'Reillys Chives
	World Cheese Awards	Bronze	O'Reillys Mustard
	Great Taste Awards	2 stars	O'Reillys Original
	Great Taste Awards	2 stars	Goats Boilíe

	Great Taste Awards	1 star	O'Reillys Mustard
2008	Great Taste Awards	1 star	O'Reillys Mustard
	Great Taste Awards	1 star	O'Reillys Chives
2007	Great Taste Awards	1 star	Ballyoak Smoked

BALLYBLUE

Milk	🐎
Style	Semi-soft, white-mould blue
Raw/pasteurised	Pasteurised
Rennet	Vegetarian
Organic	No
Reminiscent of	Blue brie
Maturation	Up to 10 weeks on shelf
Size	1.7 kg wheel, 142 g wedge, 150 g mini
Availability	Local, national, international
Fat	34.7%
Made in	Tyrone

Ballyblue

One of the first 'blues' developed on the island of Ireland, Ballyblue is a blue-veined brie handmade in the same fashion as Ballybrie. The cheese is made from pasteurised cows' milk from the creamery farmers' own local herds. Cheeses that would otherwise become Ballybrie are pierced with spiked gloves and then seeded with *Penicillium roqueforti*, which grows to produce the distinctive blue-green streaks. The result is a mild buttery brie with the piquant tang of blue running through it.

BALLYBRIE	
Milk	
Style	Semi-soft, white-mould
Raw/pasteurised	Pasteurised
Rennet	Vegetarian
Organic	No .
Reminiscent of	Brie
Maturation	Up to 10 weeks on shelf
Size	1.7 kg wheel, 142 g wedge, 150 g mini
Availability	Local, national, international
Fat	31.1%
Made in	Tyrone

Ballybrie

Ballybrie is a mild brie, handmade from pasteurised cows' milk from the creamery's local herds, with vegetarian rennet. The cheese is available in a number of shapes and sizes, including the typical Fivemiletown hexagon box and wedge. The young cheese is creamy and mild with a rich buttery brie taste and becomes richer in taste and softer with a little ageing. The pate is a rich ivory colour and the snow-white bloomy rind is edible.

BALLYOAK	
Milk	🐎
Style	Semi-soft, white-mould
Raw/pasteurised	Pasteurised
Rennet	Vegetarian
Organic	No
Reminiscent of	Smoked brie
Maturation	Up to 22 days on shelf
Size	1.7 kg wheel, 142 g wedge, 150 g mini
Availability	Local, national, international
Fat	30%
Made in	Tyrone

Ballyoak

Ballyoak is an award-winning soft smoked brie, handmade initially in the same fashion as Ballybrie, with pasteurised milk and vegetarian rennet. Each Ballyoak is slowly smoked in a kiln using sustainably foraged oak wood chips from the local Forest of Caledon. The cheese is light with a smoky, buttery taste. The bloomy white rind is edible. The smoke effect is delicate enough not to overpower the mild brie flavour. Ballyoak may be the only indigenous smoked brie available on the island of Ireland.

Boilie Cheese

BOILÍE GOATS CHEESE AND CHEESE PEARLS	
Milk	
Style	Soft
Raw/pasteurised	Pasteurised
Rennet	Vegetarian
Organic	No
Reminiscent of	Cream cheese
Maturation	Up to 5 months on shelf
Size	Grape-sized pearls in 150 g tubs, 200 g jars, 1 kg 'tugs'
Availability	Local, national, international
Made in	Tyrone

The changing face of Boilíe packaging

Boilíe Goats Cheese and Cheese Pearls

Boilíe (pronounced 'bow-lee') is a handmade cream cheese made from both pasteurised cows' and pasteurised goats' milk. The cheese is marketed in tubs and jars as grape-sized pearls suspended in garlic-infused oil and marinated with herbs and peppercorns. The pearls make an ideal snack or the whole contents, including the oil, can be added to a salad.

A Boilíe-like cheese started out in life in the 1920s in the Brodie family farmhouse in County Cavan and Boilíe was made and marketed by the Brodie family (as Ryefield Farm) until the assets of the company were purchased by Fivemiletown in 2007.

Cooneen	
Milk	
Style	Semi-soft, white-mould
Raw/pasteurised	Pasteurised
Rennet	Vegetarian
Organic	No
Reminiscent of	Goat brie
Maturation	Up to 10 weeks on shelf
Size	1.7 kg wheel, 142 g wedge, 150 g mini
Availability	Local, national, international
Fat	30.2%
Made in	Tyrone

Cooneen

Cooneen is a goats' milk brie made in a similar fashion to Ballybrie. Handmade from pasteurised goats' milk from local farms, the cheese has a mild, buttery yet distinctly goaty flavour. The pate shows an ivory colour and the texture is reminiscent of brie, yet somewhat crumbly when young. The bloomy white rind is edible, with a concentrated flavour. Cooneen is the name of a local townland about three miles from Fivemiletown Creamery.

O'REILLYS		
Milk		
Style	Soft	
Raw/pasteurised	Pasteurised	
Rennet	Vegetarian	
Organic	No	
Reminiscent of	Chèvre	
Maturation	Up to 21 days on shelf	
Size	70 g tub, 1 kg log	
Availability	Local, national, international	
Varieties	Plain; Mustard Seed; Chives	
Made in	Tyrone	

O'Reillys

O'Reillys is a fresh, soft, snow-white goats' cheese with a lemony tang. Made from pasteurised goats' milk, the cheese is ideal for adding to a salad or an omelette. O'Reillys is available in a number of varieties, including plain, rolled in mustard seed or with chives. The cheese is sold in crottin-like portions in 70 g tubs or as a 1 kg log. As with Boilíe, O'Reillys was made and marketed by the Brodie family (as Ryefield Farm) until the assets of the company were purchased by Fivemiletown in 2007.

OAKWOOD	
Milk	
Style	Semi-hard
Raw/pasteurised	Pasteurised
Rennet	Vegetarian
Organic	No
Reminiscent of	Smoked cheddar
Maturation	6 months in the creamery + up to 3 months on the shelf
Size	2 kg wheels, 167 g wedges, 1 kg bags
Availability	Local, national, international
Fat	33%
Made in	Tyrone

Oakwood

After maturing for up to six months, some of Fivemiletown's best cheddars are selected to be smoked and become Oakwood. The milk is pasteurised and made with vegetarian rennet. As with Ballyoak brie, the smoke comes from smouldering oak logs sustainably sourced from the local Forest of Caledon. The resulting taste is a tangy combination of the light smoke and the nutty cheddar taste. Grated Oakwood in a pouch is now available.

Gleann Gabhra

After twenty years in farming, Dominic and Fionnuala Gryson started making goats' cheese in 2010. Their farm is located in the Gabhra Valley near Tara, the ancient capital of Ireland, in County Meath. In consultation with the Department of Agriculture, the Grysons constructed a purpose-built facility for their goats and a dairy. They use milk (sold as Bainne Úr) solely from their own mixed herd of goats for their cheese, butter, yoghurt and fudge. The milk is pasteurised but not homogenised. Their cheese, Tara Bán, is perhaps the only goat cheddar in Ireland. The quality has already been recognised with a British Cheese Award in the New Cheese category in 2010. Gleann Gabhra is Irish for 'goat glen'.

GLEANN GABHRA	
Proprietor:	Dominic Gryson
Address:	Baile Mhae, Teamhair, Co. na Mí [Co. Meath]
Web:	www.gleanngabhra.com
Email:	info@gleanngabhra.ie
Phone:	+353 (0)46 902 6817
Cheese made:	Tara Bán
Company size:	Small
Availability:	Local, some in markets in Dublin
Other products:	Goats' milk, yoghurt, butter, ice cream, fudge

Awards

2010   British Cheese Awards   Gold   Tara Bán

TARA BÁN		
Milk		
Style	Hard	
Raw/pasteurised	Pasteurised	
Rennet	Vegetarian	
Organic	No	
Reminiscent of	Goat cheddar	
Size	15 kg block	
Availability	Local, national	
Made in	Meath	

Tara Bán

Tara Bán is a cheese new to market in 2010. It is perhaps unique in Ireland, being a goats' milk cheddar. This is a pasteurised hard goats' milk cheese made with vegetarian rennet. The grey-white pate is slightly crumbly and the flavour, for a goaty cheddar, is very mild. This is an ideal cheese for those wanting to try goats' milk products but who do not want a heavy taste or for those allergic to cows' milk. The cheese is made in the summer months only but is available, from mature stock, all year.

Fionnuala and Dominic Gryson

Glebe Brethan Cheese (Tiernan Family Farm)

David Tiernan and his wife Mairéad (Margaret) have been making the outstanding Glebe Brethan cheese since 2004 on the farm, which had, before them, been run by David's father and grandfather (David's grandmother was a dairy instructress). This hard cheese, with a subtle nutty flavour, is named after one of two monks, Brethan and Frethan, from a local fourth-century monastery. The name 'Frethan' is reserved for a potential 'brother' product to Glebe Brethan in the future. Glebe is the name of the local townland and, indeed, the old farmhouse, formerly a Church of Ireland rectory. The cheese is made in a converted coach house from raw milk from the Tiernans' own herd of about sixty Montbéliarde cows. Versatile cattle, raised for both beef and milk, the Montbéliardes look like chestnut and white versions of the more common black and white Holstein-Friesian cattle. The cheeses are handmade in a large copper-lined vat and hand turned and salted. They mature on spruce-wood shelving, as do some French and Swiss Gruyères.

Prior to 2004, David had no particular interest in cheese. With a drop in the price of milk, he developed an interest in diversifying and adding value to the milk from his Montbéliarde herd. A visit to France and a meeting with French cheese expert Julien Rouillaud planted the idea of making his own cheese. With some help from Julien and Teagasc in Moorepark, David got his cheesemaking under way. The cheese is now well established and Julien still plays a consultant's role.

Only time will tell if the couple's twin sons will take over the farm and cheese production.

David Tiernan

Glebe Brethan Cheese maturing

TIERNAN FAMILY FARM	
Proprietors:	David and Mairéad Tiernan
Address:	Glebe House, Dunleer, Co. Louth
Web:	www.glebebrethan.com
Email:	tiernans@glebebrethan.com
Phone:	+353 (0)41 685 1157
Cheese made:	Glebe Brethan
Company size:	Medium
Availability:	Local, national, international
Other products:	Raw milk
Recipe:	See p. 324 and p. 341

GLEBE BRETHAN	
Milk	
Style	Hard, thermophilic
Raw/pasteurised	Raw
Rennet	Traditional
Organic	No
Reminiscent of	Jura cheese, Comté, Gruyère, Beaufort
Maturation	1–3 years
Size	40–45 kg wheels
Availability	Local, national, international
Made in	Louth

Glebe Brethan

Glebe Brethan is a wonderful hard cheese made in the Swiss thermophilic style. The cheese is made exclusively from the raw summer milk of David Tiernan's own chocolate and white herd of Montbéliarde cattle. To the authors' knowledge, a full-size Glebe Brethan wheel, at 40–45 kg, is the largest farmhouse cheese made in Ireland. The taste is smooth, mild and slightly salty with a subtle sweet nutty overtone. Older cheeses are nuttier, earthier and a little spicy. The inviting ivory pate looks almost yellow in some lights. The natural brine-washed rind is a light brown colour. Unlike French Gruyère but like Swiss Gruyère, the pate is uniform and has no holes. Glebe Brethan is great on a cheese plate or melted in cooking.

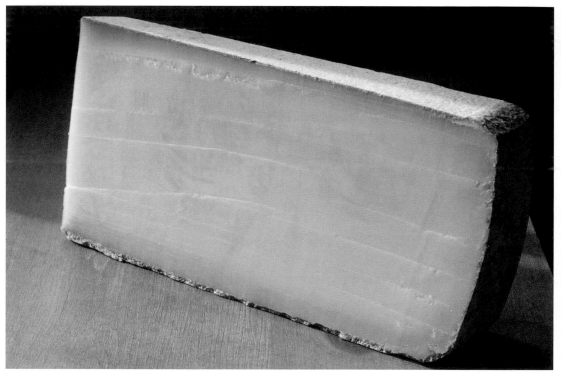

A hefty slice of Glebe Brethan

Glenilen Farm

Alan Kingston was running the family dairy farm when he married Valerie in 1997. Today they farm almost 100 acres overlooking the River Ilen, from whence their name, with over fifty Friesian cows and a few Jerseys mixed in. The cows are grass fed, producing rich, creamy milk.

Having completed a dairy science course in University College, Cork, Val spent a period working in the dairy of a large company. She took some time out to work overseas on behalf of APSO,[17] tasked with helping nomadic people in Burkina Faso to make cheese from their cows' milk to help them through the dry season when the cows were not producing.

While working with a German colleague, she learned how to make quark, a simple, versatile, low-fat cheese, not unlike thick yoghurt, that can be used in cheesecakes and other desserts as well as savoury dishes. Later, in Ireland, Val and Alan would make quark and sell it at the local farmers' market. It soon became popular with European ex-pats living in the west of Ireland.

Quark is very simple to make – pasteurised cows' milk is soured and traditional rennet added. There is no ripening process. A large sieve screen is lowered onto the curds and the whey drains away, taking most of the fat, leaving a cheese looking like a thick yoghurt, with a fat content of about 12 per cent. The quark can be eaten immediately.

Alan and Valerie Kingston

Glenilen Farm	
Proprietors:	Alan and Valerie Kingston
Address:	Drimoleague, Co. Cork
Web:	www.glenilen.com
Facebook:	GlenilenFarmDairy
Email:	val@glenilenfarm.com alan@glenilenfarm.com
Phone:	+353 (0)28 31179
Cheese made:	Glenilen Farm Low-Fat Cream Cheese
Company size:	Medium
Availability:	National, London
Other products:	Butter, cheesecakes, clotted cream, crème fraîche, double cream, mousses, yoghurts
Recipe:	See p. 343

Glenilen Low-Fat Cream Cheese/Quark	
Milk	
Style	Fresh, soft
Raw/pasteurised	Pasteurised
Rennet	Traditional
Organic	No
Reminiscent of	Cream cheese, quark
Maturation	None
Size	250 g tub
Availability	National, London
Fat	10–12% (check tub)
Made in	Cork

Glenilen low-Fat Cream Cheese

Glenilen Low-Fat Cream Cheese is a soft cheese made in the style of quark. The colour is pure white and the texture somewhat like very thick yoghurt. The cheese is made from pasteurised whole cows' milk with traditional rennet. Unlike full-fat cream cheese, no cream is added in the process. The result is a cheese with less than 12 per cent fat, suitable for those cutting back their calories. The cheese can be used as an ingredient in cheesecakes and other desserts or it can be added to savoury dishes.

The cheese is named after the glen of the nearby River Ilen.

Gubbeen Farmhouse Products

Giana Ferguson (pronounced 'jay-na') has had an interesting life. Born in London, she has Hungarian ancestry. As a child she spent time on her father's small farm in the mountains above the Pueblo Blanco of Álora near the Costa del Sol in Spain, where the family made goats' cheese. A later period spent in France added to her knowledge of cheese.

When she married Tom Ferguson, it was perhaps inevitable that she would make cheese in Ireland. She and Tom settled near Schull in west Cork and started to make cheese with the milk of their own herd in 1975. Tom is the fifth generation to farm this land. After experimenting with cottage and other soft cheeses, they settled on their recipe for washed-rind Gubbeen. They were one of the very first cheesemakers in the Irish 1970s cheese renaissance and founding members of CÁIS, the Association of Irish Farmhouse Cheesemakers (see pp. 46–7).

Today, Fingal, their son and sixth-generation Ferguson, runs the Gubbeen charcuterie business. Daughter Clovisse also has a business supplying herbs and vegetables to local shops and restaurants. Gubbeen is still handmade from the Fergusons' own cows' milk and has become an international success.

Smoked Gubbeen was introduced in 1978 and was perhaps the first smoked cheese in modern Ireland. The herd is a mix of Friesian, Kerry Black and Simmental. No chemical preservatives are used in production, only salt and traditional French and Swiss methods.

Eileen Griffin waxing a newly made Smoked Gubbeen (left)
Gubbeen cheesemaker Rose O'Donovan (right)

Gubbeen's distinctive taste can be attributed, to some extent, to the unique bacterial flora in the rind-washing process. Analysis proved at least one of the microbacteria to be previously unidentified and it has been given the name *Microbacterium gubbeenense*.[18]

It is possible to visit the dairy, but you must make an appointment in advance.

GUBBEEN FARMHOUSE PRODUCTS	
Proprietors:	Tom and Giana Ferguson
Address:	Gubbeen House, Schull, Co. Cork
Web:	www.gubbeen.com
Email:	cheese@gubbeen.com
Phone:	+353 (0)28 28231
Cheeses made:	Gubbeen, Smoked Gubbeen
Company size:	Large
Availability:	Local, national, international
Other products:	A range of dry-cured smoked meats, herbs, oatcake biscuits
Recipe:	See p.331

Awards

2010	British Cheese Awards	Gold	Gubbeen

GUBBEEN	
Milk	
Style	Semi-soft, washed-rind
Raw/Pasteurised	Pasteurised
Rennet	Traditional
Organic	No
Maturation	6 weeks min.; 6 months max.
Size	500 g round, 1.4 kg, 5 kg (mature)
Availability	Local, national, international
Fat	55.2% (Gubbeen), 54.8% (Smoked Gubbeen)
Varieties	Smoked Gubbeen; Extra Mature Gubbeen
Made in	Cork

Gubbeen and Smoked Gubbeen

Gubbeen is a washed-rind semi-soft cheese made with pasteurised cows' milk from the Fergusons' own mixed herd, using traditional rennet. The rind colour is a mix of beige and pink, while the pate itself is firm with a subtle yellow-ivory colour. The cheese is lightly cooked and lightly pressed. The flavour of even the youngest cheeses is rich and earthy, with elements of butter and nuts. The aroma is a mix of mushrooms, verdant forest and farmyard. Mature Gubbeen is worth seeking out for its particularly strong, earthy flavour.

If you are adventurous, do eat the natural rind for an extra hit of flavour, but discard the black plastic wax of Smoked Gubbeen. Smoked Gubbeen is subtly oak-smoked in the Fergusons' own kiln and is cured for about a year.

The cheese is named after the local townland, which in turn is derived from the Irish *gobín* ('small mouth'), referring to the bay to the west of the farm.

Black-waxed Smoked Gubbeen

Gubbeen waiting to be eaten

Gubbeen Cheese Oatcakes

New Gubbeens soaking in a brine bath

Hegarty's Farmhouse Cheddar (Whitechurch Foods)

When sons Dan and John Hegarty returned from study and travel to their parents' dairy farm in Whitechurch, only six miles north of Cork City, in 2000, their minds turned to farming. Both had been studying agriculture in England and in Dublin. The brothers are the fifth generation of Hegartys farming these 190 acres, which have been in the family since the mid-nineteenth century.

With the farm having to support both brothers, they looked for a way to add value to their milk. A feasibility study pointed them in the right direction – farmhouse cheese was the answer. Help came in the form of Eddie O'Neill from Teagasc Moorepark and Enterprise Ireland. Parents Jim and Elizabeth also advised. They identified a niche for an Irish clothbound cheddar. They built their cheese dairy in 2001, the brothers doing most of the work themselves. The cheddar needed at least twelve months to mature and a year is a long time to wait to see if you have it right.

By 2005, the boys had it right and the cheese has been a huge success. They use only milk produced in the 'summer' months (February/March to October) from their own herd of about ninety purebred Holstein/Friesian cows, fed on grass and home-produced barley. Between 10 and 20 per cent of their milk production goes into their clothbound cheddar. The truckles weigh about 25 kg each. This is real cheddar cheese produced directly from fresh full-fat milk and wrapped in cheesecloth, with maturation carefully monitored.

The cheese can be found at speciality delis and cheese shops around the country and the Superquinn chain. A number of Irish restaurants are now proudly using Hegarty's Cheddar too.

Dan and John Hegarty

HEGARTY'S FARMHOUSE CHEDDAR	
Proprietors:	Dan and John Hegarty
Address:	Church Road, Whitechurch, Co. Cork
Email:	whitechurchfoods@eircom.net
Phone:	+353 (0)21 488 4238
Cheese made:	Hegarty's Cheddar
Company size:	Medium
Availability:	Local, national
Other products:	Beef

HEGARTY'S FARMHOUSE CHEDDAR		
Milk		
Style	Hard	
Raw/pasteurised	Pasteurised	
Rennet	Vegetarian	
Organic	No	
Reminiscent of	Traditional cheddar	
Maturation	At least 12 months	
Size	22–25 kg	
Availability	Local, national	
Fat	36–38%	
Made in	Cork	

Hegarty's Farmhouse Cheddar

Hegarty's is a traditional cheddar made from pasteurised milk from their own herd, using vegetarian rennet. The texture is firm but slightly crumbly. The pate is a marbled ivory-yellow colour and the flavour is earthy with a cheddary bite, increasing in intensity with age. There is a pronounced saltiness on the middle palate and good length. The light beige-coloured rind has a mild flavour, but some may prefer to discard it. This cheese is matured for at least 12 months before release.

Kellys' Organic Products – Moon Shine Dairy Farm

Moon Shine Dairy Farm is an organic family farm on which products are made on a biodynamic basis, i.e. on favourable days in the moon's cycle; hence the name of the farm. Proprietors Mary and Gerry Kelly pride themselves on using a 'back-to-basics' concept and have a passionate connection with their food.

The Kellys have a mixed dairy herd of Friesian, Ayrshire and Friesian/Ayrshire cross and an Irish Moiled[19] cow and calf, a traditional rare cattle breed. The animals are fed organic hay and haylage. When meal ration is used it is organic and GM[20] free. The animals are provided with as stress-free an environment as possible and are allowed to roam freely or are kept indoors in a large straw-bedded shed.

Gerry and Mary received support from Westmeath Community Development under the LEADER+ programme when starting up their business. They decided to convert to organic farming in 1999 and were certified organic in 2002. Today they make a range of soft cream cheeses and an Emmental-like hard cheese.

KELLYS' ORGANIC PRODUCTS – MOON SHINE DAIRY FARM	
Proprietors:	Gerry and Mary Kelly
Address:	Lough Ennell, Ladestown, Mullingar, Co. Westmeath
Web:	www.kellysorganic.com
Facebook:	MoonshineOrganicDairyProducts
Email:	info@kellysorganic.com
Phone:	+353 (0)44 934 4631
Cheeses made:	Grace, Una, Moon Shine Organic Emmental
Company size:	Medium
Availability:	Local, some national
Other products:	Organic yoghurt, organic yoghurt drinks, Moon Shine Organic Milk

Rua Bawn, Irish Moiled bull on Moon Shine Dairy Farm

Awards

2010	Irish Food Writers Guild Awards Outstanding Product		Moon Shine Organic Milk
	British Cheese Awards	Bronze	Moon Shine Farmhouse
2009	Irish National Organic Awards	Best Overall Winner	Moon Shine Milk

Selected outlets: *Dublin Food Co-op (Sat.); Kennedy's of Enniskerry, County Wicklow; Mullingar Farmers' Market (Sun.); The Organic Supermarket, Blackrock, County Dublin.*

GRACE AND UNA		
Milk		
Style	Soft	
Raw/pasteurised	Pasteurised	
Rennet	Vegetarian	
Organic	Organic	
Reminiscent of	Cream cheese	
Maturation	None	
Size	300 g tubs, 1 kg tubs	
Availability	Local, Dublin	
Varieties	Plain; Sundried Tomatoes, Olives & Herbs	
Fat	17.07%	
Made in	Westmeath	

Grace and Una

This is a range of organic, soft, fresh-cream cheeses with a number of additives. The cheeses are made with organic pasteurised cows' milk and vegetarian rennet. Grace is the plain soft cream cheese version. Una has added sundried tomatoes, olives and herbs on the surface. Brid and Aine have now been discontinued.

The colour is slightly off-white and the texture is smooth and creamy. The flavour is fresh, milky and tangy. The cheeses make an ideal addition to a salad or can be used in cooking.

MOON SHINE ORGANIC EMMENTAL	
Milk	
Style	Semi-hard
Raw/pasteurised	Pasteurised
Rennet	Vegetarian
Organic	Organic
Reminiscent of	Emmental
Maturation	6 weeks
Size	5 kg wheel
Availability	National
Fat	26.67%
Made in	Westmeath

Moon Shine Organic Emmental

This is a semi-hard organic Emmental-like cheese made in 5 kg wheels. The cows' milk is organic and pasteurised and the rennet is vegetarian. The artificial wax rind is a beige-yellow colour and can be discarded. The pate shows a rich yellow-ivory. The pate is firm but elastic with large Swiss cheese-style holes and a pleasant rubbery squeak on the teeth. The aroma is mild and cheesy and the flavour is mild yet complex, reflecting both savoury and sweet notes. This is an excellent cheese for sandwiches.

Kilbeg Dairy Delights

Husband and wife team Kieran and Jane Cassidy have been making cheese and other cultured dairy products on their farm near Kells, County Meath, since 2005. Today they make three soft cheeses: Kilbeg Quark (and Fat-Free Quark), Kilbeg Cream Cheese and Kilbeg Mascarpone. Jane gave up a career as a nurse following a cheesemaking course with the Teagasc Moorepark Food Research Centre, Fermoy, County Cork. She and Kieran set up with smallholder equipment sourced in the UK. By 2008 they had given up their own cattle and now buy in their milk. Kilbeg Quark (and Fat-Free Quark) is one of the very few quark cheeses being made for retail in Ireland (as of early 2011) and the low percentage of fat in these products is proving very popular with the slimming community across Ireland. Kilbeg Mascarpone is also one of the very few mascarpone cheeses produced in Ireland.

The cheese, and indeed the rest of the product range, is becoming increasingly available in large retail outlets across Ireland as demand increases. The cheeses are used in restaurants, in the catering industry and in the manufacture of high-quality food products.

As well as cheese, the Cassidys also produce crème fraîche, sour cream, Greek-style yoghurt, natural yoghurt, smoothies and fruit yoghurt muesli pots.

Tourist visits to Kilbeg are accommodated, but you must call ahead. Kilbeg is named after the local townland.

Bainne clabair, today called clabber or clabbered milk, was a type of soured milk product that may have been similar to modern quark. This was popular in Ireland and Scotland and was later brought to the US by emigrants. It can still be found in parts of the southern states and New England, where it is sometimes known as bonny clabber.

Jane and Kieran Cassidy

KILBEG DAIRY DELIGHTS	
Proprietors:	Kieran and Jane Cassidy
Address:	Horath, Carlanstown, Kells, Co. Meath
Web:	www.kilbegdairydelights.ie
Facebook:	Kilbeg-Dairies
Email:	info@kilbegdairydelights.ie
Phone:	+353 (0)46 924 4687
Cheeses made:	Kilbeg Quark, Kilbeg Fat-Free Quark, Kilbeg Cream Cheese, Kilbeg Mascarpone
Company size:	Medium
Availability:	National
Other products:	Crème fraîche, sour cream, Greek-style yoghurt, natural yoghurt, smoothies and fruit yoghurt muesli pots
Recipe:	See p. 342

KILBEG QUARK AND FAT-FREE QUARK	
Milk	
Style	Soft
Raw/pasteurised	Pasteurised
Rennet	Traditional
Organic	No
Reminiscent of	German quark
Maturation	2 months
Size	200 g, 2 kg, 10 kg
Availability	National
Fat	11% (Full-Fat Quark); 0.009% (Fat-Free Quark)
Made in	Meath

Kilbeg Quark and Fat-Free Quark

Kilbeg Quark is a handmade pasteurised soft cows' milk cheese, in the German quark style, made with traditional rennet[21] and probiotic[22] culture. The cheese is produced throughout the year. The colour is slightly off-white and the taste is fresh, subtle and ever so slightly sweet and sour. The texture is creamy and smooth. As a low-fat or indeed fat-free cheese, quark is sought after by the slimming industry and can be used as a breakfast spread or on top of fruit. It is also used in baking and cooking. The word 'quark' is from German and means 'curd'.

KILBEG CREAM CHEESE AND KILBEG MASCARPONE	
Milk	
Style	Soft
Raw/pasteurised	Pasteurised
Rennet	Traditional
Organic	No
Reminiscent of	Cream cheese, mascarpone
Maturation	2 months
Size	200 g, 2 kg
Availability	National
Fat	30% (Cream Cheese); 11% (Mascarpone)
Made in	Meath

Kilbeg Cream Cheese and Kilbeg Mascarpone

These two creamy cheeses made by Kilbeg are primarily used for cooking, but do make a refreshing snack on their own. Amongst other things, mascarpone is used to make the Italian dessert tiramisu. Cream cheese is used to make cheesecakes and other confectionery and is a natural twin with bagels, which are now well established in Ireland. Both cheeses are slightly sweet. Cream is added to the cream cheese at the start of the production process, while cream is added towards the later stages of mascarpone production. The colour is slightly off-white.

Killeen Farmhouse Cheese

Growing up on a farm and witnessing her mother following in her grandmother's footsteps in producing cheese from their dairy herd, the young Marion Roeleveld had an early exposure to cheesemaking. Her first proper job was with an artisanal cheese producer, though the actual cheesemaking was jealously guarded and she had to make do with cleaning out the tanks and other assorted tasks around the dairy.

A period as a journalist for a small agricultural periodical followed, but all was to change when she moved to Ireland in 2001 following husband Haske.

Haske, having moved to Ireland in the early 1990s, had established a farm on the northern shore of Lough Derg, near Portumna, County Galway. Wanting to have more involvement with the end product of their labours, both in terms of financial reward and for something to do, Marion decided to turn her hand to cheesemaking.

The first problem was that while she had seen others making cheese at close quarters, she didn't actually know how to make it herself. Undaunted, and a number of courses in the techniques of production later, she took her first steps by making cheeses to order for third parties. Enormous encouragement, though scant acknowledgement, was derived when only the second cheese she'd ever made scooped gold at the World Cheese Awards. On the back of this she made the decision to strike out and make cheese in her own right.

Marion Roeleveld

Her Dutch upbringing led to the decision to produce gouda, and since they had a herd of goats already, the first cheese to be produced was a goats' gouda. This was followed rapidly by a cows' gouda produced from milk sourced from a local supplier. In addition to the plain cheeses, Marion makes a range of herb- and spice-flavoured cheeses.

Today they have a herd of over 200 goats. The task of milking falls to Haske, and the milk is piped directly from the milking parlour to the adjoining dairy in the purpose-built premises constructed in early 2010. Marion single-handedly produces all the cheese. The other feature of the new premises is a greatly expanded maturation area, where she hopes to be able to build up a selection of cheeses of various levels of maturity to cater for demand from all sections of the market. With production in 2009 of around 9 tonnes, the expanded storage facilities will permit her to increase this over the course of the next few years. Sixty per cent of the milk production is dedicated to the cheese at present, with the remainder being sold to various third parties, including Glenisk, who produce a range of goats' milk products.

KILLEEN FARMHOUSE CHEESE	
Proprietor:	Marion Roeleveld
Address:	Killeen Millhouse, Ballyshrule, Ballinasloe, Co. Galway
Web:	www.irishcheese.ie/members/killeen.html
Email:	killeen.cheese@gmail.com
Phone:	+353 (0)90 974 1319
Cheeses made:	Killeen Goat Gouda, Killeen Cow Gouda
Company size:	Medium
Availability:	Local, national
Other products:	Goats' milk (sold to other parties)

Gouda production
Gouda is produced by heating the cultured milk to separate the curd from the whey. At this point, some of the whey is removed and replaced with water in a process known as washing the curd. This removes some of the lactic acid, resulting in a sweeter cheese.

After being shaped in a mould, the new cheese passes some time in a brine solution, which contributes to the cheese's characteristic taste. After drying for a couple of days, the cheese is coated to prevent it from drying out.

Awards

2010	British Cheese Awards	Silver	Cow Basil & Garlic
	British Cheese Awards	Bronze	Goat
	British Cheese Awards	Silver	Mature Cow
	World Cheese Awards	Silver[23]	Goat
2009	SHOP Awards	Gold	Goat Fenugreek
	SHOP Awards	Silver	Goat
2008	Irish Farmhouse Cheese Awards	Silver	Goat
2007	Irish Farmhouse Cheese Awards	Best Goat Cheese	Goat

KILLEEN GOAT GOUDA

Milk	
Style	Semi-hard, hard when mature
Raw/pasteurised	Pasteurised
Rennet	Traditional
Organic	No
Reminiscent of	Goat gouda
Maturation	2–12 months, mainly sold at 2 or 5 months
Size	5 kg wheel
Availability	Local, national
Made in	Galway

Killeen Goat Gouda

First produced in 2004, deriving its name from the locality, Killeen Goat Gouda is an excellent example of a pressed gouda cheese style.

Produced year round from pasteurised whole milk from their own herd, the pate is a light cream colour when young, with a very creamy texture, and pocked with small air holes. As the cheese matures, the pate darkens, becoming a brownish beige colour by the time the cheese is a year old, at which point the texture has become dry and crumbly, with whitish crystals flecked throughout – reminiscent of a mature Parmesan. The rind progresses from a cream colour when young to a wrinkled brown on maturity.

At six weeks the cheese is wonderfully sweet on the nose, creamy, with a slight saltiness on the palate. As it matures, it develops nutty and earthy notes, with a long finish. At one year, the nose has become quite pungent and the palate just on the right side of aggressive. It is much earthier on the palate, with forest notes and an enormously long finish. Indeed, the Parmesan comparison extends to this being a fine cheese to grate onto pasta or risotto dishes.

To date, most cheese has been sold at a maturity of around two months, simply by necessity through lack of space, as more mature specimens are in demand. With the new maturation facilities, Marion hopes to be able to offer a full range of mature cheeses.

She also produces a range of goats' cheeses flavoured with the addition of various herbs and spices. These are typically sold at around two months and prove particularly popular in farmers' markets, with specialist shops tending to prefer the plain variety.

Selected outlets: *McCambridge's, Galway; On the Pig's Back, English Market, Cork; Sheridans; farmers' markets throughout the country.*

Eleven-month-old Killeen Goat Gouda

KILLEEN COW GOUDA

Milk	
Style	Semi-hard, hard when mature
Raw/pasteurised	Pasteurised
Rennet	Traditional
Organic	No
Reminiscent of	Gouda
Maturation	2–12 months, mainly sold at 2 or 5 months
Size	5 kg wheel
Availability	Local, national
Made in	Galway

Killeen Cow Gouda

Like the goats' cheese, this was also first produced in 2004. As they don't have their own dairy herd, the cheese is produced from pasteurised whole milk from a local supplier.

The pate of the young cheese is a creamy yellow colour, darkening very slightly towards the rind, and pocked with small air holes.

On the nose, the cheese has fruity, sweet notes. On the palate it is sweet and buttery, with a pronounced nuttiness and decent length. These flavours intensify as the cheese ages, though most of it is sold at between two and five months.

Selected outlets: *McCambridge's, Galway; On the Pig's Back, English Market, Cork; Sheridans; farmers' markets throughout the country.*

Kilshanny Cheese

In the 1980s, Peter Nibbering was living with his family in the Netherlands. He had never been to Ireland. As his family expanded, he needed more living space. A Dutch newspaper advertised a property for sale in Ireland, owned by another Dutchman. By 1989, after a visit to check out the property, Peter and family had moved to Derry House in the townland of Kilshanny, near Ennistymon, County Clare. Amongst other things, Peter inherited the cheese business of his new house's previous occupier. Peter continued making Kilshanny Cheese and is still making it over twenty years later.

The cheese is in the gouda style and Peter makes a number of varieties: plain, Garlic, Cumin, Mixed Herbs, Greek Mix, Nettle and Green Pepper. Raw milk from a neighbour's Friesian cows is used, with traditional rennet. The cheese is produced only in the summer months.

The cheese is named after the local village of Kilshanny (*Cill Seanaigh*, 'Church of Senan/Senach').

The cheese can only be found locally at a number of farmers' markets and in a few local shops, but has a cult following in the area.

KILSHANNY CHEESE	
Proprietor:	Peter Nibbering
Address:	Derry House, Kilshanny, Lahinch, Co. Clare
Phone:	+353 (0)65 707 1228
Cheeses made:	Kilshanny and varieties
Company size:	Small
Availability:	Local

Maturing Kilshanny

Peter Nibbering

Plain Kilshanny ready to eat

Kilshanny	
Milk	
Style	Semi-hard
Raw/pasteurised	Raw
Rennet	Traditional
Organic	No
Reminiscent of	Gouda
Maturation	11 days – 6 months
Size	round 4–5 kg, 454g
Availability	Local
Varieties	Plain; Garlic; Cumin; Mixed Herbs; Greek Mix; Nettle; Green Pepper
Made in	Clare

Kilshanny

This is a semi-hard cheese in the gouda style. Handmade with raw milk from a local herd of Friesian cows and traditional rennet, the pate is firm, with a few holes. The cheese shows a creamy yellow colour, with a fresh aroma and a mild gouda flavour. The rind is covered with yellow plastic wax and should be discarded. Several herbed varieties are available.

Knockalara Farmhouse Cheese

Wolfgang and Agnes Schliebitz arrived in Ireland in late 1989 with the intention of making sheep's cheese, having been visitors to Ireland since the mid-1970s from their native Germany. By 1982 Wolfgang, a motor mechanic by trade, had decided that he could not see himself spending the rest of his life working on cars.

Both lovers of good food, in particular sustainably produced organic food, they decided to try their hand at making cheese, encouraged by a friend who at the time was making sheep's cheese. Above all, they wanted to be as self-sufficient as possible. In the tight grip of recession in the mid-1980s, Ireland was still a cheap place to buy property. The only problem was how to finance it.

Their house, which they owned, needed a lot of work done on it to be able to raise enough to make the move. Wolfgang did the majority of the work himself. It would be almost five years before it was complete, and a further two for the sale to be finalised.

Finally, they arrived in Ireland in the summer of 1989 with their three young daughters, giving themselves six weeks to find a property. Initially they concentrated on the west coast, ranging from west Cork as far north as Sligo. A contact in Roscommon advised them to look east of the Shannon, due to the amount of rain they suffered from (looking at a rainfall map showed that particular spot to be among the wettest in the country!). They also discounted west Cork on the basis that there was no point in coming to Ireland only to have German neighbours.

This led them to look around the southeast. They had decided that they wanted a two-storey farmhouse, with 10–20 acres of land, but just could not find a place that met all

Agnes and Wolfganag Schliebitz

their requirements. An estate agent in Dungarvan proposed a farmhouse with outbuildings near Cappoquin, west Waterford. A bit of negotiation secured a 5-acre field beside the house as well (and they would go on to rent additional land as they needed it).

Now they had a house – albeit one with no running water, which had been uninhabited for more than five years and which was in need of total renovation. After moving into the house in December 1989, they faced long months of hard work to make the place habitable.

Their neighbours were also sceptical of the notion of somebody making sheep's cheese, and in fact were convinced that they were confusing sheep with goats. Nevertheless, the German friend who had planted the idea in the first place had himself arrived in Ireland a couple of years previously. He had found three Friesland sheep for sale, which he bought and was keeping for the Schliebitzes, so they had a flock even before they had a roof over their heads. When the initial three turned out not to be prodigious breeders (at least of ewe lambs), they set about importing five further sheep, all in lamb, from a reputable dealer in Germany. Despite causing consternation when one gave birth to twin lambs while Wolfgang was waiting for the Fishguard to Rosslare ferry, and having paperwork only for the five ewes and not the two lambs, these would form the basis of their flock for years to come. In time this would stabilise at around forty, although it did climb to twice that at one point.

The location turned out to be well chosen. On arrival, they were aware of the conservative nature of Irish tastes at the time, but realised that sheep's milk cheese could represent a niche. They were banking on chefs in top restaurants having an awareness of food culture elsewhere in Europe, and thus having an openness to a unique home-grown sheep's milk cheese. This belief turned out to be well founded, and Wolfgang was soon plying the road between Waterford and Cork – both less than an hour away – making contacts in restaurants and hotels.

They made their first cheese in the summer of 1990, after managing to get a fourth wall and a roof on the dairy. The sheep were entirely hand-milked, which became time-consuming as the size of the flock increased. Furthermore, with sheep's milk, they could not just get a break by letting somebody in to milk them, as there was no other ready outlet for the milk. When the flock at one point reached seventy to eighty strong, they made the decision to contract out the milking. This turned out to be disastrous.

One of the flock developed mastitis, which went undetected. As the sizeable flock, further augmented in size to about 120, were now being milked by machine, the infection spread like wildfire. Catastrophe was narrowly averted, and this led to a couple of important changes. Up to this point the cheese had been produced from raw milk. Following the outbreak, having brought the milking back under their control, they had to pasteurise the milk. Since they did not have the facilities to mix raw and pasteurised cheesemaking, they had to switch to pasteurising their entire output. The other major consequence was that they felt the need to diversify in order to give themselves some fallback should something similar recur. Thus, Comeragh, a cows' milk cheese, was born.

By 2007, though they had always got enormous satisfaction from it, the twice-daily milking was becoming a chore and they felt they would like to be able to take a break every now and then. Henry Clifton Brown, with his flock of around 300 Friesland sheep on his farm near Cashel, was supplying milk at the time to Louis Grubb for Crozier Blue as well as Helen Finnegan at Knockdrinna in Kilkenny. An arrangement was made which saw him extend supply to the Schliebitzes.

Today the cheese is handmade exclusively by Agnes. Wolfgang had been cheesemaker in the early years, but since he was also doing all the travelling, this devolved over time. Despite the fact that their original cheese, the soft Knockalara, remains enormously popular to this day, Agnes is forever experimenting. Alongside the other regular cheeses, Comeragh and Mature Knockalara, she produces small batches of other sheep's and cows' milk cheeses. Production generally starts around the beginning of March and continues until the end of September. At the time of writing, Agnes wants to step up production of the hard cheeses to ensure higher levels of stock throughout the year, but also to allow them to have cheeses of greater maturity.

The Schliebitzes sell their own and other cheeses and produce at markets throughout the region. Since starting this in the wake of the explosion in farmers' markets in the mid-2000s, they have found it a very rewarding experience. They are able to present their produce in peak condition and talk to their customers about it, and for the more experimental cheeses they have a loyal customer base that can provide feedback.

Aside from the market, their main customers are restaurants where the soft cheese particularly finds favour, the mature cheese being more popular in the markets. Some national availability is provided by Sheridans, and small amounts are also exported to the UK and Germany.

KNOCKALARA FARMHOUSE CHEESE	
Proprietors:	Wolfgang and Agnes Schliebitz
Address:	Knockalara, Cappoquin, Co. Waterford
Web:	www.irishcheese.ie/members/knockalara.html
Phone:	+353 (0)24 96326
Cheeses made:	Knockalara, Knockalara Mature, Knockalara Hard, Comeragh, Dromana
Company size:	Medium
Availability:	Local, national (supermarkets and multiples), UK, Germany
Recipe:	See p. 318

Cheese for sale at the Schliebitzes' market stall

KNOCKALARA	
Milk	
Style	Soft
Raw/pasteurised	Pasteurised
Rennet	Vegetarian
Organic	No
Reminiscent of	Creamy Feta
Maturation	6 weeks – 4 months
Size	Rounds, wedges
Availability	Local, national, international (UK, Germany)
Made in	Waterford

Knockalara

The first cheese the Schliebitzes ever produced remains a firm favourite to this day. Although it can benefit from a bit of ageing, up to about four or five months when protected by its foil, this is generally a cheese to be consumed relatively young, usually from around six weeks.

Somewhat resembling a Feta, but much creamier in texture and less salty, the cheese is uniformly brilliant white. On the nose there is a distinct sweet creaminess. The creaminess is carried through to the palate, with slight citrus notes, and a pleasant, slightly sweet/sour finish.

It is an excellent cheese for Mediterranean-style cookery, being well suited to pasta dishes in particular. It is sold in individual foil-wrapped wedges as well as larger rounds. It is also sold in jars with olive oil and herbs.

KNOCKALARA MATURE	
Milk	
Style	Semi-hard, washed-rind
Raw/pasteurised	Pasteurised
Rennet	Vegetarian
Organic	No
Reminiscent of	Ossau Iraty, Tomme
Maturation	9+ months
Size	1.5 kg wheels
Availability	Local, national, international (UK, Germany)
Made in	Waterford

Knockalara Mature

Other than the fact that it is a sheep's milk cheese, Knockalara Mature bears no other relation to its sibling.

A semi-hard washed-rind cheese, it is aged for a minimum of around nine months, but more typically around twelve months, before being offered for sale. It spends part of its early stages of maturation wrapped in foil to prevent it becoming very hard and dry as it ages.

The rind ranges in colour from yellow through orange to brown, with white patches. The pate is creamy white in colour, darkening to brown close to the rind, and flecked with tiny holes throughout. The texture is firm and, while fairly elastic, exhibits a degree of crumbliness.

On the nose there are vegetal notes, and on the palate, following a slightly sour attack, there are barnyard notes and a well-balanced acidity with good length.

KNOCKALARA HARD	
Milk	
Style	Hard
Raw/pasteurised	Pasteurised
Rennet	Vegetarian
Organic	No
Reminiscent of	Tomme
Maturation	9+ months
Size	1.5 kg wheels
Availability	Local, national, international (UK, Germany)
Made in	Waterford

Knockalara Hard

This cheese is aged for a minimum of twelve months. It has a thick, wrinkled rind, brown in colour and flecked with white. The pate is brownish yellow in colour, darkening gradually towards the rind, firm, but with a slight elasticity in texture and liberally flecked with elongated holes.

On the nose there are barnyard notes, but also mushrooms and damp cellars. On the palate the cheese is quite crumbly, salty and has noticeable fungal notes. The finish has a slightly yeasty tingle and good length.

At the time of writing this cheese is a work in progress, as Agnes is still tweaking it. She is, however, confident that it will become a permanent part of their range.

Other Knockalara cheeses

Comeragh

Comeragh is a Knockalara staple, but at the time of writing was out of season, so was not available for tasting. It is a firm cows' milk cheese, made from milk sourced from a local supplier, produced in a method broadly similar to cheddar and matured for a minimum of eight months, but usually longer. It is produced in 2.5 kg rounds, but is also sold as vacuum-packed consumer wedges. One development they would like to pursue is to produce a vintage version, aged for around eighteen months.

Dromana

Dromana is a range of small, round, fresh sheep's milk cheeses packed in sunflower oil and herbs that is sold exclusively in the markets.

Cappagh

Agnes is also in the process of developing a second cows' milk cheese, at the moment called Cappagh, which, like the Knockalara hard cheese, will in time become part of the range. As it stands at the moment, the cheese is a washed-rind cheese, in size somewhat similar in thickness to the rounds of Comeragh. The rind is golden yellow in colour, the pate creamy yellow at the core and darkening gradually towards the rind with well-dispersed holes. The texture is firm and elastic. On the nose there is a buttery note and the palate is tangy with salty/sour notes and a long finish.

Cappagh

Round of Comeragh cows' milk cheese

Knockanore Farmhouse Cheese

Eamonn Lonergan made his first cheese in October 1987. Having trained as an accountant and worked in industry for a number of years, Eamonn made the decision to return to the family farm at Ballyneety in the picturesque Blackwater Valley in County Waterford in the late 1970s. Marrying in 1984, Eamonn began to look at ways of getting added value from his raw materials.

At about this time he saw an RTÉ documentary on Veronica and Norman Steele of Milleens Cheese, who had left jobs in Dublin and set out to make cheese on a hillside in west Cork. Inspired by what they were achieving in a relatively difficult environment, Eamonn wondered what he could do given the lush pastures of his farm at Ballyneety, near Tallow in west Waterford. With the support of the recently formed Tallow Enterprise Centre, Eamonn set about learning how to make cheese. At the time, University College, Cork, was running a course in cheesemaking and the Teagasc Moorepark Research and Innovation Centre at nearby Fermoy was just establishing a training programme for aspiring cheesemakers. Eamonn thus learned his craft between the two, describing the UCC approach as more academic, while Moorepark was much more hands on.

Thus began what Eamonn describes as a twenty-five-year ongoing experiment. An early attempt at making a washed-rind cheese was abandoned due to the labour-intensive nature of having to turn the cheeses every day as they ripened. He finally gravitated towards a cheddar style.

All Eamonn's cheeses are made from raw milk from his own 120-strong herd of Friesians. The herd has been managed from the herd he took over from his father, thus minimising the risk of exposure to TB, for which regular testing is carried out. However, tests are not infallible, so as a precaution, he has installed a pasteuriser should the day arrive when an initial test might return positive. This would allow him to continue making cheese during the time it would take to repeat the test.

Eamonn has worked hard to build up a market for his cheese. As he says, 'You're never going to make millions. It is hard work, but very satisfying – you have to be passionate about it. All in all it makes for an interesting voyage through life.'

The explosion of farmers' markets came too late for Eamonn, although he does currently supply some markets (Wolfgang and Agnes Schliebitz of nearby Knockalara regularly sell Eamonn's cheeses from their market stall). By the early 2000s Eamonn was already engaged with supermarkets. Dealing with supermarkets has its advantages and disadvantages. Although it opens up a large market, the burden of paperwork is considerable. According to Eamonn, dealing with supermarket chains has improved markedly over the past decade. The buyers today are much more knowledgeable and the supermarket chains themselves are more open to the idea of local, sustainable produce, as their customers are demanding it.

A stroke of luck gave Eamonn a big break in the US market. Whole Foods Market is a US chain of food stores devoted to organic and sustainable production, having in the order of 400 stores throughout the US and a handful in the UK. One of their buyers, Tom Slattery, was on his way to a large food fair in Germany and stopped off in Ireland to see a farmhouse cheesemaker he'd heard about who was using local wine as a flavouring. His contact in Ireland was Glenstal Foods in Limerick, and when they pointed out that the 'local wine' was in fact wine bought in the local supermarket, Tom lost interest. Since he was there already, he asked them who else he could see. Glenstal had been exporting small amounts of cheese to the US for Eamonn up to this point and they suggested that Tom go and meet him. As Eamonn describes it: 'Tom, a fairly large gentleman, got out of the car outside the front door, and having shook hands, his next words were, "Now, show me these cows that make the cheese." He wasn't one bit interested in seeing the dairy and our gleaming stainless-steel equipment – he figured he could walk into any cheese plant anywhere in the world and see that. All he wanted to do was see happy cows eating green grass, and that's what he got. As a result, Whole Foods are now a substantial export market for us.'

Eamonn is also opening up Continental markets. Glenstal are also exporting some cheese to France, Germany and Belgium. Knockanore Oakwood Smoked is introducing Parisian palates to smoked cheese (smoked cheeses are almost entirely unknown in France) through fromager François Priet in his shop in the 18ème.

On the recessionary state of the Irish economy at the dawn of the 2010s, Eamonn is circumspect. He started his business in the midst of the 1980s recession and sees things as having come full circle. The distinguishing factor this time is that the Irish palate has become much more adventurous as a result of the explosion in foreign travel over the past fifteen years. The fact that there is a sentiment of support for local enterprise

will also help to see them through this period. On the perception that Irish farmhouse cheese is relatively expensive, Eamonn points out that the raw material is expensive to start with. It's difficult to guarantee a year-round supply of top-quality milk, given the wet nature of our winters.

Eamonn makes cheese between late February/early March and early December, when the cows are able to spend considerable amounts of time on the pasture.

KNOCKANORE FARMHOUSE CHEESE	
Proprietor:	Eamonn Lonergan
Address:	Ballyneety, Knockanore, Co. Waterford
Web:	www.knockanorecheese.com
Email:	eamonn@knockanorecheese.com
Phone:	+353 (0)24 97275
Cheeses made:	Plain White, Plain Red, Smoked and various flavoured
Company size:	Medium
Availability:	Local, national, international (US, Europe)

Awards

2010	World Cheese Awards	Gold	Crushed Chilli with Peppers
2009	World Cheese Awards	Gold	Oakwood Smoked
	International Cheese Awards	Gold	Oakwood Smoked
	World Cheese Awards	Silver	Smoked Cheddar
	SHOP 2009	Gold	White Cheddar
	SHOP 2009	Gold	Oakwood Smoked

KNOCKANORE PLAIN WHITE/RED

Milk	
Style	Semi-hard
Raw/pasteurised	Raw
Rennet	Vegetarian
Organic	No
Reminiscent of	Cheddar
Maturation	6 months – 2 years
Size	150 g portion, 3 kg wheel
Availability	Local, national, international
Varieties	White; Red; Garlic & Herb; Garlic & Chive; Black Pepper & Chive
Made in	Waterford

Knockanore Plain White and Red

Eamonn's main cheeses are Knockanore Plain White and Red. These are cheddar-style cheeses matured for a minimum of six months. Both cheeses are rindless. The pate is firm, with some elasticity, and is a buttery yellow in the plain white, orange in the red. In both cases the pate is even and closed.

The two samples tasted differed significantly. The red, being the younger of the two, had a grassy nose with buttery notes. On the palate there was a slightly mealy mouthfeel, with the butteriness carrying through, together with a mild nuttiness and medium length.

The white sample had an intense buttery nose, which carried through to the palate. Nuttiness followed this and there is a slight saltiness on the finish. It has well-balanced acidity, a smooth mouthfeel and very good length.

Eamonn also produces a trio of flavoured versions – Garlic & Herb, Garlic & Chive and Black Pepper & Chive. These are typically released earlier.

KNOCKANORE OAKWOOD SMOKED	
Milk	
Style	Semi-hard
Raw/pasteurised	Raw
Rennet	Vegetarian
Organic	No
Reminiscent of	Smoked cheddar
Maturation	6 months – 2 years
Size	150 g portion, 3 kg wheel
Availability	Local, national, international
Made in	Waterford

Knockanore Oakwood Smoked

Select wheels of the plain white cheddar are used for the Oakwood Smoked. The cheeses are smoked for a period of ten days in an on-premises kiln using oak chips sourced in nearby Lismore, developing a brownish-yellow rind. The pate also takes on a slightly brown appearance. On the nose the cheese is sweetly smoky, though it's subtle and not at all overpowering. A slight nuttiness also comes through.

Tasted in isolation, the pate has a sweet attack on the palate, with light hints of smoky flavour following on. Tasting the rind gives a meaty, robust attack, although the smokiness never overwhelms. There is enormous length and a very complex flavour profile.

Knockatee Natural Dairy

Peter Ireson, with the help of his wife Olga, makes a number of excellent farmhouse cheeses on his farm on the startlingly beautiful Beara Peninsula. The name 'Knockatee' is taken from the hill behind their farm. Peter, originally from England, has been farming in Ireland since the early 1990s and making cheese since 2002, with the aid of a grant from the EU LEADER project. He now produces three cheeses: a cheddar, a gouda and a gorgeous blue called Kerry Blue, all made from raw cows' milk. The cheeses were originally made from the milk of his own Jersey herd but now he takes milk from a number of neighbouring shorthorn cow herds, producing only in summer, from May to October. The cheeses can be bought from the Iresons' farm directly or from a few local markets and shops. You'll be doing well to find it outside Kerry, but the cheeses, especially the Kerry Blue, are worth going out of the way for.

In 2010 Peter started experimenting with a new cheese, which he has called Beara Blue. This cheese is made with raw cows' milk and traditional rennet, like the Kerry Blue, but has a natural rind and a completely different production process. Beara is creamier and less crumbly, perhaps more Stilton-like, and has a lot more blue! Mature Beara has a pleasantly intense flavour. Production is labour intensive and only small quantities are made, but it is worth seeking out.

Peter Ireson and cheese

KNOCKATEE NATURAL DAIRY	
Proprietors:	Peter and Olga Ireson
Address:	Lehid Upper, Tuosist, Killarney, Co. Kerry
Email:	knockateedairy@eircom.net
Phone:	+353 (0)64 668 4236
Cheeses made:	Kerry Blue, Knockatee Cheddar, Knockatee Gouda, Beara Blue
Company size:	Small
Availability:	Local

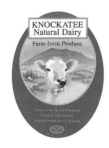

KERRY BLUE		
Milk		
Style	Semi-hard	
Raw/pasteurised	Raw	
Rennet	Traditional	
Organic	No	
Reminiscent of	Shropshire Blue	
Maturation	4–18 months	
Size	2 kg rounds	
Availability	Local	
Made in	Kerry	

Kerry Blue

Ireland is not blessed with many home-produced blue cheeses. One of the rarest, Kerry Blue, is one of the best and worth seeking out. The bright orange wax of this cheese immediately marks it as different; most blue cheeses are wrapped in foil. The orange wax is matched by the slight orange base colour of the pate, achieved through the addition of natural annatto dye. The texture is both moist and crumbly. The colour is subtle, compared to the apparently similar but hard Shropshire Blue, which has a much deeper colour. The wax keeps the Kerry Blue cheese moist and retains its wonderfully fresh raw-milk blue-cheese flavour. Not unlike the dog of the same name, this cheese has bite. Unlike some blues, however, the salt content is not overpowering. The blue veins develop from the added *Penicillium roqueforti*. The cheese is pressed under its own weight. This is a cheese to be sought out and discovered. It won't disappoint.

KNOCKATEE CHEDDAR	
Milk	
Style	Hard
Raw/pasteurised	Raw
Rennet	Traditional
Organic	No
Reminiscent of	Real English cheddar
Maturation	Average 10 months
Size	10 kg truckle
Availability	Local
Made in	Kerry

Knockatee Cheddar

Peter Ireson makes his hard cheddar cheese with old-fashioned methods imported from Lancashire. Raw shorthorn milk is used with traditional rennet. The 40 kg in a batch take about twelve hours to make. The cheddaring process is long and complex and Peter wraps his cheddar truckles in linen cloth. The cheese is scalded and pressed under its own weight. Each truckle weighs in at about 10 kg and matures, on average, for about ten months. The result is a classic cheddar with a rich real-cheddar bite. The rind is a dull brown colour while the pate is a dull yellow.

KNOCKATEE GOUDA	
Milk	
Style	Hard
Raw/pasteurised	Raw
Rennet	Traditional
Organic	No
Reminiscent of	Gouda
Maturation	3+ months
Size	4–5 kg wheel
Availability	Local
Varieties	Plain; Garlic; Nettles
Made in	Kerry

Knockatee Gouda

Knockatee Gouda is a hard cheese with a pale yellowish pate, made in a 4–5 kg wheel. The milk is raw and the rennet is traditional. This rich-tasting cheese is scalded, not cooked, and is pressed under its own weight and matured for a minimum of three months. Three varieties are available: Plain, Garlic and Nettles. The texture is firm, with lots of holes.

Knockdrinna Farmhouse Cheese

Having spent fifteen years as a civil servant, with the final two spent in frustration trying to influence policy while trying to balance life with a young family, Helen Finnegan decided that there had to be a better way to make a living.

Instilled with a lifelong interest in good food, in 2004 she began to experiment with cheese production in the kitchen of the family farm in Stoneyford, County Kilkenny. The first efforts with cows' milk proved encouraging and, having a fondness for goats' cheese, Helen decided to try her hand at that. Sourcing milk locally from Hugh Daniels, who at the outset had a small herd of six goats, the first result of the experiment was Knockdrinna Snow, a small camembert-style cheese, followed by Knockdrinna Gold, a harder goats' cheese. Hugh still supplies all Helen's goats' milk, and as time has passed, and Knockdrinna's popularity and production levels have grown, so has his herd, currently numbering in excess of 100 animals.

Initial sales at farmers' markets around Kilkenny/Carlow proved very positive and encouraged Helen to invest in a purpose-built cheese plant on the farm, which came into production in 2006, allowing her to broaden her horizons.

As the success of the cheeses grew, Helen began to receive enquiries about sheep's cheese. Sourcing milk from Henry Clifton Brown, already producing milk for Crozier Blue from his farm between Cashel and Tipperary, she produced a sheep's cheese in the same style as Knockdrinna Gold, naming it Knockdrinna Meadow.

An unexpected twist came at the end of 2007. Lavistown cheese, produced at nearby Lavistown House by Olivia Goodwillie, had long been a venerable name in Irish cheese,

having been in production for around twenty-five years at that point. Its popularity in the run-up to Christmas meant that Olivia was struggling to meet demand, so she turned to Helen for assistance. At the time, Lavistown was also growing and developing its popular range of courses, running the gamut from mushroom picking to basket weaving, and Olivia found that there weren't enough hours in the day to concentrate on both this activity and cheesemaking. Seeing a capable pair of hands in Helen on the back of the pre-Christmas production run, she agreed to sell the Lavistown name and recipe to her, which Helen is bringing forward and has made her own.

In mid-2009 Helen opened a farm shop and café in the main street of Stoneyford, right beside the farm. This provides an outlet not only for the cheeses, but also for their range of free-range pork products produced from their herd of whey-fed rare-breed pigs and the Knockdrinna range of jams, chutneys and pesto as well as other products sourced from local suppliers. What has emerged is fantastic local support, as the recent opening of the nearby motorway has had a negligible effect on passing trade (Stoneyford had previously been on the main road from Waterford to Kilkenny).

From time to time, capacity permitting, Helen and her cheesemaker Edel Foley do small batches of other cheeses. A Feta-like brined goats' cheese is a staple, as it is ready to be sold after a week. Also notable is Abbot, a delicious cows' milk cheese somewhat in the style of Munster, or nearer to home, Ardrahan. All are available in the farm shop.

KNOCKDRINNA FARMHOUSE CHEESE	
Proprietor:	Helen Finnegan
Address:	Stoneyford, Co. Kilkenny
Web:	www.knockdrinna.com
Email:	Helen.Finnegan@knockdrinna.com
Phone:	+353 (0)56 772 8886
Cheeses made:	Knockdrinna Snow, Knockdrinna Gold, Knockdrinna Meadow, Lavistown, Knockdrinna Brined Goat. Also occasional small batches of other cheese
Company size:	Medium
Availability:	Local, some national distribution
Other products:	Pork products, range of jams, chutneys, pestos (all available in the Knockdrinna Farm Shop)

Awards

2010	Irish Foodwriters Guild	Outstanding Product	Knockdrinna Meadow
	British Cheese Awards	Silver	Knockdrinna Meadow
	British Cheese Awards	Bronze	Knockdrinna Snow
2008	Great Taste Awards	1 star	Knockdrinna Meadow

KNOCKDRINNA SNOW

Milk	
Style	Soft, surface-ripened, white-mould
Raw/pasteurised	Pasteurised
Rennet	Traditional
Organic	No
Reminiscent of	Goat camembert
Maturation	2–8 weeks
Size	180 g wrapped rounds
Availability	Local, national
Made in	Kilkenny

Knockdrinna Snow

Their first commercially produced cheese, Knockdrinna Snow, is a small camembert-style cheese produced from pasteurised goats' milk.

In appearance, the rind is brilliant white with a penicillin mould. The pate is white, with a soft, elastic texture, becoming creamy from the outside as the cheese matures.

On the nose, the cheese is creamy, developing forest notes as it ages. On the palate, the young cheese has a mild, creamy taste with citrus notes. As the cheese matures, the taste profile becomes more complex, developing a full range of vegetal, gamey, camembert flavours.

It is a cheese designed to be eaten relatively young, being ready from between two to eight weeks, depending on preference.

KNOCKDRINNA GOLD		
Milk		
Style	Semi-hard, washed-rind	
Raw/pasteurised	Pasteurised	
Rennet	Vegetarian	
Organic	No	
Reminiscent of	Goat Tomme	
Maturation	Min. 2 months, but generally sold at 3–8 months	
Size	3.5 kg wheels	
Availability	Local, national	
Made in	Kilkenny	

Knockdrinna Gold

Gold is a semi-hard Tomme-style cheese from pasteurised goats' milk and vegetarian rennet. It is produced in medium-sized 3.5 kg wheels. Originally produced as a washed-curd cheese in a gouda style, this has since been abandoned. The natural rind, washed in a mix including organic white wine, is a reddish beige colour. The pate is firm, slightly crumbly and creamy white in colour, darkening slightly towards the rind, with small air holes.

On the nose, the cheese has a mild, sweetish, goaty aroma. In the young cheese, this follows through on the palate, with a slight saltiness and mild nutty flavour. The cheese becomes more crumbly and develops bite as it ages. It is ready to eat at two months, but is in general matured for at least three months, becoming fully mature at around eight months.

KNOCKDRINNA MEADOW		
Milk		
Style	Semi-hard, washed-rind	
Raw/pasteurised	Pasteurised	
Rennet	Vegetarian	
Organic	No	
Reminiscent of	Sheep Tomme	
Maturation	Min. 2 months, but generally sold at 3–8 months	
Size	3.5 kg wheels	
Availability	Local, national	
Made in	Kilkenny	

Knockdrinna Meadow

On the back of the success of Gold, a number of customers made enquiries about the availability of a similar sheep's milk cheese. This led Helen to the door of Henry Clifton Brown just outside Cashel, who agreed to supply milk. Henry was already supplying milk to Louis Grubb for the production of Crozier Blue. Thus, Knockdrinna Meadow was born.

A semi-hard sheep's milk cheese made to the same recipe and size as Gold, Meadow has a similar reddish beige washed rind. The pate is a very light creamy yellow, with small holes throughout, darkening slightly towards the rind.

On the nose, the cheese is more subtle than Gold, with a sweet, creamy aroma. On the palate, the young cheese is mild and creamy. The predominantly sweet attack is followed by a pleasant tangy sourness in the aftertaste. There's a pronounced nuttiness, and as the cheese ages it takes on more earthy notes and becomes more crumbly.

As with Knockdrinna Gold, the cheese is ready to eat at two months, but is generally matured for at least three months.

LAVISTOWN	
Milk	
Style	Semi-hard, washed-rind
Raw/pasteurised	Pasteurised
Rennet	Vegetarian
Organic	No
Reminiscent of	Caerphilly, Tomme de Vache
Maturation	Min. 2 months up to 12 months. Most commonly sold at 5–6 months.
Size	3.5 kg wheels
Availability	Local, national
Made in	Kilkenny

Lavistown

Produced to a Caerphilly-style recipe from pasteurised cows' milk, but more reminiscent of a southern French Tomme de Vache, Lavistown has a long history behind it.

This is a semi-hard cheese produced in 3.5 kg rounds. The washed rind is beige in colour. The crumbly pate is a uniformly rich yellow in colour, with no significant darkening towards the edge, and pocked with small holes.

On the young cheese, there isn't a very pronounced nose. On the palate there's a tangy, buttermilk sour attack with good length. As the cheese ages, it becomes drier and more crumbly, and this flavour profile becomes more pronounced.

Original Lavistown

Some mention should be made of the Lavistown in its original form. Produced by Olivia Goodwillie at Lavistown House just outside Kilkenny since 1983, it was one of the original classics of Irish farmhouse cheese. In terms of flavour profile, it differed markedly from the current cheese. Most of the cream was skimmed off the milk, resulting in quite a low-fat cheese with a noticeable buttermilk tang. Seasonal variation was also quite noticeable: the winter cheese tended to be firmer, while the summer cheese tended to be richer and had a pinker rind.

KNOCKDRINNA BRINED GOAT		
Milk		
Style	Soft	
Raw/pasteurised	Pasteurised	
Rennet	Vegetarian	
Organic	No	
Reminiscent of	Feta	
Maturation	1 week	
Size	1 kg blocks	
Availability	Local	
Made in	Kilkenny	

Knockdrinna Brined Goat

This is a tangy goats' milk cheese similar to Feta. Rindless, as it is sold after a week, the pate is brilliant white and crumbly in texture.

There is a creaminess to the nose, which follows through on the palate with a fresh, zingy taste. The saltiness is not intrusive and there is a real depth of flavour.

The cheese is available only from Knockdrinna Farm Shop and local markets.

Milleens Cheese

In the far southwest of Ireland are the counties of Cork and Kerry. The far west of these counties manifests itself as a series of fingers of land, places of extraordinary beauty stretching out into the Atlantic Ocean. One hour's drive down one of these fingers, the Beara Peninsula, towards its northern coast, almost in Kerry but just tucking itself in behind the Cork border, near the hamlet of Eyeries and hiding from the world perhaps, you will find Milleens Cheese.

Veronica and Norman Steele have been making cheese in one form or another since 1972. Milleens Cheese itself, having been made and sold since 1978, qualifies as the first cheese of the cheese revival in Ireland. Norman Steele first came to Ireland to study philosophy. He became a farmer in west Cork and married Veronica. For years he played a dual role of farmer and university philosophy lecturer.

Making cheese was a way of storing milk through the winter months and, in doing so, Veronica and Norman made a connection with the ancient ways of Ireland. Having experimented with cheddar and Emmental-like cheeses, the Steeles settled on a soft washed-rind cows' milk cheese. Such cheeses ripen from the surface inwards.[24] They are small, to give a high surface-to-volume ratio. The ripening is bacterial and the surface is tacky to the touch.

Initially the cheese was made from their own herd of mixed Friesian and Kerry cows, but they later moved their focus to cheese production itself, selling their own cows and taking milk from local farms. These local cows were, and still are, feeding on the same

One-day-old Milleens beginning the maturation process

Milleens 'O'

rich, mixed-foliage west Cork diet. A chance tasting by Myrtle Allen and restaurateur Declan Ryan first led to the excellence of Milleens being recognised and Veronica and Norman started selling the cheese to Declan's first restaurant. The cheese also played a starring role on RTÉ's celebrated *Hands* crafts programme. Everybody wanted some of this new, rich-tasting, very Irish cheese and Milleens has gone from strength to strength across Ireland and on the international market. Such was the success that Veronica and Norman began to train many other local cheesemakers, including some of today's well-known and established makers. While still around to advise, Veronica and Norman have stepped back from day-to-day cheesemaking and put the reins in the very capable hands of their son, Quinlan.

For her role in kicking off the Irish farmhouse cheese renaissance, Veronica has been referred to as mother, grandmother and matriarch of Irish farmhouse cheese.
Selected outlets: *Ireland: On the Pig's Back, English Market, Cork; Sheridans; Superquinn. London: Neal's Yard. Scotland: Ian Mellis.*

MILLEENS CHEESE	
Proprietor:	Quinlan Steele
Address:	Milleens, Eyeries, Beara, Co. Cork
Web:	www.milleenscheese.com
Facebook:	Milleens-Cheese
Email:	milleens@eircom.net; info@milleenscheese.com
Phone:	+353 (0) 27 74079
Cheeses made:	Milleens, Milleens Dote, Milleens 'O'
Company size:	Medium
Availability:	Local, national, international
Recipe:	See p. 325

Awards

2010	British Cheese Awards	Silver	Milleens 'O'
	British Cheese Awards	Silver	Milleens Dote
	Great Taste Awards	1 star	Milleens Dote
2009	World Cheese Awards	Silver	Milleens Dote
	Great Taste Awards	2 stars	Milleens
	SHOP Awards	Silver	Milleens

MILLEENS	
Milk	
Style	Semi-soft, washed-rind
Raw/pasteurised	Pasteurised
Rennet	Traditional
Organic	No
Reminiscent of	Reblochon, Munster, Trappist cheeses
Maturation	3–5 weeks (12 days in spring)
Size	250 g (Dote), 1 kg, 1.5 kg wheel
Availability	Local, national, international
Fat	26% (52% fat in dry matter)
Made in	Cork

Milleens

Milleens is a semi-soft washed-rind cheese with a heady farmyard aroma and a rich, complex flavour. The rind is sticky to the touch and the whole cheese can be seen as a living organism. Washed with local mountain-spring water, the cheese matures from the outside inwards and naturally acquires the bacterium *Brevibacterium linens* that contributes considerably to the cheese's flavour. The cheese is neither cooked nor pressed.

Made from the milk of local Friesian herds with traditional rennet, the earthy flavour reflects the local grass and heathers on which the cows graze. While previously made from raw milk, the milk is now pasteurised. The texture is smooth, creamy and somewhat elastic. The mottled peach-coloured rind is probably best avoided, but can reward the adventurous with an intense taste and crystalline texture. Milleens is excellent on the cheeseboard. The 250 g retail variety is called the Dote. A new wheel, with a round piece removed from the centre, Polo mint fashion, is called the Milleens 'O'. The 'O' shape not only looks good but also provides a bigger surface-area-to-volume ratio, aiding in the surface-ripening process.

Millhouse Cheese

Beni Gerber trained as a chef in his native Switzerland and, while head chef in a restaurant in the spectacular Swiss Alps, he became fascinated by the production of the cheese typical of this mountainous region.

Moving to Ireland in 1997 with his wife Elfie, he wondered whether he could reproduce this type of cheese in his rather flatter new surroundings near Tullamore, County Offaly.

Not wishing to make life too easy for himself, he decided to apply the techniques he'd learned in Switzerland to making a hard sheep's milk cheese – Swiss cheeses being almost exclusively made from cows' milk.

While the quality of grazing and water in County Offaly ensured first-rate milk from the herd of pedigree east Friesian sheep they invested in, Beni soon discovered that the recipes that had been making superb cows' milk cheese in the Alps for centuries didn't translate at all to the somewhat different properties of sheep's milk. He would spend almost two years tinkering with the recipe before he had a result he was happy with. In the meantime, the passable experiments ended up either on his plate or those of close friends, but at the same time a lot of other batches wound up in the bin. At the end of this process he was producing a subtly flavoured hard sheep's cheese capable of long periods of maturation.

Beni Gerber with a wheel of Millhouse cheese
(his manual cheese press can be seen on the left)

He initially sold his produce largely on his own in markets around Ireland's midlands, with some sales via local shops, and a small but significant amount being exported to Switzerland.

Success followed when he entered his cheese at the Listowel Food Fair in 2003, where it won a silver medal and Best New Cheese trophy. Gold medals followed in the same competition in the following two years, and in 2006 he won a bronze medal for Pastorello ('little shepherd boy') – a soft-textured sheep's milk cheese sometimes flavoured with herbs and spices.

As time went by, however, Beni lost the Swiss market following a restructuring at the importer and was forced to curtail his market presence due to time pressures. He has also had to cease production of Pastorello, as he found that he had to turn over a significant portion of his small production to satisfy the regulatory demands for testing. (When a 2 kg wheel is cut, its maturation ceases and it cannot be sold if it is too young, making the cheese uneconomic.)

Describing himself as a 'micro' artisanal producer, Beni makes and matures his cheese in an ingenious premises fashioned from a refrigerated container. Elfie takes care of managing the herd, which at the time of writing is around twenty milking animals, down from almost forty when production was at its peak.

In addition to cheese production, Beni and Elfie have a small number of self-catering units onsite to let to tourists.

MILLHOUSE CHEESE	
Proprietors:	Beni and Elfie Gerber
Address:	Killeenmore, Tullamore, Co. Offaly
Web:	www.millhouseireland.com
Email:	info@millhouseireland.com
Phone:	+353 (0)57 934 4334
Cheese made:	Millhouse
Company size:	Small
Availability:	Local, Dublin

Selection of Beni Gerber's cheese

MILLHOUSE SHEEP'S CHEESE	
Milk	🐏
Style	Hard
Raw/pasteurised	Raw
Rennet	Vegetarian
Organic	No
Reminiscent of	Manchego, mature Spanish/Portuguese sheep's cheese
Maturation	3 months min., usually up to around 1 year, but can take more
Size	1 or 2 kg wheels
Availability	Local, some national
Varieties	Plain; Caraway; Garlic; Caraway, Coriander & Fennel
Made in	Offaly

Eleven-month-old Millhouse

Four-year-old Millhouse

Millhouse Sheep's Cheese

Millhouse sheep's cheese is handmade from raw milk, to which a starter and vegetarian rennet are added.

The young cheeses are pressed in a manual press and then washed in a brine bath. Initially the cheeses are washed daily, then after a while every second day, then every three days etc. until eventually they are washed weekly for the more mature cheeses.

The minimum maturation period is three months, with the cheese being at its prime at about nine to twelve months. It is, however, capable of much longer ageing and Beni has examples of four- and six-year-old cheeses in his storage room.

The most usual size for the cheese is 2 kg wheels, though Beni produces smaller cheeses of around 1 kg at the end of a batch if only a small amount of curds remain. Current production totals around 0.5 tonnes annually.

When young, the cheese has a supple, elastic pate, which becomes harder in texture as the cheese ages and, though retaining a degree of suppleness, it is quite hard by eleven months.

At eleven months the pate is a rich, creamy yellow colour, darkening towards the rind, with a sprinkling of small holes. The edible rind itself is a yellowish red colour. On the nose the cheese is nutty, with slight vegetal notes. The nuttiness follows through on the palate, where the aftertaste is decently long. There is also a slight saltiness, but this is in no way overpowering and is very much in harmony with the flavour of the cheese. Acidity is not pronounced.

With a four-year-old sample, the pate is very hard and is reminiscent in colour and texture to a chunk of hard dark caramel. The colour is uniform throughout and the pate is flecked with white crystals, which form when the cheese is around two years old. The nose is intense and this follows through on the palate with a complex taste that seems to linger forever. The intensity is not, however, coupled with the caustic notes that can sometimes overwhelm cheeses of a similar vintage.

In addition to the plain cheese, Millhouse is available flavoured with caraway, garlic or caraway, coriander and fennel. These varieties tend to be sold at around one year of age.

Selected outlets: *Natural Stuff, Tullamore; Sheridans (occasionally); Wrights of Howth, Dublin Airport; various farmers' markets.*

Hobelkäse
Hobelkäse refers to a hard, mature cheese which is sliced very thinly on a mandolin or Hobel (plane), which permits it to release its taste.

Mossfield Organic Farm

Since 2004 Ralph Haslam has been making cheese on his farm near Birr, County Offaly, at the foot of the Slieve Bloom Mountains, in the very centre of Ireland. He has farmed the land for dairy since 1982, inheriting the farm from his father. Now he farms a herd of about eighty-five red and white German Rotbunt/Friesian cows on 350 acres of land, 240 of which are his own. The farm consists mostly of limestone pasture, which produces lush grass dotted with wild herbs and clover. The milk from this grass-fed breed, high in fat and protein, makes Ralph's rich, handmade Mossfield cheese. The Rotbunt breed may include the bloodline of the old Irish Moiled cow, which was brought to Germany by Irish monks in the distant past.

Like many Irish cheesemakers, Ralph was hit by the low price of milk and wanted a way to add value. He originally thought about making ice cream, but cheese won the day. Six years before his foray into cheesemaking, Ralph had converted to organic production for environmental reasons. He was fully converted to organic by 2001. Now Ralph's Mossfield Cheese, made in a broadly gouda style, is making a name for itself. He has an impressive dairy built with financial aid from the organic section of the Irish Department of Agriculture. As well as cheese, he sells buttermilk, cream and surplus milk and is working on a new cheese in the Feta style.

Mossfield, half-eaten already

MOSSFIELD ORGANIC FARM	
Proprietor:	Ralph Haslam
Address:	Clareen, Birr, Co. Offaly
Web:	www.mossfield.ie
Facebook:	MossfieldOrganicCheese
Email:	info@mossfield.ie
Phone:	+353 (0)57 913 1002
Cheeses made:	Mossfield and varieties
Company size:	Medium
Availability:	Local, national
Other products:	Buttermilk, cream, surplus milk

Awards

2010	Irish National Organic Awards	Best Overall Winner	Mossfield Mature
	British Cheese Awards	Silver	Mossfield Mature
	British Cheese Awards	Bronze	Mossfield Mediterranean
	British Cheese Awards	Bronze	Mossfield Cumin
	Great Taste Awards	1 star	Mossfield Young Cheese
2008	Great Taste Awards	3 stars	Mossfield Mature
	Great Taste Awards	1 star	Mossfield Cumin

MOSSFIELD ORGANIC CHEESE	
Milk	
Style	Semi-hard to hard
Raw/pasteurised	Pasteurised
Rennet	Vegetarian
Organic	Organic
Reminiscent of	Gouda, cheddar, Gruyère, Emmental (mature like Parmesan)
Maturation	6, 9, 12 months, 2 months (young and herbs)
Size	4.5 kg–5 kg, 170 g –200 g, vacuum packs
Availability	Local, national
Fat	48%
Varieties	Plain (young); Mature; Mediterranean Herbs; Cumin; Garlic & Basil
Made in	Offaly

Mossfield Organic Cheese

Mossfield is an organic cheese made broadly in the gouda style. The cheese is made with vegetarian rennet from pasteurised cows' milk of the red and white Rotbund/Friesian breed. The curd is cooked and pressed and the pate shows a creamy ivory colour. The cheese is available in a number of varieties: plain (young), Mature, Mediterranean Herbs, Cumin and Garlic & Basil. The young cheese has a mild aroma and flavour. Older cheeses develop a zingy aftertaste and have a crystalline texture. The very mature cheese has a distinct nutty taste. The variable beige-coloured plastic-wax rind should be discarded.

Young Mossfield

Mossfield Garlic & Basil

Mossfield Cumin

Mossfield Mature

Mossfield

Mount Callan Farmhouse Cheese

In 1996 Lucy Hayes left behind the sunny climes of Australia for Ireland, with Irish husband Michael and four small children in tow. They bought a dairy farm in the west of County Clare. When Michael began farming, Lucy needed something to do with her time. She learned the basics of cheesemaking from a local Dutchman, read some books and started making cheese in her kitchen. Advice from the Department of Agriculture and Teagasc helped, as did a grant from the LEADER fund. A number of high-quality soft cheeses and goudas were being made in Ireland at the time and Lucy wanted to do something different. She experimented with and adapted a number of cheddar recipes she had received. Because of cheddar's long maturation time, it can take a while to know whether you've got it right or wrong, but the hens benefited from the mistakes. She took the first lot of traditional muslin-wrapped cheddar cheese to Sheridans in 1999. It sold out rapidly. Lucy had got it right and began to develop. Her cheese production has grown every year since. The cheese is made from April to September with raw milk, now mostly from neighbouring herds, and matured in stone cabins.

Mount Callan Cheese is used in the manufacture of O'Donnell's Tipperary Crisps (www.odonnellscrisps.com).

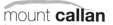

MOUNT CALLAN FARMHOUSE CHEESE	
Proprietor:	Lucy Hayes
Address:	Drinagh, Ennistymon, Co. Clare
Web:	www.irishcheese.ie/members/mountcallan.html
Email:	mtcallancheese@eircom.net, mtcallan@oceanfree.net
Phone:	+353 (0)65 707 2008
Cheese made:	Mount Callan Cheddar
Company size:	Medium
Availability:	Local, national, international (UK, Germany)
Recipe:	See p. 323

Awards

Several British Cheese Awards over many years

2005	Listowel Food Fair	Gold
2005	Irish Champion	

MOUNT CALLAN		
Milk		
Style	Hard	
Raw/pasteurised	Raw	
Rennet	Traditional	
Organic	No	
Reminiscent of	Cloth-bound cheddar	
Maturation	9–12 months (18 months max.)	
Size	12–15 kg truckle	
Availability	Local, national, international	
Made in	Clare	

Mount Callan

The cloth-bound cheddar-style Mount Callan is named after a local landmark visible from Lucy Hayes's farm. The cheese is made only in summer from the raw milk of local Friesian and Montbéliarde cows, using traditional rennet. It is cooked and pressed and the large cheesecloth-bound truckles, weighing up to 15 kg, are matured from between nine to twelve months on wood in a stone cabin. The result is a cheddar-style cheese with a rich, earthy, nutty flavour. A limited amount of Mount Callan is matured to eighteen months and develops a powerful, tangy flavour. The tightly pressed pate shows a creamy yellow colour, while the natural rind is a dusty grey, with a mushroomy aroma.

Mount Callan can be found at a number of gourmet restaurants and outlets around Ireland, including Sheridans and On the Pig's Back in the English Market, Cork. A little makes its way to the UK and Germany.

Old MacDonnell's Farm

Brian and Wendy MacDonnell, along with son Paddy, make a range of fresh soft cows' and goats' milk cheeses on their farm near the woody glades of the Glen of the Downs in County Wicklow, the 'garden county' of Ireland. Along with the cheese, a range of probiotic yoghurts and hummus is made. The milk, from their own herds of Holstein/ Friesian cattle and Saanen goats, is pasteurised and the rennet is vegetarian. The cheese is sold in small plastic tubs, ranging in weight from 150 g to 270 g. The range includes a goats' milk Mini Chèvre (12.4 per cent fat) in olive oil with chilli, black peppers, herbs and garlic; a Herbs de Provence & Garlic Probiotic Cheese (10.4 per cent fat) made from cows' milk in sunflower oil, herbs, garlic and parsley; and a 'Greek' Tzatziki Probiotic Yoghurt Cheese (10.7 per cent fat), made from cows' milk in sunflower oil, with cucumber, garlic, mint, roasted red peppers, rosemary and olives.

OLD MACDONNELL'S FARM	
Proprietors:	Brian and Wendy MacDonnell
Address:	Glen of the Downs, Bray, Co. Wicklow
Web:	www.oldmacdonnellsfarm.ie
Email:	sales@oldmacdonnellsfarm.ie
Phone:	+353 (0)1 282 9707/+353 (0)86 244 5150
Cheeses made:	Cows' soft cheese range; goats' soft cheese range
Company size:	Medium
Availability:	Local, national
Other products:	Probiotic yoghurt, hummus

Orchard Cottage Dairy (was Magpie Cottage Dairy)

Having already attended The Organic College at Dromcollogher, near Limerick, Joseph Desmond undertook a number of courses in cheesemaking with Judy Wotton at Ardagh Castle near Baltimore, Cork, and with Teagasc. He joined Chris and Phil Rhodes in early 2010 at Magpie Cottage Dairy, where he learned his trade. By the end of the year he had bought the business, moved it to his family's organic cattle farm at Ballinhassig, County Cork, and renamed it Orchard Cottage Dairy. Joe has fourteen goats this year, will have twenty-four next year and is aiming for thirty. He plans to try his hand at a hard goats' cheese next year. He is in conversion to organic farming and hopes to get certification in 2012.

Chris and Phil had established Magpie in the mid-1990s with a small herd of pure-bred Anglo-Nubian goats and had been among the founders of the Mahon Point Farmers' Market, which provided an outlet for their produce.

At the moment Joseph produces a fresh cheese from raw goats' milk and vegetarian rennet. The plain cheese is sold in 150 g balls. He also sells the cheese in jars of sunflower oil with herbs – somewhat similar to Boilíe. Some are flavoured with thyme and garlic or sundried tomato, basil and garlic.

The cheeses are available through local farmers' markets.

ORCHARD COTTAGE DAIRY	
Proprietor:	Joseph Desmond
Address:	Rigsdale, Ballinhassig, Co. Cork
Email:	josephdesmond@hotmail.com
Phone:	+353 (0)86 303 7871/+353 (0)21 488 5540
Cheeses made:	Cáis Cruinn – plain fresh goats' cheese, goats' cheese balls in jars of oil with herbs
Company size:	Small
Availability:	Local

St Tola (Inagh Farmhouse Cheese)

When Siobhán Ní Gháirbhith was a young girl, she would sometimes visit her neighbour's goat farm to get goats' milk to help her sisters' asthma. She probably never imagined that she would one day take over the operation and produce St Tola goats' cheese herself.

Those neighbours were Meg and Derrick Gordon in the townland of Inagh in County Clare. When Siobhán took over the reins in 1999, the Gordons had been making St Tola for nearly twenty years. Now Siobhán and her family have their own herd of over 200 goats on their 65-acre farm, producing an array of high-quality handmade goats' cheeses to certified organic principles. The mixed flock of Saanen, Toggenburg and British Alpine goats produce the rich, characteristic St Tola taste.

The cheeses are named after St Tola of Clonard, a seventh/eighth-century Irish saint who established a monastic community in County Clare.

St Tola (Inagh Farmhouse Cheese)	
Proprietor:	Siobhán Ní Gháirbhith
Address:	Inagh, Co. Clare
Web:	www.st-tola.ie
Email:	info@st-tola.ie
Phone:	+353 (0)65 683 6633
Cheeses made:	St Tola Fresh Log, St Tola Mature Log, St Tola Original, St Tola Crottin, St Tola Divine, St Tola Hard, St Tola Greek Style
Company size:	Large
Availability:	Local, national

Awards

2010	Irish National Organic Awards	Best Organic Retail Product	St Tola Original
	Irish Cheese Awards	Best New Cheese	St Tola Original
	Irish Cheese Awards	Gold	St Tola Divine
	British Cheese Awards	Silver	St Tola Divine
	Irish National Organic Awards	Best Organic Retail Product	St Tola Original
	Great Taste Awards	2 stars	St Tola Hard
2009	Irish National Organic Awards	Best Organic Export Product	St Tola Original
	SHOP Awards	Supreme Champion	St Tola Original
2008	Great Taste Awards	1 star	St Tola Original

Siobhán Ní Gháirbhith and her son outside her goat-muralled house.

St Tola cheesemaker

St Tola Log (Fresh and Mature) and St Tola Original	
Milk	
Style	Fresh, Soft, *geotrichum* mould rind
Raw/Pasteurised	Raw
Rennet	Traditional
Organic	**Organic**
Reminiscent of	Chèvre
Maturation	6 weeks shelf life (Fresh), 5–8 weeks shelf life (Mature)
Size	1 kg log (Fresh and Mature), 150 g pot, 120 g (Original Mature slice)
Availability	Local, national
Varieties	Fresh, Mature, Original
Made in	Clare

St Tola Log showing the *geotrichum* 'brainy' folds

St Tola Log (Fresh and Mature) and St Tola Original

St Tola Log Fresh is an unmatured goats' cheese with a fresh, tangy flavour and rich, almost whipped texture. The pate and rind are snow white. The cheese is ideal in a salad or in cooking. If this cheese is allowed to mature, it becomes St Tola Log Mature. The distinctly patterned 'brainy' rind matures to a beautiful golden colour under the influence of *geotrichum*[25] mould. The texture becomes creamier and the flavour matures to a rich medley of zesty farmyard tastes. This cheese has a lot going on, with a caramel-like quality to the liquidy bit contrasting with the lemony tang and fluffy texture. The mature cheese is great for the cheeseboard, in salads or even toasted.

St Tola Crottin	
Milk	
Style	Soft
Raw/pasteurised	Raw
Rennet	Traditional
Organic	**Organic**
Reminiscent of	Crottin
Maturation	Shelf life 4 weeks
Size	120 g crottin
Availability	Local, national
Varieties	Ash-covered
Made in	Clare

St Tola Crottin

St Tola Crottin is the result of a similar process to that of St Tola Log, but more moisture is retained in the cheese. The result, not much bigger than a golf ball, is quite reminiscent of a French goats' crottin.[26] The melting texture of the cheese makes it ideal for a cheeseboard or as a starter. It is an excellent complement to honey. The rind is natural and the pate is white. The cheese can be matured to individual requirements and the natural rind yellows with age. Some are covered with ash.

ST TOLA DIVINE		
Milk		
Style	Soft	
Raw/pasteurised	Raw	
Rennet	Traditional	
Organic	**Organic**	
Reminiscent of	Cream cheese	
Size	120 g, 1 kg (catering)	
Availability	Local, national	
Made in	Clare	

St Tola Divine

Divine is the latest addition to the St Tola range and is a classic goats' milk cream cheese. The cheese is creamy, mild and spreadable and goes well with fruit, honey and, of course, the classic salmon.

ST TOLA HARD		
Milk		
Style	Hard	
Raw/pasteurised	Raw	
Rennet	Traditional	
Organic	**Organic**	
Reminiscent of	Gouda, cheddar	
Size	200 g, 450 g, 2.2 kg round	
Availability	Local, national	
Made in	Clare	

St Tola Hard

St Tola Hard is a goats' cheese reminiscent of both gouda and cheddar. The cheese is covered with a yellow wax rind. The pate shows a pale, somewhat marbled cream colour. The flavour is nutty with a bit of zing. The cheese is ideal for the cheeseboard, perhaps with a little fruit and a glass of wine.

ST TOLA GREEK STYLE		
Milk	🐐	
Style	Semi-hard	
Raw/pasteurised	Raw	
Rennet	Traditional	
Organic	Organic	
Reminiscent of	Feta	
Size	150 g slice, 1 kg block	
Availability	Local, national	
Made in	Clare	

St Tola Greek Style

This cheese has a salty, zingy, lemony taste somewhat reminiscent of (Greek) Feta. The texture is firm but crumbly. The rind is natural and the pate is snow white. The cheese is ideal in a salad or in cooking as it retains its shape well.

Sunview Goats (Kilmichael Soft Goats' Cheese)

Sunview Farm is situated in the herb-rich grasslands of Cork – ideal *terroir* for the goat herd of Anne and Brian Bond. The Bonds have been making goats' cheese from their surplus milk as something of a hobby in their retirement. After several attempts, and with encouragement from friends, the Bonds began producing more and more cheese and had to build a dedicated goat dairy. Now their cheese is a sought-after delicacy in the locality and can be found at a number of local farmers' markets. They also sell goats' milk and yoghurt.

The name 'Kilmichael' is from the Irish *Cill Mhichíl* ('St Michael's Church').

SUNVIEW GOATS	
Proprietors:	Anne and Brian Bond
Address:	Sunview House, Terelton, Co. Cork
Phone:	+353 (0)26 46967
Cheese made:	Kilmichael Soft Goats' Cheese
Company size:	Small
Availability:	Local
Recipe:	See p. 346

KILMICHAEL SOFT GOATS' CHEESE

Milk	
Style	Soft
Raw/pasteurised	Raw
Rennet	Vegetarian
Organic	No
Maturation	None to a few weeks
Size	100–120 g topped pyramid
Availability	Local
Varieties	Plain; Parsley & Chives
Made in	Cork

Kilmichael Soft Goats' Cheese

Kilmichael is a cultured soft goats' cheese made with vegetarian rennet. The appearance is somewhat reminiscent of a topped pyramid. When young, the cheese is mild and spreadable and almost cream cheese-like in texture. The pate and natural rind are white. The flavour is clean tasting and mildly goaty. With age, the cheese firms up and yellows somewhat. A plain variety and a variety with a layer of parsley and chives are available. The cheese has both sweet and savoury applications.

Toonsbridge Dairy

Toby Simmonds already runs the Real Olive Company in Ireland but is going into business with local farmer John Lynch. And the business they're going into? Buffalo farming. These are Asian water buffalo (*Bubalus bubalis*) and John has about fifty animals; these are probably the only water buffalo in Ireland. They are kept for dairy and, as of early 2011, the business is just getting off the ground. Toby and John are making high-quality buffalo mozzarella from raw buffalo milk and traditional rennet, the sort you might find in its home territory around Naples. They are also making buffalo ricotta and a hard grana-type cheese with both raw semi-skimmed buffalo milk and cow's milk. With time, buffalo cream cheese and yoghurt may follow. Sean Ferry, of Desmond and Gabriel cheese fame, is also helping with the cheese production.

TOONSBRIDGE DAIRY	
Proprietors:	Toby Simmonds and John Lynch
Address:	Macroom, Co. Cork
Phone:	+353 (0)26 41471
Cheeses made:	Buffalo mozzarella, buffalo ricotta
Company size:	Small
Availability:	Local

Triskel Cheese

Since late 2009 Anna Lévêque has been making cheese at Killowen Orchard on the banks of the River Suir, near Portlaw in County Waterford. Initially arriving in Ireland via a Teagasc placement with the object of improving her English, she took her first steps in cheesemaking with Helen Finnegan at Knockdrinna and subsequently with Frank Shinnick at Fermoy.

When Fermoy reduced their number of cheesemaking days per week, Anna had to look for another outlet. By chance, an acquaintance at Killowen Farm had a unit with cold storage which he offered for setting up a dairy. Anna undertook most of the preparation herself, putting up and then scrubbing by hand plastic panelling which had gone green from having been stored outside.

Anna took inspiration for the name of her cheese from a box of biscuits received as a birthday present. A triskel, or triskelion, is an ancient Celtic symbol involving three points in the form of spirals, legs or arms. Anna began by producing creamy Loire Valley-style goats' cheeses and in summer 2010 began production of a Morbier-style cows' milk cheese, which is showing great promise.

As the milk for all her cheeses is sourced locally, Anna can get the milk straight from the milking parlour to her dairy at its natural temperature without having to chill it.

Despite her relative newcomer status, Anna is already achieving recognition, having been awarded the Bridgestone Guide's Artisan of the Year award for 2010 in their Megabytes Awards.

Anna can accommodate visitors, depending on her availability, but advance notice is essential.

TRISKEL CHEESE	
Proprietor:	Anna Lévêque
Address:	Killowen Orchard, Portlaw, Co. Waterford
Email:	triskelcheese@hotmail.com
Phone:	+353 (0)86 074 4534
Cheeses made:	Triskel Pyramid, Triskel Dew Drop, Triskel Gwenned
Company size:	Small
Availability:	Local, some national

TRISKEL DEW DROP		
Milk		
Style	Soft, fresh	
Raw/pasteurised	Raw	
Rennet	Traditional	
Organic	No	
Reminiscent of	Crottin	
Maturation	None	
Size	100 g	
Availability	Local, national	
Made in	Waterford	

Triskel Pyramid and Dew Drop

Anna Lévêque makes several goats' cheeses, seasonally, during the spring and summer months from milk sourced from a local herd of Alpine/Anglo-Nubian crosses. The youngest and freshest is a crottin-style cheese (shown above) sold in farmers' markets throughout the south. These are typically sold at less than a week old and primarily by a market colleague who will often sell them dressed in olive oil with herbs.

TRISKEL PYRAMID

Milk	
Style	Soft to hard
Raw/pasteurised	Raw
Rennet	Traditional
Organic	No
Reminiscent of	Valençay
Maturation	2–4 weeks
Size	120 g
Availability	Local, national
Made in	Waterford

The cheese is brilliant white throughout and is so young that there is no rind as such. It is fresh and creamy on the nose, which follows through on the palate with the taste of creamy goats' milk, which of course is exactly what it was just a few days previously.

Dew Drop is essentially the same cheese, though formed in the shape of a drop.

Pyramid is reminiscent of a Valençay goats' cheese from the Loire Valley. It is in the shape of a truncated pyramid and coated with ash that, in addition to giving it its distinctive appearance, helps promote the ripening of the cheese. The cheese has a wrinkled bluish-grey appearance. When cut, the pate is a brilliant white with a thin yellowish rind (under the ash coating). It has a fresh, herb-scented, slightly goaty nose. On the palate, the pate is moist, very creamy, fresh and soft.

Pyramid is matured for two to four weeks before being sold.

Ash in cheesemaking *Ash is sometimes used for aesthetic reasons, as in Triskel Gwenned and Morbier, although it serves an important function in the production of certain soft cheeses. The ash (actually a very fine food-grade charcoal) helps to neutralise the surface acid of the cheese and to promote the Penicillium candidum and other ripening moulds, which prefer lower-acid environments, while inhibiting growth of the unwanted kind. It is mixed with salt before application. It works especially well with goats' cheeses, which are naturally high in lactic acid, and will promote the development of a nutty texture with a strong creamy flavour.*

Triskel Gwenned	
Milk	
Style	Semi-hard
Raw/pasteurised	Raw
Rennet	Traditional
Organic	No (but made with organic milk)
Reminiscent of	Morbier
Maturation	6–12 weeks
Size	1 kg wheel, 200 g portions
Availability	Local
Made in	Waterford

Triskel Gwenned

In the summer of 2010 Anna started to produce this cheese from cows' milk locally sourced from an organic herd. She settled on the organic milk after experimenting with both organic and non-organic milk. She found that the properties of the milk from the organic herd made it much easier to work with, reacting very well with the starter and rennet she was using.

It is similar in style to Morbier, with a distinctive line of ash in the centre. In a young, immature cheese the pate is a creamy yellow colour and the rind a reddish brown. At four weeks of maturation the cheese has a creamy nose and, while lacking length on the palate at this stage, has a wonderful fresh flavour and melts very well over potatoes. As the cheese matures, the pate becomes softer and the flavour develops pronounced barnyard notes.

Tullynascreena Goats' Cheese

Michael Tolksdorf and wife Monika run a small cheese operation in Dromahair, Carrick-on-Shannon, County Leitrim, having arrived from Germany in 1995. They don't make cheese all the time but intend to start again in 2011. The Tolksdorfs have a mixed herd of about twenty goats and make soft cheese from raw milk and vegetarian rennet. One of the cheeses is made with herbs and garlic and the other is sold in oil in somewhat similar fashion to Fivemiletown's Boilíe. The quality of the cheese has been recognised in the past through a number of British cheese awards. The cheese is sold in local restaurants and shops. Tullynascreena is named after a local mass rock (*Tulach na Scrin*, 'the hill of the shrine').

TULLYNASCREENA GOATS' CHEESE	
Proprietors:	Michael and Monika Tolksdorf
Address:	Dromahair, Carrick-on-Shannon, Co. Leitrim
Email:	dromahair@arcor.de
Phone:	+353 (0)71 916 4590
Cheese made:	Soft goats' cheese
Company size:	Small
Availability:	Local

Wicklow Farmhouse Cheese

Wicklow Farmhouse Cheese has been run by John and Bernie Hempenstall and their family since 2005, but their ancestors have been farming here for generations. The dairy farm lies at Curranstown, near Croghan Mountain, just outside Arklow in County Wicklow. The family make a range of handmade cheeses from pasteurised milk, produced from their own herd of about sixty Friesian cows. They also make a number of goats' cheeses from pasteurised milk from a local herd. The cows are fed a quality feed during winter, so the Hempenstalls make high-quality cheese throughout the year.

In 2005 John wanted to supplement his farm's income and, with an interest in cheese, he set about looking at how to convert part of his farm to cheese production. With the help of a course and expertise from Teagasc, he invested in a small cheesemaking facility. He saw a niche for blue cheese in the Irish market and soon set about producing Wicklow Blue cheese. He took it upon himself to promote and market his cheese locally and the quality of his product soon began to tell. Local popularity quickly became national. Now Wicklow Blue is widely available across Ireland in local shops, supermarkets, delicatessens, farmers' markets and restaurants. The early success of the cheese was marked by a bronze medal awarded at the British Cheese Awards in 2005, the same year that production started. Many more awards have followed, including a gold medal at the Nantwich International Cheese Awards in 2009.

A selection of Wicklow cheeses

John Hempenstall with awards

Following the success of Wicklow Blue, the Hempenstalls produced a second cheese, Wicklow Baun, a rich, delicately flavoured brie-like cheese, made from double-cream cows' milk, which is also making its mark. John is continuously developing new cheeses with a view to providing a full, balanced cheeseboard. To that end, he now produces a cheddar-like cheese, Wicklow Gold, for the consumer, and a brie, St Kevin, for the catering industry. He also produces soft goats' cheese and goats' gouda with milk from a neighbour's herd. With the company going from strength to strength and establishing its brands within Ireland, John and the family are not sitting on their laurels. They are looking to expand into the UK market and have a number of ideas for exciting new cheeses in the pipeline.

WICKLOW FARMHOUSE CHEESE	
Proprietors:	John and Bernie Hempenstall
Address:	Curranstown, Arklow, Co. Wicklow
Web:	www.wicklowfarmhousecheese.ie
Facebook:	Wicklow-Farmhouse-Cheese
Email:	wfcheese@eircom.net
Phone:	+353 (0)402 91713
Cheeses made:	Wicklow Blue, Wicklow Baun, Wicklow Gold, Wicklow Goats' Gouda, Wicklow Goats' Log, St Kevin Brie
Company size:	Medium
Availability:	Local, national
Other products:	(Cultured) buttermilk
Recipe:	See p. 337 and p. 345

Awards

2010	British Cheese Awards	Bronze	Wicklow Blue
	British Cheese Awards	Gold	Wicklow Gold
	British Cheese Awards	Silver	St Kevin Brie
	British Cheese Awards	Gold	Wicklow Baun
	World Cheese Awards	Gold	Wicklow Baun
	World Cheese Awards	Bronze	Wicklow Gold
2009	World Cheese Awards	Bronze	St Kevin Brie
	World Cheese Awards	Bronze	Wicklow Blue
	British Cheese Awards	Bronze	Wicklow Baun
	International Cheese Awards	Gold	Wicklow Farmhouse Cheese
	SHOP Awards	Gold	Wicklow Baun

WICKLOW BLUE

Milk	
Style	Soft, blue
Raw/pasteurised	Pasteurised
Rennet	Vegetarian
Organic	No
Reminiscent of	Blue brie, Bleu de Bresse, Cambozola
Maturation	3 weeks
Size	150 g and 1.2 kg
Availability	Local, national
Fat	27.3%
Made in	Wicklow

Wicklow Blue

One of the few Irish-made blue cheeses, Wicklow Blue's reputation is firmly established in Ireland. This beautifully mild handmade cheese is somewhat reminiscent of brie, notwithstanding the tangy blue veins. Like Wicklow Baun, the double-cream pasteurised milk gives it a rich, creamy, buttery taste. The delicate mouldy white rind is edible. The pate colour is a deep ivory with rich blue *Penicillium roqueforti* veins. It is somewhat reminiscent of both French Bleu de Bresse and German Cambozola. Since its appearance in Ireland in 2005, this cheese has rapidly established itself as a market leader. A versatile cheese, it can be used as a starter, in a salad, on a cheeseboard or just as a special treat. It is rapidly becoming an Irish classic, winning several medals, including Best Irish Cheese at the World Cheese Awards in 2008, and several medals at the International Cheese Award and the British Cheese Awards in 2008 and 2009.

WICKLOW BAUN		
Milk		
Style	Soft, white-mould	
Raw/pasteurised	Pasteurised	
Rennet	Vegetarian	
Organic	No	
Reminiscent of	Brie	
Maturation	4 weeks	
Size	150 g and 1.2 kg	
Availability	Local, national	
Made in	Wicklow	

Wicklow Baun

Wicklow Baun is an award-winning brie-like cheese from the same stable as Wicklow Blue. Following the success of Wicklow Blue, the Hempenstall family began to produce this soft white-rind cheese in 2006. The pasteurised full-fat double-cream milk used in the cheese gives it its rich, creamy, buttery taste. It is somewhat of an understatement to say that this cheese is brie-like, as it leaves many bries in its wake. It is delicious as a standalone cheese, in a sandwich or to end a meal. A similar cheese, St Kevin Brie, is also produced for the catering industry in 1 kg bricks. The origin of the name 'baun' is from the Irish *bán*, meaning 'white'. The surface-ripening white mould is a typical *Penicillium candidum*.

Wicklow Gold	
Milk	
Style	Hard
Raw/pasteurised	Pasteurised
Rennet	Vegetarian
Organic	No
Reminiscent of	Sweet cheddar
Maturation	4 months – 1½ years
Size	200 g and 3 kg
Availability	Local, national
Varieties	Plain; Dillisk; Nettle & Chives; Basil & Garlic; Tomato & Herbs
Made in	Wicklow

Wicklow Gold

Wicklow Gold is a mild, sweet cheddar from the makers of Wicklow Blue and Wicklow Baun. Having successfully developed the brie range, the Hempenstalls turned to production of hard cheeses. Their first, produced since 2007, is a delicious cheddar made from pasteurised milk from their own herd of Friesian cows, with vegetarian rennet. The pate has a light gold colour and is sold rindless. The cheddar is available in several varieties: Dillisk (seaweed), Nettle & Chives, Basil & Garlic and Tomato & Herbs. Deeply flavoured aged varieties are also becoming available.

WICKLOW GOATS LOG	
Milk	
Style	Soft
Raw/pasteurised	Pasteurised
Rennet	Vegetarian
Organic	No
Reminiscent of	French log
Maturation	4 weeks
Size	150 g and 1 kg
Availability	Local, some national
Made in	Wicklow

WICKLOW GOATS GOUDA	
Milk	
Style	Semi-hard
Raw/pasteurised	Pasteurised
Rennet	Vegetarian
Organic	No
Reminiscent of	Goat gouda
Maturation	3 months min.
Size	150 g and 5 kg
Availability	Local, some national
Made in	Wicklow

Wicklow Goats Log and Goats Gouda

The Hempenstalls started making goats' cheeses in 2009. So far, two cheeses are produced, a soft goats' log and a semi-hard goats' gouda. Both are made from pasteurised goats' milk sourced from a neighbour, using vegetarian rennet. *Penicillium candidum* gives the white-bloom rind to the goats' log, while the gouda is covered in red wax. The log pate is pure white when young. The gouda has a cream-coloured pate and is cooked and pressed. The gouda was introduced to the market towards the end of 2009. Both are available from deli counters and farmers' markets locally, with some nationwide availability.

Wilma's Killorglin Farmhouse Cheese

Wilma Silvius came to Ireland in 1980 and married husband John O'Connor in 1983. When the recession hit in the 1980s and she was laid off from her teaching job, she turned to cheesemaking. Leveraging her Dutch heritage, she started making gouda-style cheese in her kitchen. Success led to sales in local grocery stores and country markets. Expansion continued and her cheese became well known outside the locale of Killorglin, County Kerry. When her husband became involved in politics in the early 2000s, Wilma cut back her production somewhat, but her cheese is still sought out and favoured by locals and tourists alike.

Wilma produces cheese only in the summer months, from the pasteurised milk of her twenty-four Holstein cows. She makes a little raw-milk cheese on demand but there are extra overheads involved in raw-milk cheese production that prove prohibitive with a small-scale operation such as Wilma's. Only natural rennet is used to make the cheese range. As well as the plain gouda, Wilma also makes a cumin-infused cheese in the Leiden style and some with cloves in the Friesland style. She also makes some with garlic and a soft quark cheese and some yoghurt. Most of the cheese is released after six weeks, but some of the gouda is aged for up to three years, developing a rich, nutty flavour and used, sometimes, in place of Parmesan.

Her produce can be found at local markets in Kerry and at selected outlets around the country, including Cavistons in Dublin, On the Pigs Back in the English Market, Cork, Peter Ward's Country Choice in Nenagh, and from her house. Wilma does accommodate tourist visits to her farm, but large groups must call ahead.

WILMA'S KILLORGLIN FARMHOUSE CHEESE	
Proprietor:	Wilma O'Connor
Address:	Ardmoniel, Killorglin, Co. Kerry
Email:	killorglincheese@eircom.net
Phone:	+353 (0)66 976 1402/ +353 (0)87 978 7944
Cheeses made:	Plain Gouda, Gouda with cumin, cloves or garlic, Quark
Company size:	Small
Availability:	Local
Other product:	Yoghurt

Yeats Country Foods

In the late 1980s, in the heart of Yeats Country in County Sligo, the Higgins and Molloy families formed Yeats Country Foods. Initially they made soft cream cheese, fromage frais, yoghurt, pasteurised milk, cream and buttermilk. As the quality of the products became known, the company expanded. Now they have a state-of-the-art production factory in the rolling hills of Donegal and are certified organic, producing the same range of dairy products: soft cheese, low-fat soft cheese, sour cream, crème fraîche, cheese dips, fresh milk, low-fat milk and buttermilk.

Yeats Country is named after a region encompassing County Sligo and parts of Leitrim and Roscommon, renowned for its beauty and named after the Irish poet William Butler Yeats, who grew up in this area and wrote about it in his poetry.

YEATS COUNTRY FOODS	
Proprietor:	John Molloy
Address:	Carraroe, Sligo, Co. Sligo. (Green Pastures Donegal, Creamery Road, Convoy Lifford, Co. Donegal)
Web:	www.yeatscountryfoods.com www.greenpasturesdonegal.com
Facebook:	YeatsCountryFoods
Email:	info@yeatscountryfoods.com info@greenpasturesdonegal.com
Phone:	+353 (0)74 914 7193 +353 (0)74 914 7463
Cheeses made:	Organic Soft Cheese, Organic Light in Fat Soft Cheese, Organic Light in Fat Soft Cheese Mini Pots, 3 cheese dips
Company size:	Large
Availability:	National
Other products:	Sour cream, crème fraîche, fresh milk, 1% milk, buttermilk

Awards

2010	World Cheese Awards	Bronze	Organic Full Fat Soft Cheese
	Great Taste Awards	1 star	Organic Low Fat Soft Cheese
	Great Taste Awards	1 star	Organic Full Fat Soft Cheese
2009	World Cheese Awards	Silver	Organic Full Fat Soft Cheese
	World Cheese Awards	Bronze	Organic Low Fat Soft Cheese
	Great Taste Awards	1 star	Organic Full Fat Soft Cheese
	Great Taste Awards	1 star	Organic Low Fat Soft Cheese
	Great Taste Awards	1 star	Organic Mascarpone
2008	Great Taste Awards	2 stars	Full Fat Soft Cheese
	Great Taste Awards	1 star	Soft Cheese

YEATS COUNTRY ORGANIC SOFT CHEESE

Milk	
Style	Soft
Raw/pasteurised	Pasteurised
Rennet	Vegetarian
Organic	Organic
Reminiscent of	Cream cheese
Size	150 g
Availability	National
Fat	28% (Full Fat) 16% (Light in Fat)
Made in	Sligo, Donegal

Yeats Country Organic Soft Cheese

Yeats Country Organic Soft Cheese is a light, soft cheese made from cows' milk with vegetarian rennet. Typically the cheese is available in 150 g tubs. A Light in Fat version is also available.

This is real cream cheese with that substantial, rich cream cheese taste.

3. Other Irish Cheesemakers

This section describes some Irish cheesemakers who perhaps do not fit the stricter guidelines on farmhouse and artisanal cheeses by virtue of their size or the fact that they source their milk, cheese or curd from other cheesemakers or from overseas or they repackage cheese. These producers are not industrial block cheese makers; they still retain at least an artisanal element in their cheesemaking. Some of them are quite small, but some of their production may be outside the stricter definitions of farmhouse or artisanal cheeses, as discussed on pp. 11–14. Nonetheless, the cheese produced can be of the highest quality.

Abbey Cheese Co. (Paddy Jack Cheese)

The Abbey Cheese Company was founded in the early 1990s by Pat Hyland – Paddy Jack to his friends and loyal customers – as a means of maximising revenue from his milk supply. Abbey produces a range of brie-style cheeses.

His first cheese was a risky proposition, Abbey Blue Brie – similar in style to Cambozola. It proved to be a success and Pat added a plain and a smoked brie to the range, a goats' cheese, St Canice, and a cows' cheese, Paddy Jack.

Pat has been selling his cheeses from his stall in the Temple Bar Farmers' Market for a decade now and there is some local availability in supermarkets.

Abbey Cheese Co.	
Proprietor:	Pat Hyland
Address:	Cuffsborough, Ballacolla, Co. Laois
Email:	abbeycheese@eircom.net
Phone:	+353 (0)57 873 8599
Cheeses made:	Abbey Blue Brie, Abbey Brie, Abbey Smoked Brie, Abbey Goats' Cheese, St Canice, Paddy Jack
Company size:	Small
Availability:	Local

Abbey Blue Cheese

Abbey Smoked Brie

Bandon Vale Fine Cheese Co.

Bandon Vale was founded in 1994 by Andy and Margaret Mahon to revive the art of 'territorial' cheesemaking and expanded over the course of a decade to become a major supplier of ingredients to the food industry.

Today, in association with Newmarket Creamery, Bandon Vale source and hand pack a range of speciality cheeses made from pasteurised cows' milk, aimed primarily at the hamper market. These are Vintage, a nutty, mature cheddar; Murragh, a full-flavoured Irish cheddar; and Glandór, a mellow-flavoured Red Leicester style. They are available as large waxed cheeses, 250 g prepack, and small 200 g waxed varieties.

BANDON VALE FINE CHEESE CO.	
Proprietors:	Andy and Margaret Mahon
Address:	Lauragh Industrial Estate, Bandon, Co. Cork
Web:	www.bandonvale.ie
Email:	info@bandonvale.ie
Phone:	+353 (0)23 884 3334
Cheeses made:	Vintage, Murragh, Glandór
Company size:	Medium
Availability:	National

Cahill's Cheese

Dan Cahill presides over Cahill's Cheese, inherited from his father, David, who retains a great pride in the family business. David inherited the farm from his father, William, who inherited it from his uncle, David. Old great-grand-uncle David had emigrated to Massachusetts in the 1860s. When he returned to Ireland in 1902, he bought the 64-acre dairy farm. Today the Cahills have a successful international business hand-crafting cheese, with a range of additives, from cheddar curds. Dan's father, David, studied dairy science at UCC and not only worked the family farm but worked as a government dairy inspector at the local Golden Vale creamery. Around 1979, together with wife Marion, David started making yoghurt and a little cream and cottage cheese, and later branched into cheddar manufacture. The small quantities produced were sold in local shops. By 1985 they were producing what was probably the first porter cheese in the world. Today, through a number of distributors, Cahill's is sold across Ireland, the UK and perhaps their largest market, the US.

CAHILL'S CHEESE	
Proprietor:	Dan Cahill
Address:	Newcastle West, Co. Limerick
Web:	www.cahillscheese.ie
Facebook:	Cahill's Cheese
Email:	info@cahillscheese.ie
Phone:	+353 (0)69 62365
Cheeses made:	Ardagh Wine Cheddar (red), Ballintubber Cheddar with Chives (black), Ballyporeen Cheddar with Herbs (green), Whiskey Cheese (yellow), Original Irish Porter Cheddar (brown, with Guinness)
Company size:	Large
Availability:	Local, national, international (US)
Recipe:	See p. 333

(Top, l–r): Cahill's Ardagh Castle Wine Cheese, Dan Cahill; (middle): Cahill's Porter, Ballintubber and Ballyporeen cheeses; (bottom, l–r): Cahill's Wine Cheese, Cahill's Porter Cheese.

Cahill's is a range of cheeses made from pasteurised cows' milk and vegetarian rennet. A number of flavours are available, colourfully sealed in natural wax: Ardagh Wine Cheddar (red), Ballintubber Cheddar with Chives (black), Ballyporeen Cheddar with Herbs (green), Whiskey Cheese (yellow) and Original Irish Porter Cheddar (brown). The whiskey used is Irish Kilbeggan whiskey (www.kilbegganwhiskey.com) and the porter used is Guinness (www.guinness.com).

Herbs were historically mixed into cheeses in the seventeenth century in the Galtee Mountains, as it was believed that the herbs had health-promoting properties. Adding whiskey to cheese was a monastic activity in Ireland, allegedly later brought to Scotland by Irish monks.

Ardagh Wine Cheddar is named after Ardagh in west Limerick, where this medieval monastic cheese was revived about a hundred years ago from an old Limerick Palatine recipe.

JOD – Old Irish Creamery

JOD is an award-winning family cheese manufacturing firm based in Kilmallock, County Limerick.

Founded in 1992 by Jim O'Doherty, a former cheesemaker with Golden Vale Food Products in nearby Charleville, JOD specialises in flavoured cheddar-style cheeses (they also produce unflavoured varieties), which have brought a host of awards to their door over the years – three silver medals at the World Cheese Awards; gold, silver and three bronze medals at the International Cheese Awards; and silver at the SHOP awards – all in 2010 alone.

This is truly a family business, as Jim is assisted by wife Lulu and son James. Pat Kinnane looks after the commercial side and there is a staff of four to manufacture the cheese.

JOD – OLD IRISH CREAMERY	
Proprietor:	Jim O'Doherty
Address:	JOD Foods, Effin Creamery, Kilmallock, Co. Limerick
Web:	www.oldirishcreamery.com

Email:	info@oldirishcreamery.com
Phone:	+353 (0)63 71209
Cheeses made:	Old Irish Creamery plain and flavoured cheddar-style cheeses
Company size:	Medium
Availability:	National, international

Oisín Farmhouse Cheese

Rochus van der Vaard grew up in the Netherlands in the surroundings of the beautiful Biesbosch National Park. As an adult he kept a little goat farm, but the authorities decided that the land on which he lived needed to be returned to the water! When his land was bought out, Rochus looked to Ireland, where land was cheap at the time.

Having moved to Ireland in 1997 with his wife and young daughter, he runs his cheesemaking operation near Kilmallock, south of Limerick City, in the lush Golden Vale. Rochus and wife Rose's cheesemaking operation is certified organic by IOFGA. In the summer months they make gouda-style cheese from the milk of local goats and sheep. Some of the goat gouda is flavoured with garlic and nettles and some is smoked. All the cheese is made from pasteurised milk with GM-free vegetarian rennet.

In winter, when milk supply is hard to come by, Rochus imports milk and cheese from his native Netherlands and from Italy. The Dutch cheese is made by his sister, an expert and fanatical cheesemaker. Rochus sells imported Chevretta, a Greek-style cheese, and a delicious blue goat gouda from his sister, a Feta from Greece and a Parmesan from Italy. This imported cheese is organic, high quality and low in price.

Rochus had his own goats from 1997 to 2004, when he found, as have many Irish farmhouse cheesemakers, that it was impossible to be both a full-time farmer and full-time cheesemaker, so now his herd has been taken over by a neighbour and Rochus buys back the milk.

Rochus is investing in new farmland some six miles away and intends to use native Irish Dexter cattle to make cheese. These 'mini-cattle' are usually black in colour and the smallest in Europe, producing creamy milk not unlike that of the Jersey breed. They probably date back to the nineteenth century in Ireland. Rochus will make cows' gouda and cheddar.

Oisín cheese is named after the local townland of Glenosheen (*Gleann Oisín*, 'Oisín's glen') in the Ballyhoura Mountains.

OISÍN FARMHOUSE CHEESE	
Proprietors:	Rose van de Graff and Rochus van der Vaard
Address:	Glenosheen, Kilmallock, Co. Limerick
Email:	oisinfarmhouse@gmail.com
Phone:	+353 (0)63 91528
Cheeses made:	Goats' and sheep's gouda
Company size:	Medium
Availability:	Local, national

Round Tower Farmhouse Cheese

Round Tower is a distributor of a range of cheeses, including Dingle Gold Cheddar and other sliced and grated cheddar and artisanal gouda, branded as Round Tower and available as young, matured or with herbs. The company also distributes a number of other Irish cheeses.

ROUND TOWER FARMHOUSE CHEESE	
Proprietors:	Nan and Michael O'Donovan
Address:	Farranmareen, Enniskeane, Co. Cork
Email:	gkmr@eircom.net
Phone:	+353 (0)23 47105/+353 (0)87 273 1329
Company size:	Small

4. Irish Farmhouse Cheese Recipes

What happens to the holes
when all the cheese has been eaten?
Anon.

Cheese can be used in every course: hot and cold starters, soups and salads, main courses and sides, and even in desserts. It is a key constituent in a number of classic snack recipes: cheese on toast, macaroni cheese, lasagne, potatoes dauphinois, aligot, breaded cheese sticks, deep-fried cheese, French onion soup, blue cheese salad, goats' cheese salad, fondue, cauliflower cheese, cheese soufflé, cheese bread and four-cheese pizza, to name but a few. Irish artisanal cheeses are found in the best restaurants right across Ireland and international chefs are beginning to recognise the exceptional quality of Irish cheeses. We are delighted to reproduce a number of cheese recipes provided by some of the best chefs that Ireland has to offer. These recipes are chosen to show the versatility of cheese in cooking. While not all Irish farmhouse cheeses are represented here, those used are a good cross-section of the current range of Irish artisanal cheeses, from the very soft to the very hard. Readers should use their own discretion in replacing one cheese with another in these recipes; cooking is about experimentation, but be aware that the chefs have chosen some of these cheeses carefully for their complementary flavours, textures and even melting points.

Before the recipes, we present a few tips and guidelines for cooking with cheese.

Cooking with cheese

Cheese is composed of water, fat and milk protein. As a general rule, if you heat cheese beyond 60°C (140°F) or expose cheese to lower heat for a prolonged period, the protein coagulates and separates from the fat and water. This coagulate is tough and stringy. The process is irreversible and should be avoided.

Cheeses with higher moisture levels (60–80 per cent – soft cheese) tend to melt at lower temperatures, around 30°C (86°F), while cheeses with lower moisture levels (30–35 per cent – hard cheese) melt at higher temperatures, around 70–75°C (158–167°F). Others will melt at 40–45°C (104–113°F). All cheeses have an identifiable melting point for which you can test. For example, cream cheese melts at about 30°C (86°F), blue cheese at about 45°C (113°F), camembert and brie at about 40°C (104°F), Parmesan at about 70°C (158°F). The melting point of hard cheeses like cheddar and gouda increases with the age of the cheese.[1]

Guidelines for cooking with cheese

- Do not be tempted to cook with bad cheese. If it is bad, throw it out. On the other hand, if you have leftover cheese which is still perfectly good but might not look so appetising, you can freeze it with a view to cooking with it later.
- Freezing cows' milk cheese dries it out, making it dry and crumbly when thawed – not good to eat directly but fine for cooking. Goats' and sheep's milk cheeses freeze better.
- Cheese and high heat do not mix well. Minimise exposure to heat in terms of duration and degree.
- Add the cheese towards the end of cooking and off the main heat.
- Sometimes the heat of the food alone is enough to melt the cheese.
- Exposure can be controlled better with a microwave (at reduced power) – brown briefly under the grill if necessary.
- Grate, crumble or shred the cheese before adding – the cheese will melt more quickly and will be exposed to heat for a shorter time.
- Lower-fat cheeses and fresh cheeses such as cottage cheese, ricotta, Feta or mascarpone have a higher proportion of protein and will not stand heat as well as a higher-fat cheese. Fresh cheeses can 'curdle' very easily. When heated gently, these cheeses are excellent for making sauces.
- Washed-rind and soft-ripened cheeses (like Taleggio, Reblochon and St André) can exude oil in an unpleasant way when heated too much. When heated gently, they are excellent on pizzas.
- Very low-fat and non-fat versions of full-fat cheeses like 'block' cheddar often do not melt properly.
- Very high-fat cheeses such as mozzarella or provolone will melt more easily and mix in sauces better if there are other fat-rich ingredients in the sauces (the fats blend well).
- Very hard cheeses (e.g. Parmigiano-Reggiano, Pecorino, aged gouda) can turn pleasantly crispy and crunchy when heated. They are also excellent for grating on pasta, soups and quiches.

- Hard cheeses like cheddar are excellent for grilled cheese sandwiches and to add flavour to soufflés and gougères.
- Lemon juice helps prevent coagulation.
- Starch added to a cheese sauce mix helps the cheese to bind and stay bound.
- Cooking mollifies the taste of cheese, so choose a stronger-tasting cheese than you think you need.
- Do not be tempted to cook with processed cheese. Although it may melt better, the flavour will be mollified and artificial.
- Cooking with alcohol and cheese together can destabilise the cheese. If the alcohol is added slowly and allowed to evaporate, the effect on the cheese will be minimised.

Derry Clarke's carpaccio of beef with grated Gabriel Cheese and watercress salad, horseradish mayonnaise

Reproduced with the permission of Derry Clarke, chef patron of L'Ecrivain, Dublin (www.lecrivain.com).

'Carpaccio of beef is surprisingly popular in the restaurant. The thinner you can slice the beef, the better. I am serving it with Gabriel cheese, which is a lovely mature, hard cheese from the west of Cork.'

Serves 4

Ingredients
400 g beef fillet, trimmed of all fat

1 tablespoon Dijon mustard

1 tablespoon black peppercorns, crushed

1 tablespoon sea salt

1 tablespoon chopped parsley

Cheese and watercress salad
1 bunch watercress, washed

200 g Gabriel or Parmesan

285 ml mayonnaise

1 tablespoon horseradish mixed with the juice of 1 lemon

Method

Rub the beef on all sides with the mustard. Roll in the pepper, salt and parsley mixture. Roll the beef tightly in clingfilm and place in the freezer for three hours. Slice very thinly on a slicing machine or with a very sharp carving knife. Add the horseradish/lemon mixture to the mayonnaise and mix.

Lay the beef on a plate. Arrange the cress on top. Season with sea salt and pepper. Grate the cheese over the dish and serve with the horseradish mayonnaise on the side.

Denis Cotter's strawberry, watercress and Knockalara Sheep's Cheese salad with honey-raspberry dressing and spiced walnut crumb

Reproduced with the permission of Denis Cotter, owner/chef of the fabulous vegetarian Cafe Paradiso, Cork City, and author of several books, including For the Love of Food: Vegetarian Recipes from the Heart (Collins, London, 2011) (www.cafeparadiso.ie).

Serves 4

Ingredients
2 slices of day-old bread

2 tablespoons walnuts

4 dried birdseye chillies, crushed

2 tablespoons fresh parsley, chopped

2 tablespoons olive oil

Dressing
2 tablespoons raspberry vinegar

1 tablespoon honey

10 fresh raspberries

200 ml sunflower oil

Salad
250 g watercress

12 strawberries, quartered lengthways

150 g Knockalara Sheep's Cheese, crumbled

Method

Put the bread in a food processor with the walnuts, chillies and parsley, and pulse to get a coarse crumb. Heat the olive oil in a frying pan over medium heat, add the crumb and fry it for 5 minutes, stirring, until browned and crisp. Drain on kitchen paper.

Blend all the dressing ingredients to get a slightly thickened dressing. Mix all the salad ingredients gently with enough of the dressing to lightly coat the leaves.

Divide the salad between four plates and drizzle a little more of the dressing around the plate. Scatter some of the spiced walnut crumb over the top.

Darina Allen's salad of Crozier Blue Cheese with char-grilled pears and spiced candied nuts

Reproduced with the permission of Darina Allen. Copyright © 2011 Ballymaloe Cookery School (www.cookingisfun.ie).

Serves 8

Ingredients

Salad
A selection of salad leaves (include curly endive and watercress if possible)

3–4 ripe pears, depending on size (Bartlett or Anjou)

sunflower oil for grilling

110–175 g ripe Crozier Blue or Cashel Blue Cheese

Spiced candied nuts
100 g walnut halves

75 g sugar

½ teaspoon freshly ground cinnamon

½ teaspoon freshly ground coriander

¼ teaspoon freshly ground star anise

Dressing
2 tablespoons red wine vinegar

6 tablespoons extra virgin olive oil (we use Mani or extra virgin organic olive oil from Greece)

salt and freshly ground pepper

Garnish
chervil sprigs

Method

Preheat the oven to 180°C/350°F/gas mark 4.

Gently wash and carefully dry the salad leaves. Put into a bowl, cover and refrigerate.

Spread the walnuts in a single layer on a baking tray and toast them for 4 or 5 minutes, just until they smell rich and nutty. Meanwhile, mix the sugar with the spices. Spread over the base of a frying pan in an even layer. Scatter the walnut halves on top. Cook over a medium heat until the sugar melts and starts to colour. Carefully rotate the pan until the walnuts are completely coated with the amber-coloured spicy caramel. Turn out onto a Silpat® mat or silicone paper or an oiled baking tray. Allow to cool and harden. Store in an airtight container until later if necessary.

Whisk all the ingredients together for the dressing, pour into a jam jar, cover and store until needed.

Heat a grill-pan on a high flame. Peel, quarter and core the pears. Toss in a little sunflower oil, grill on both sides and then on the rounded side.

Cut the cheese into cubes or small wedges. Sprinkle the salad leaves with the dressing and toss gently until the leaves glisten. Taste and add more seasoning if necessary.

Divide the salad between the plates, making a little mound in the centre. Slice each char-grilled pear in half and tuck three pieces in between the leaves. Scatter with a few cubes of Crozier Blue and some spiced candied walnuts. Sprinkle with a few sprigs of chervil and serve. Bellingham Blue, Stilton or Gorgonzola cheese would also be delicious.

Potato and Bellingham Blue Cheese soup

Contributed by George Philips.

Serves 4–6

Ingredients

3 tablespoons olive oil

1 onion, peeled and chopped

1 kg potatoes, peeled and cut into small cubes

1 litre vegetable or chicken stock

2 garlic cloves, peeled and chopped

sea salt and black pepper to taste

1 cauliflower, trimmed and cut into small pieces

3 sprigs of thyme

200 g Bellingham Blue cheese

150 ml single cream

Garnish
parsley, finely chopped (optional)

Method

When cooking with blue cheese, taste the cheese for salt content and adjust added salt accordingly.

Heat the olive oil in the pan, add the onion and cook until soft. Stir every minute. Turn the heat up to medium and add the potatoes, stock, garlic, salt and pepper. Let the soup cook for 20 minutes, until the potatoes are soft. Add the cauliflower and thyme and season lightly with sea salt and black pepper.

Cut and crumble the cheese so that it will melt easily when added to the soup. Cut off any hard rind that may stay solid.

Liquidise the soup or mash, then return it to the pan at a low heat.

Add the cream and cook over a low heat until the cheese has melted. Remove from heat, cool, then blend until really smooth.

Return the soup to the heat. When it is thoroughly warmed, re-season and serve in hot bowls with crusty bread. Garnish with parsley or any other edible herb if you have any to hand.

Roasted pepper with Ardrahan Cheese

From Ardrahan Cheese.

Serves 2

Ingredients

2 large sweet red peppers

4 large tablespoons of mixed salad leaves (young spinach or lambs' lettuce)

227 g Ardrahan Cheese

garlic croûtons, heated

4 tablespoons vinaigrette dressing

Method

Put the peppers in a roasting tin and bake in a very hot oven (230°C/450°F/gas mark 8) for 15 minutes, until the skin has blistered and blackened. Cool and peel away the skin, removing the seeds and stalk ends. Cut into slices.

Wash and dry the salad leaves and tear them into bite-sized pieces. Put in a dish with the peppers. Cut the cheese into wafer-thin slices and add to the dish. Add the hot garlic croûtons and toss in the dressing.

Serve immediately.

Deep-fried St Killian

Copyright © 2011 John McLaughlin.

Serves 6

Ingredients

1 young St Killian

1 egg, beaten

breadcrumbs

sunflower oil for deep-fat frying

redcurrant jelly

Method

Refrigerate the cheese before starting, to make sure that it is firm.

Put the egg into a bowl and spread the breadcrumbs in a thick layer on a plate or shallow bowl. Cut the cheese into six wedges. Coat with the egg and roll in the breadcrumbs until well coated. Arrange on a plate. Put the wedges into the freezer for about 15–20 minutes to ensure they are well chilled (though not frozen) for the next step.

Heat the oil in the fryer. Deep-fry the wedges until the breadcrumbs are crispy and golden brown. Do them in two or three batches so that the oil doesn't cool down.

Serve immediately with redcurrant jelly on the side. Rocket salad with balsamic dressing would be a good accompaniment.

Carrigaline thatched pork chops

From Carrigaline Farmhouse Cheese.

Serves 4

Ingredients
4 pork loin chops

salt and ground
black pepper

2 cooking apples, peeled,
cored and chopped

125 g Carrigaline Cheese,
grated

Method

Season the chops and grill for 10–15 minutes on each side.

Place the apples in a saucepan with 3 tablespoons of water. Cover and cook gently until the apples form a thick pulp. Mix in half of the Carrigaline Cheese.

Spread the apple mixture over the cooked chops. Sprinkle the remaining cheese over the top. Return the chops to the grill and cook until the cheese melts.

Mount Callan Cheese and leek soufflé

From CÁIS – originally from Bord Bia.

Serves 6

Ingredients
butter for greasing

2 tablespoons olive oil

3 leeks, chopped

2 tablespoons butter

3 tablespoons plain flour

350 ml warm milk

100 g Mount Callan
Cheese, grated

1 tablespoon lemon
thyme leaves

cracked black pepper

3 egg yolks

4 egg whites

425 ml cream

Method

Brush six 1-cup-capacity soufflé ramekins with butter. Heat the olive oil in a frying pan over a medium heat. Add the leeks and cook for 6 minutes or until golden. Set aside.

Place 2 tablespoons of butter in a saucepan over a medium heat and melt. Add the flour and cook, stirring for 1 minute. Whisk the milk into the flour mixture and then stir until the mixture has boiled and thickened. Remove the mixture from the heat and stir through the cheese, thyme, pepper, leeks and egg yolks.

Beat the egg whites until soft peaks form. Fold the egg whites through the cheese mixture and spoon into the ramekins. Place the ramekins in a baking dish and fill the dish with enough water to come halfway up the sides of the ramekins.

Bake at 180°C/350°F/gas mark 4 for 20 minutes or until the soufflés are puffed and set. Remove the baking dish from the oven and allow the soufflés to fall and cool slightly.

To serve, invert the soufflés onto deep serving dishes and coat each with cream. Return to the oven and bake for a further 15 minutes or until the soufflés are puffed and golden. Serve with a rocket salad.

Glebe Brethan fondue

From Glebe Brethan Cheese.

Serves 4–6

Ingredients
300 ml dry white wine

500 g Glebe Brethan cheese, diced

1 garlic clove, crushed

freshly ground black pepper

1 tablespoon cornflour

1 loaf of country or wheaten bread cut into cubes, each with a crust

Method

Reserve 3 tablespoons of the wine and add the rest to a heavy saucepan and heat to simmering. Add the cheese, garlic and pepper, stirring with a wooden spoon until melted. Blend the cornflour with the reserved cold wine, adding to the fondue mixture until creamy. Season to taste.

Serve hot with chunks of bread speared on forks.

Durrus/Milleens tartiflette

Tartiflette is a great staple of the French Savoie region. It is traditionally made with Reblochon, but Durrus or Milleens make excellent stand-ins.

Serves 6

Ingredients
1 kg waxy potatoes
(e.g. Charlotte, Nicola, Désirée)

25 g butter/2 tablespoons
sunflower oil or a mixture
of both

2 large onions, peeled
and thinly sliced

200 g lardons*

1 clove of garlic, peeled
and halved

salt and pepper

250 g tub crème fraîche

100 ml dry white wine
(optional)

1 young Milleens Dote**
or small Durrus

Method

Preheat the oven to 210°C/410°F/gas mark 6.

Bring the potatoes to the boil in their jackets, reduce the heat and boil for about 10 minutes – they should not be fully cooked. Remove from the heat, drain, and when cool enough to handle, peel them and cut them into 5 mm slices.

Heat the butter and/or oil in a large heavy frying pan. Add the onions and lardons and sweat over a low-medium heat until soft.

Rub the inside of an ovenproof dish with the cut side of the clove of garlic. Arrange a layer of potato slices on the bottom, followed by a layer of the onions and lardons. Season with salt and pepper (beware if the lardons are from a salty joint of bacon!). Repeat this layer upon layer until all are used up – finish with an onion/lardon layer.

Spread the crème fraîche over the top of the layers. Add the white wine if using.

Cut the Milleens in half and then split each half horizontally. Arrange the cheese cut side down on top of the mixture. Transfer to the oven. Cook for around 10 minutes.

Reduce the oven to 180°C/350°F/gas mark 4 and continue to cook for another 15–20 minutes or until the cheese is well melted over the potato mixture.

Serve with a green salad.

Notes

With washed-rind cheeses, the rind can become quite strong and, though edible, may not be to the taste of all. If this is the case, the rind can be trimmed from the cheese before putting it in the oven.

*   *To make lardons, cut 5 mm slices from a smoked streaky bacon joint, removing the skin if necessary. Cut the slice(s) into 5 mm wide strips. If the slices come from a thick joint, or if you prefer cubed lardons, you may cut the strips further into rough 5 mm cubes.*

**   *A Dote is the small individual Milleens cheese. If you can only find pieces sold from the larger cheese, simply cut them into slices and proceed with the recipe.*

Aligot (with Fermoy St Gall)

Aligot is a hearty potato and cheese dish from the L'Aubrac region of central France. It is delicious enough to eat on its own, but makes an excellent accompaniment to a good steak or, for the ultimate comfort food, some good-quality sausages.

Serves 6

Ingredients

500 g floury potatoes (e.g. Kerrs Pinks, Golden Wonder)

salt

2 cloves garlic, peeled

50 g butter

200 ml crème fraîche

300 g young St Gall

salt and pepper

Method

Peel the potatoes and put them in a pot of cold salted water with the cloves of garlic. Bring to the boil and simmer until cooked. Remove from the heat and drain. Add the butter and crème fraîche and mash the potatoes.

While the potatoes are cooking, trim the rind from the cheese and cut it into thin slices. Add the cheese to the mashed potato and return the pot to a very low heat. Season to taste.

Using a wooden spoon, stir continuously until the mixture becomes very elastic and forms long strings when the spoon is removed from the pot.

Serve piping hot as a side dish with steak or good-quality sausages.

Darina Allen's Ardsallagh Goats Cheese croquettes with rocket leaves, roast pepper and tapenade oil

Serves 5

Ingredients
285 g Ardsallagh Soft Goats Cheese (or a similar fresh mild goat cheese)

seasoned flour

1 egg, beaten

flaked almonds to coat cheese

white breadcrumbs to coat cheese

2 large red peppers

extra virgin olive oil

Tapenade oil
110 g black olives, stoned

1 tablespoon capers

1 teaspoon lemon juice, freshly squeezed

160 ml olive oil

freshly ground pepper

Dressing
4 tablespoons extra virgin olive oil

1 tablespoon balsamic vinegar

½ clove garlic, peeled and crushed

salt and freshly ground pepper

Salad
selection of lettuce and rocket leaves

Garnish
wild garlic flowers in season

Method

First divide the Ardsallagh Goats Cheese into 25 balls and chill.

Next make the tapenade oil. Coarsely chop the olives and capers and add the lemon juice. Whisk in the olive oil and process to a coarse or smooth purée as you prefer. Season with freshly ground pepper.

Coat the cheese in seasoned flour, egg, flaked almonds and breadcrumbs. Arrange in a single layer on a flat plate. Cover and chill well.

Roast the peppers in a preheated oven 200°C/400°F/gas mark 6 for approximately 20 minutes. Put into a bowl, cover the top with clingfilm and allow to steam for 5–10 minutes. Peel, remove seeds and cut into strips.

Next make the dressing. Whisk all the ingredients together in a bowl. Heat the oil in a deep-fat fryer or a pan to 200°C/400°F. Fry the croquettes in batches until crisp and golden. Drain on kitchen paper.

Toss the salad leaves in a bowl with just enough dressing to make the leaves glisten.

Divide between the five plates. Put five croquettes on each plate, decorate with strips of red pepper, rocket leaves and a drizzle of tapenade oil. Scatter some wild garlic flowers over the top and serve immediately.

Indian potatoes topped with Castlefarm Shamrock Cheese

From Jenny Young of Castlefarm Cheese.

'This is my version of an Indian recipe. The Golden Wonders are dry and fluffy and tasty and work really well with the spices. The addition of our cheese and organic eggs completes the dish, making it a meal in one.'

Serves 4

Ingredients

4 Golden Wonder potatoes

1 large onion, peeled and chopped

2 tablespoons olive oil

½ teaspoon black mustard seeds

½ teaspoon chilli flakes

½ teaspoon garam masala

6 curry leaves

115 g Castlefarm Shamrock Cheese, cut into slivers

2 Castlefarm organic eggs

Method

Preheat the oven to 200°C/400°F/gas mark 6.

Boil and mash the potatoes. Fry the onion in a tablespoon of olive oil until soft and translucent. Keep this warm in the oven. Meanwhile, fry the black mustard seeds in the remaining olive oil until they start to pop. Add the chilli, garam masala and curry leaves and mix. Then add the potato and mix again. Top with the onion and add slivers of Castlefarm Shamrock. Put the frying pan into the top part of the oven until the cheese has melted, which takes about 5 minutes. Place the eggs on top of the potato mixture and bake for 4–8 minutes, depending on how you like your eggs. Serve immediately.

Claire Nash's Ardsallagh Goats Cheese, golden beetroot and roasted onion frittata

From Claire Nash of the wonderful Nash 19 Restaurant, Cork City (www.nash19.com).

Serves 4–6
as a starter or lunch

Ingredients
3 medium free-range eggs

80–100 ml single cream

250 g beetroot, cooked

250 g Ardsallagh Goats Cheese

2 medium red onions, roasted in rosemary and a little sea salt

Method

Preheat the oven to 170°C/340°F/gas mark 4. Line a pan 24 cm x 4 cm deep with greaseproof paper.

Crack the eggs into a small jug, beat, top up to 250 ml with cream and mix together.

Put half the beetroot into the pan. Layer half the cheese, followed by half the onion. Repeat the process. Add the egg mixture and cook for 12–15 minutes.

Serve with Nash 19 Fig Confit or Nash 19 Relish and organic leaves.

Claire's top tips
You can substitute milk for some of the cream, but it will take longer to cook and is not as decadent. Do not overcook; the custard centre should be a little loose, as it will continue to cook once resting.

Denis Cotter's roast aubergine parcels of Coolea Cheese, black kale and hazelnuts with warm cherry tomato and caper salsa

Reproduced with the permission of Denis Cotter, owner/chef of the fabulous vegetarian Cafe Paradiso, Cork City, and author of several books, including For the Love of Food: Vegetarian Recipes from the Heart *(Collins, London, 2011) (www.cafeparadiso.ie).*

'This Cafe Paradiso classic was created with Coolea in mind, not only for its buttery, nutty flavour that seems both intense and subtle at the same time, but mostly to feature the way it softens into a luscious pillow just before it melts. Serve with some crushed or mashed potato.'

Serves 4

Ingredients

3 medium aubergines

olive oil to brush aubergines

300 g black kale

60 g hazelnuts, toasted and finely chopped

160 g mature Coolea Cheese

Sundried tomato paste
4 sundried tomatoes, soaked

100 ml olive oil

Sauce
250 g cherry tomatoes, halved

1 clove garlic, peeled and finely chopped

1 fresh green chilli, thinly sliced

1 tablespoon small capers

3 tablespoons olive oil

salt

Method

Preheat the oven to 200°C/400°F/gas mark 6.

Cut and discard both ends and a slice from two sides of each aubergine. Cut the remaining flesh into long slices of about ½ cm thick. Brush these lightly with olive oil on both sides and place them on a parchment-lined baking tray. Roast in the oven for 10–12 minutes, until fully cooked and lightly coloured. You will need three slices per portion.

Put the soaked sundried tomatoes in a food processor with 100 ml olive oil and blend to get a thick paste.

Bring a large pot of water to the boil, drop in the kale and cook it for 5–7 minutes, then cool it in a bowl of cold water. Squeeze out as much water as possible and chop the kale finely. Stir in the chopped hazelnuts and 2–3 tablespoons of the sundried tomato paste.

Use a vegetable peeler to slice the cheese into thin shavings.

Lay the roasted aubergines on a work surface, best-looking sides down. Place three layers of cheese shavings to evenly cover the centre third of each slice, and cover these with a tablespoon of the kale mixture, again shaping it to cover the cheese evenly. Fold over the uncovered parts of the aubergine slices and press gently to get a flat-topped parcel.

Place the aubergine parcels on a parchment-lined oven tray. Bake them in the oven for 7–8 minutes, until the cheese has just begun to melt into soft pillows.

While the aubergine parcels are cooking, make the sauce. Place the cherry tomatoes, garlic, chilli and capers in a small pan with 3 tablespoons of olive oil and a pinch of salt. Heat gently for 5–6 minutes, until the tomatoes are beginning to soften and release their juices.

Serve the aubergine parcels immediately, three to a portion, with the salsa poured over.

Clodagh McKenna's baked Gubbeen Cheese with thyme and rosemary

Reproduced with the permission of Clodagh McKenna (www.clodaghmckenna.com).

This recipe originally appeared in *The Irish Farmers' Market Cookbook* (HarperCollins, London, 2006). This recipe was given to Clodagh by her dear friend Giana Ferguson. Gooey, warm and delicious, it takes about two minutes to prepare and will take less than one minute to devour.

Serves 4

Ingredients
1 baby Gubbeen

1 tablespoon chopped mixed fresh herbs, such as thyme and rosemary

2 cloves of garlic, peeled and chopped

black pepper

crusty loaf of bread

Method

Preheat the oven to 180°C/350°F/gas mark 4. Cut the cheese in half horizontally to make two rounds. Sprinkle the herbs, garlic and black pepper on the bottom half of the cheese. Replace the top disc of cheese and place the wheel on a large piece of tinfoil. Wrap the foil around the cheese, forming a chimney hole on top with the excess foil. The chimney will let out the moisture while the cheese bakes. Place the cheese on a baking sheet and bake for 20 minutes, or until the cheese is soft and runny.

Spread on slices of chunky bread while the cheese is still warm.

Derry Clarke's boudin of Clonakilty black pudding with Cashel Blue Cheese and cider sorbet, crisp cured bacon and stout jus

Reproduced with the permission of Derry Clarke, chef patron, L'Ecrivain, Dublin (www.lecrivain.com).

Serves 4

Ingredients

Boudin of Clonakilty black pudding

300 g Clonakilty black pudding

1 breast of chicken

25 g butter

1 shallot, peeled and diced

1 sprig of thyme, chopped

salt and freshly ground black pepper

1 tablespoon olive oil

Cashel Blue Cheese and cider sorbet

300 ml stock syrup

juice of ½ lemon

90 g Cashel Blue Cheese, crumbled

100 ml cider

Crisp cured bacon

1 teaspoon vegetable oil

4 rashers streaky bacon

Stout jus

200 ml Guinness

200 ml demi-glaze

Method

Boudin of Clonakilty black pudding

Remove skin from black pudding and crumble into a bowl. Blend the chicken breast in a food processor until it is puréed. Heat the butter in a saucepan and gently cook the shallot with the thyme and allow to cool.

Combine the black pudding, chicken and cooked shallot mixture in a bowl and season with salt and freshly ground black pepper. Form the mixture into a sausage shape 5 cm in diameter. Roll the sausage in clingfilm and then in tinfoil. Place in a pot of simmering water and poach for 45 minutes. Allow to cool.

Cashel Blue Cheese and cider sorbet

Bring the stock syrup to the boil. Remove from the heat, add the lemon juice and allow to cool. Transfer to an ice-cream maker and churn as per instructions. Just as the sorbet reaches its soft stage, add the crumbled cheese and cider. Mix until the cheese and cider are incorporated and freeze.

Alternatively, pour the mixture into a shallow container and freeze to a slush. Whisk well so that the sorbet becomes very light and fine-grained. Add the cheese and cider just before it is firm.

Crisp cured bacon

Preheat the oven to 180°C/350°F/gas mark 4. Grease an oven tray with the vegetable oil; lay the rashers flat on the tray without overlapping. Grease the underside of another tray and place it on top. Bake for 15–18 minutes, until crisp.

Stout jus

In a heavy-bottomed saucepan, boil the Guinness to reduce it by half. Add the demi-glaze and warm through.

To serve, slice the boudin in 1 cm pieces and pan fry in a little olive oil for 1 minute on each side, ensuring that it is heated throughout. Place on four warmed plates and top each one with a scoop of Cashel Blue Cheese and cider sorbet. Arrange the crisp cured bacon on the sorbet. Finally, dribble the stout jus around the plate.

Derry Clarke's Ardagh Cheese in an herb crust, butternut squash, honey dressing

Reproduced with the permission of Derry Clarke, chef patron, L'Ecrivain, Dublin (www.lecrivain.com).

Serves 4

Ingredients
4 x 60 g circles of
Ardagh Cheese
(alternative: Crottin
de Chèvre)

100 g breadcrumbs

50 g chives and parsley,
chopped

60 g Parmesan, grated

2 eggs, beaten

100 ml milk

50 g plain flour

olive oil for frying

Butternut squash
2 butternut squash

2 tablespoons honey

1 teaspoon thyme, chopped

6 sage leaves, thinly sliced

sea salt

Method

Preheat the oven to 200°C/400°F/gas mark 6.

To prepare the Ardagh Cheese
Mix together the breadcrumbs, herbs and Parmesan. Beat the egg and milk together. Slice by slice, place the cheese in the flour, then the egg wash. Coat lightly with the herb and Parmesan mix. Set aside until required.

Butternut squash
Cut the squash in half, deseed and cut into thin strips. Using a round cutter, cut out four circles of squash slightly larger than the cheese circles. Sprinkle with honey, thyme, sage and sea salt. Bake in the oven for 10 minutes, until soft. Retain the contents of the baking tray to dress the goats' cheese.

To cook the cheese
In a hot pan, fry the coated cheese in olive oil until golden brown.

To assemble the dish, place a circle of butternut squash on each of four plates, place a round of cheese on top and drizzle the remaining honey from the tray over the cheese.

Derry Clarke's Carrigbyrne Cheese pithiviers

Reproduced with the permission of Derry Clarke, chef patron, L'Ecrivain, Dublin (www.lecrivain.com).

Serves 4

Ingredients

50 g celery, diced

50 g apple, diced

1 tablespoon chives, finely chopped

280 g Carrigbyrne (St Killian) Cheese

200 g spinach leaves, blanched

200 g puff pastry

1 egg, beaten

Method

Preheat the oven to 180°C/350°F/gas mark 4.

Blanch the celery until tender and place in a bowl with the apple and chives. Add the cheese and mix until soft. Place in the fridge to rest. Lay out the spinach leaves and place one tablespoon of the cheese mix in the centre of each spinach leaf and wrap carefully (the spinach keeps the moisture from soaking into the pastry).

Roll out the pastry to ½ cm thickness and cut it into 30 cm squares, allowing one square per portion. Put a heaped teaspoon of spinach-wrapped cheese mixture in the middle of each pastry square. Brush the edges with beaten egg and pull in the four corners towards the centre to form a parcel. Seal the edges by pinching the pastry together and brush the top with the remaining egg.

Bake for 15 minutes or until golden brown. Serve the pithiviers warm.

Ross Lewis's Ardsallagh Goats Cheese, red pepper basquaise, artichoke, tomato confit, black olive oil

Serves 4

Ingredients

Tomato confit

8 vine-ripened baby plum tomatoes

2 sprigs of basil, chopped

salt and pepper

Black olive oil

100 g stoned black olives

150 ml olive oil

Red pepper basquaise

75 ml olive oil

1 banana shallot, peeled and thinly sliced

1 clove garlic, peeled and chopped

pinch saffron threads

pinch Espelette pepper

3 plum tomatoes, skinned, deseeded, julienne

6 red peppers, skinned, deseeded, julienne

1 sprig of thyme

1 sprig of basil

salt and pepper

20 ml sherry vinegar

Method

Tomato confit

The confit should be made two days ahead. Cut the baby plum tomatoes in two lengthways and remove the stalks. Place them on a greaseproof-lined oven tin, scatter over the chopped basil and season. Leave above the oven for 48 hours or until they become semi-dried. Discard the basil.

Black olive oil

Place the stoned olives on a tray with greaseproof and place above the oven or other warm place. Allow to become dry and brittle. Place in a blender and start the machine – they will turn into a powder. Add 150 ml olive oil and blend until a thick consistency is reached. Pass through a chinois and store in a bottle.

Red pepper basquaise

Heat 75 ml olive oil lightly in a heavy-bottomed pan. Add the shallot, garlic, saffron and Espelette pepper and cook until soft. Do not colour. Add the 3 plum tomatoes, peppers, thyme and basil. Season lightly and cook on a very low heat for 20–30 minutes. Check seasoning, add the sherry vinegar and place in a container.

Cont'd on the next page

Ross Lewis's Ardsallagh Goats Cheese recipe cont'd

Artichokes

500 ml water

100 ml olive oil

juice of 1 lemon

1 sprig of rosemary

4 baby globe artichokes

Dressing

100 ml Chardonnay vinegar

150 ml olive oil

25 ml walnut oil

juice of ½ lime

Asparagus and broccoli

4 asparagus spears, blanched

8 florets sprouting broccoli, blanched

4 croûtons baked in oven, rubbed with garlic

4 x 40 g slices of Ardsallagh Goats Cheese

Artichokes

Place the water, 100 ml olive oil, lemon juice and rosemary in a saucepan. Trim the artichokes and place in the pan. Bring to the boil and allow to simmer for about 15 minutes or until cooked. Remove from the heat and allow to cool. Cut in half.

Dressing

Combine all ingredients and shake well.

To serve, combine the asparagus tips, sprouting broccoli, tomato confit and artichoke in a bowl. Season with salt and pepper and the dressing. Divide the vegetables between four plates. Place the croûtons on top with some basquaise, and then the slice of cheese. Drizzle black olive oil around.

Catherine Fulvio's Ballyknocken walnut and Wicklow Blue Cheese bruschetta

Serves 4

Ingredients

2 lemons
(zest of 1 and juice of 2)

4 teaspoons honey

pinch of salt, or to taste

pinch of black pepper,
or to taste

200 ml extra virgin olive oil

8 x 1½ cm-thick ciabatta slices,
sliced diagonally

1 large garlic clove, halved
crosswise

12 walnut halves

4 slices of pancetta

6–8 cherry tomatoes

250 g salad leaves, including
fresh garden herbs if available

180 g Wicklow Blue Cheese,
cubed into 1 cm pieces

Garnish
edible flowers

Method

Remove the zest from one of the lemons in large strips with a vegetable peeler and cut any white pith from the strips with a sharp knife. Then cut into narrow strips – julienne. Blanch the zest in boiling water for 1 minute, then drain in a sieve and plunge into a bowl of cold water to stop cooking. Drain and pat dry.

Squeeze enough juice from the lemons to measure 6 tablespoons. Whisk together the lemon juice, honey, salt and pepper, then add 150 ml of the olive oil in a slow stream, whisking until emulsified.

Prepare the grill. Brush both sides of the bread slices with the remaining olive oil and season with salt and pepper. When the grill is hot, toast the bread on the lightly oiled grill rack, turning once, until golden, about 3 minutes total. Immediately rub one side of each slice with garlic.

Meanwhile, toast the walnut halves by dry-pan frying them. When the walnuts have cooled, break into smaller pieces. Fry the pancetta and, when cooled, cut into 1 cm pieces. Halve the tomatoes.

Toss the salad leaves with half of the lemon zest and enough dressing to coat, then season with salt and pepper.

Put the toasts on salad plates and spoon some of the remaining dressing over each. Place some salad on top, then bruschetta, then salad and top with the blue cheese cubes. Sprinkle the pancetta and walnut pieces around the bruschetta/salad tower. Place 3 tomato halves around the plate. Then scatter the remaining lemon zest and droplets of the remaining salad dressing.

Finally, garnish with edible flowers.

Aoife Cox's Irish potato 'risotto' with Desmond Cheese

This recipe is an Irish slant on the classic rice dish risotto, replacing the rice with potatoes.

Serves 2

Ingredients

butter for frying

200 g chestnut mushrooms, sliced (or use a mixture of chestnut and shiitake mushrooms)

2 largeish potatoes (about 400 g once peeled), preferably floury

approx. 400 ml vegetable stock

olive oil for frying

1 medium onion (about 150 g), peeled and finely chopped

½ teaspoon dried thyme

¼ teaspoon dried sage

salt

2 cloves garlic, peeled and finely chopped

150 ml Guinness or other stout

25 g Desmond Cheese if you can lay your hands on it, or use Parmesan, finely grated

approx. 4 tablespoons flat-leaf parsley, chopped

¼ teaspoon lemon zest or more to taste

freshly ground black pepper

You will also need a deep-sided frying pan; mine was about 26 cm wide.

Method

Place your pan over a medium heat and add about 1 tablespoon of butter. When the butter has melted, add the sliced mushrooms. Avoid stirring until the mushrooms have shrunk and released their juices. Fry until well browned and the mushrooms have reabsorbed any liquid, around 12–15 minutes. Remove the mushrooms from the pan and set aside.

While the mushrooms are frying, scrub and peel the potatoes. Cut into slices around 2 mm thick. Stack the slices and cut into sticks about 2 mm wide and then into approximately 1 cm lengths.

Place the stock in a small saucepan and keep at a simmer over a low heat.

Using the same pan that you used for the mushrooms, return the pan to a medium heat, add about 2 teaspoons of butter and 2 teaspoons of olive oil. When hot, add the onion, thyme, sage and a pinch of salt. Stir and fry for 3–4 minutes or until the onions are translucent. Add the garlic and stir and fry for another minute or so.

Add the potato pieces, stir briefly, then add the Guinness. Stir until the liquid has mostly been absorbed. Add a ladle of stock to the potatoes and continue stirring, again until the liquid has mostly been absorbed. Continue adding ladles of stock and stirring until the potato pieces are just tender, around 25–30 minutes.

Stir in the fried mushrooms and cook for about another minute.

Remove from the heat, stir in about half the grated cheese, half the chopped parsley and the lemon zest. Add freshly ground black pepper to taste and additional salt if you think it needs it.

Serve sprinkled with the remaining grated cheese and chopped parsley.

Variations

As with a regular risotto, the variations are, I think, endless. You can certainly use white wine in place of the beer and make any number of potato-friendly additions.

Aoife Cox's tricoloured Irish vegetable terrine (with St Gall Cheese)

'Marrowfat peas, parsnips and carrots – all familiar occupants of the Irish dinner plate. Here they are baked into a terrine with the wonderfully nutty St Gall cheese from Cork and, yes, a lot of eggs.'

Serves 8–10 as a starter

Ingredients

300 g carrots, peeled and very finely sliced

300 g parsnips, peeled and chopped into small chunks

1 packet (125 g) no-soak marrowfat peas

1 tablespoon mint, finely chopped

1 teaspoon Dijon mustard

2 tablespoons flat-leaf parsley, finely chopped

1 tablespoon orange juice

salt and freshly ground black pepper

150 g St Gall cheese, grated (or Emmental)

6 eggs, separated

Method

Preheat the oven to 190°C/375°F/gas mark 5 and line a 2-lb loaf tin with parchment paper.

Using two separate saucepans (or a steamer with two separate baskets), boil or steam the carrots and parsnips until tender (around 10 minutes for the parsnips, longer for the carrots). Drain each and, in separate bowls, mash well.

Meanwhile, in another small saucepan, add the marrowfat peas to about 500 ml boiling water. Bring back to the boil and simmer gently for 15–20 minutes, until tender. Drain any excess liquid (you should end up with about 300 g cooked weight) and mash well.

Add the mint to the peas, the Dijon mustard to the parsnips and the parsley and orange juice to the carrots. Mix each well and season to taste with salt and black pepper.

Divide the cheese evenly amongst the peas, parsnips and carrots. Likewise, divide the 6 egg yolks amongst the three mixtures, adding 2 egg yolks to each. Mix well.

Whisk all 6 egg whites to soft peaks, then divide amongst the three bowls and fold gently into each mixture.

Fill your loaf tin, starting with the peas, then the parsnips and finally the carrots. Bake the terrine until it is firm to the touch and a skewer comes out fairly cleanly. This took about 1 hour and 15 minutes for me. You will need to cover the top of the terrine with foil after about 30 minutes to prevent the top from burning.

Remove from the oven and allow to cool slightly before turning out of the tin. Slice and serve at will. It is good warm, at room temperature or chilled.

Variations

I am sure that you could make an equally good (and even greener) version of this by substituting fresh or frozen garden peas for the marrowfats.

Aoife Cox's Raclette au St Gall

Serves as many people as you care to feed

Ingredients

waxy potatoes – allow around 200–300 g per person

selection of green fruit and vegetables, e.g. asparagus, courgettes, Romanesco cauliflower,[2] broccoli, spring onions, green apple

olive oil

a nice melty cheese – I used St Gall

You will also need, ideally, a table-top Raclette grill, which makes it easier for everyone to do their own grilling, though you could grill the vegetables separately using your grill/broiler and then top with the cheese and serve. More work for you, though.

Method

Scrub the potatoes and boil them in salted water until fork-tender – this may take around 15 minutes for baby potatoes, longer if you are using larger spuds. Drain, cover with a tea towel and allow to dry off for 5 minutes or more.

Wash and pat dry any other vegetables you are using. Chop the broccoli or Romanesco into bite-sized pieces. Slice the courgettes in pieces around ½ cm thick. Slice the spring onions. Chop the apple into small chunks. Leave asparagus spears whole.

Most of the vegetables for grilling can be placed directly on the heated grill. You can toss them in the barest amount of olive oil beforehand if you like.

Guests fill their little grill pans with their choice of potato, spring onions, apple and grilled vegetables, top it all with cheese, let it melt under the grill, then eat and repeat.

Variations

The variations on Raclette are limited only by your imagination. If it goes well, grilled or otherwise, with cheese, then it is a candidate for Raclette.

Rachel Allen's baked eggs with creamy kale (with Glebe Brethan Cheese)

Reproduced, with permission, from Rachel Allen's Entertaining at Home (Collins, London, 2010).

'This is delicious for brunch. If you can't get kale, use spinach. I love to use the Irish farmhouse cheese Glebe Brethan for its delicious flavour and melting texture.'

Serves 6

Ingredients

25 g butter

450 g kale (about 175 g with stalks removed)

salt and ground black pepper

350 ml single or regular cream

pinch of freshly grated nutmeg

6 eggs

350 g Glebe Brethan cheese, grated (or Gruyère if you can't find Glebe Brethan)

You will need six 100 ml ramekins or ovenproof dishes.

Method

Preheat the oven to 180°C/350°F/gas mark 4.

Add the butter to a large, wide frying pan and place over a medium heat. Add the kale and season with salt and pepper. As soon as the kale wilts and becomes tender, add the cream and nutmeg, then allow to bubble for 3–5 minutes, until thickened.

Divide the kale between the ramekins or dishes, placing it around the inside of each dish and leaving a small well in the centre.

Break one egg into each dish and sprinkle the grated cheese over the top. Bake in the oven for 8–10 minutes or until golden on top and bubbling around the edges. Scatter over a little pepper and serve immediately with a little toast on the side.

Kilbeg fruit trifle

From Kilbeg Dairy Delights.

Serves 8

Ingredients

7 sponge fingers

2 tablespoons sweet sherry

2 tablespoons apple juice

1 pack strawberry
sugar-free jelly

280 g mixed fruit (such as
strawberries, raspberries,
pomegranate seeds or
tinned fruit in juice)

255 g Kilbeg Fat-Free Quark

150 g low-fat custard

1 vanilla pod

Method

Arrange the sponge fingers in the bottom of a trifle bowl. Mix together the sherry and apple juice and drizzle over. Set aside to soak for about 10–15 minutes.

Meanwhile, make the jelly according to packet instructions. (If you are using tinned fruit, replace the water with the juice and make up to the correct amount with boiling water.) Allow to cool slightly before pouring over the sponge fingers. Scatter over half the mixed fruit and chill overnight or until set.

Mix the quark with the low-fat custard. Split the vanilla pod in half lengthways, remove the seeds and stir them into the quark/custard mixture. Pour this over the jelly and chill for a further 20 minutes before serving topped with the remaining fruit.

Glenilen Farm lemon cheesecake

Reproduced with the permission of Glenilen Farm.

Serves 6

Ingredients

Base

225 g digestive biscuits
(or HobNobs, ginger nuts
or a combination)

85 g butter

Topping

1 lemon

1 tablespoon gelatine powder

285 ml double cream

370 g Glenilen Low-Fat
Cream Cheese

85 g sugar

Method

Base

Process the biscuits into crumbs. Melt the butter and combine. Press into a greased 20 cm round deep tin.

Topping

Squeeze the lemon. Place the juice in a bowl and sprinkle the gelatine powder over it. Stir in the gelatine and place in a microwave on 'defrost' until gelatine is dissolved – do not boil.

Whip the cream softly. Add the cream cheese and sugar, whipping all the time. Add the dissolved lemon gelatine mixture in a steady stream to get a smooth mix.

Pour onto the biscuit base. Refrigerate until set.

Murphys' Bluebell Falls Goats Cheese ice cream

Reproduced with the permission of Kieran Murphy, owner of blog www.icecreamireland.com and Murphy's Ice Cream Shops in Kerry (Dingle, Kenmare and Ballyferriter) and Dublin (Wicklow Street and Temple Bar) (www.murphysicecream.ie).

Serves 8

Ingredients
5 egg yolks

130 g sugar

200 ml milk

½ teaspoon vanilla

150 g Bluebell Falls Cygnus Honey or Cygnus Plain, or other excellent goats' cheese

240 ml cream

Method

Combine the egg yolks and sugar and beat until thick. Bring the milk to a low simmer. Beat the milk into the egg/sugar mixture in a slow stream. Pour the mixture back into the pan and place over a low heat. Stir continuously until the custard thickens slightly (around 65–70°C/150–158°F) and just coats the back of a spoon. Do not overheat, though, because at around 76°C/169°F you will scramble the eggs.

Immediately remove from the heat. Allow to cool, then mix in the vanilla and goats' cheese, using a blender or processor just until smooth. Whip the cream until it has doubled in volume (you should have soft peaks – do not overwhip). Fold (gently stir) in the custard.

Freeze using a domestic ice cream machine or cover and place in the freezer. If you are using a domestic ice cream machine, transfer to a freezer-proof covered container when the ice cream has achieved a semi-solid consistency (around 15 minutes). Place it in the freezer and continue to freeze until it is solid.

Note

To pasteurise the eggs, heat the custard to 73°C/163°F and maintain that temperature for at least 5 minutes. Use a cooking thermometer, though, and keep stirring. If the custard goes any higher than 76°C/169°F, the eggs will scramble. Immediately cover and place in the freezer until cool.

Murphys' Wicklow Blue Cheese and caramelised shallot ice cream

Reproduced with the permission of Kieran Murphy, owner of blog www.icecreamireland.com and Murphy's Ice Cream Shops in Kerry (Dingle, Kenmare and Ballyferriter) and Dublin (Wicklow Street and Temple Bar) (www.murphysicecream.ie).

Serves 6

Ingredients

2 banana shallots, peeled

1 tablespoon butter or oil

2 tablespoons sugar
(for shallots)

125 g sugar
(for custard)

5 egg yolks

200 ml milk

50 g Wicklow Blue Cheese

210 ml cream

Method

Quarter the shallots lengthwise and chop into fine pieces. Fry over a medium-high heat with the butter or oil, stirring constantly until they are golden. Stir in the 2 tablespoons of sugar and continue to fry until the sugar has melted and the shallots have turned a dark golden brown. Spread on a tray to cool.

Beat the rest of the sugar and egg yolks together until thick and pale yellow. Bring the milk to a low simmer. Beat the milk into the eggs and sugar in a slow stream. Pour the mixture back into the pan and place over a low heat. Stir continuously until the custard thickens slightly (around 65–70°C/150–158°F) and just coats the back of a spoon. Do not overheat, though, because at around 76°C/169°F you will scramble the eggs. Immediately remove from the heat and allow to cool completely.

Break up or chop the blue cheese and put in a blender with half of the custard, pulsing until smooth. Stir the blue cheese/custard mix back into the rest of the custard, cover, return to the refrigerator and allow to sit for at least two hours.

Whip the cream until it has doubled in volume (you should have soft peaks – do not overwhip). Fold the cream (gently stir) into the custard.

Freeze using a domestic ice cream machine, adding the caramelised shallots when the ice cream is already quite solid. Otherwise, cover and place in the freezer, again adding the shallots when it has become semi-solid.

If you are using a domestic ice cream machine, transfer to a freezer-proof covered container when the ice cream has achieved a semi-solid consistency (around 15 minutes). Place it in the freezer and continue to freeze until it is solid.

Notes

This ice cream will only be as good as the blue cheese you use. Find one you like!

To pasteurise the eggs, heat the custard to 73°C/163°F and keep at that temperature for 5 minutes. Use a cooking thermometer. If the custard goes any higher than 76°C/169°F, the eggs will scramble. Immediately cover and place in the freezer until cool.

Pashka (with Kilmichael Soft Goats' Cheese)

Provided by Sunview Farm.

Pashka is a traditional Eastern European Easter cheese dessert often made in a Christmas pudding-style mould. It works well with Kilmichael Soft Goats' Cheese.

Serves 6

Ingredients

450 g very fresh Kilmichael Soft Goats' Cheese (quark or other liquidy curd cheese can be substituted)

75 g caster sugar

75 ml double cream

50 g almonds, blanched and chopped

50 g plump sultanas

50 g glacé fruits, chopped

Method

Line a 900 ml basin with a double layer of cotton, ideally muslin or cheesecloth. Beat the cheese and sugar together until smooth. Lightly whip the cream and fold into the cheese mixture with the almonds, sultanas and half the glacé fruits. Spoon into the basin. Fold over the cloth and cover with a plate with a weight on top. Chill overnight in the fridge. Remove the weight and plate, unfold the cloth and invert the pudding on to a serving dish. Peel away the cloth. Decorate with the remaining glacé fruits.

Appendix 1: Irish Farmhouse Cheeses

Key to abbreviations

HT	Heat-treated
Org	Organic
Past	Pasteurised milk
Raw	Raw or unpasteurised milk
S	Smoked
SH	Semi-hard
SS	Semi-soft
Trad	Traditional
Var	Variety
Veg	Vegetarian
VH	Very hard

Cheesemaker	Cheese	County	Raw / Past	MILK (Cow / Goat / Sheep)	RENNET (Veg / Trad)	Style	Blue / Smoked / Organic
Abbey Cheese Co. (Paddy Jack Cheese)	Abbey Blue Brie	Laois	Past	Cow	Veg	SS *white-mould*	Blue
Abbey Cheese Co. (Paddy Jack Cheese)	Abbey Smoked Brie	Laois	Past	Cow	Veg	SS *white-mould*	S
Ardagh Castle Goats Cheese	Ardagh Castle Goats Cheese	Cork	Raw	Goat	Veg	Hard	
Ardrahan Farmhouse Cheese	Ardrahan (+ smoked)	Cork	Past	Cow	Veg	SS *washed-rind*	S
Ardrahan Farmhouse Cheese	Duhallow	Cork	Past	Cow	Veg	SH	
Ardsallagh Cheese	Ardsallagh Soft Goats Cheese (+ varieties)	Cork	Past	Goat	Veg	Soft	
Ardsallagh Cheese	Ardsallagh Hard Goats Cheese (+ smoked)	Cork	Past	Goat	Veg	SH	S
Bay Lough Cheese	Bay Lough (+ varieties)	Tipperary	Raw & past	Cow	Veg	Hard *waxed*	S
Béal Organic Cheese	Raw Milk Handmade Mature Béal Organic Cheese	Kerry	Raw	Cow	GM-free Veg	Hard	Org
Béal Organic Cheese	Pasteurised Handmade Mature Béal Organic Cheddar	Kerry	Past	Cow	GM-free Veg	Hard	Org
Bellingham Blue Cheese (Glyde Farm Produce)	Bellingham Blue	Louth	Raw	Cow	Veg	SH	Blue
Bellingham Blue Cheese (Glyde Farm Produce)	Boyne Valley Blue	Louth	Raw	Goat	Veg	SH	Blue
Bluebell Falls Goats Cheese	Cygnus (+ varieties)	Clare	HT	Goat	Veg	Soft	
Bluebell Falls Goats Cheese	Orion	Clare	HT	Goat	Veg	SH	

Cheesemaker	Cheese	County	Raw / Past	MILK (Cow / Goat / Sheep)	RENNET (Veg / Trad)	Style	Blue / Smoked / Organic
Bluebell Falls Goats Cheese	Pegasus	Clare	HT	Goat	Veg	Soft *white-mould*	
Boyne Pastures	Toto	Meath	Past	Sheep	Veg	SH	
Boyne Pastures	Toto Blue	Meath	Past	Sheep/Cow	Veg	SH	Blue
Burren Gold (Aillwee Cave Farm Shop)	Burren Gold (+ varieties)	Clare	Raw, Past	Cow	Trad	Hard *waxed*	S
Cahill's Cheese	Ardagh Wine Cheddar	Limerick	Past	Cow	Veg	Hard *waxed*	
Cahill's Cheese	Ballintubber Cheddar with Chives	Limerick	Past	Cow	Veg	Hard *waxed*	
Cahill's Cheese	Ballyporeen Cheddar with Herbs	Limerick	Past	Cow	Veg	Hard *waxed*	
Cahill's Cheese	Whiskey Cheese	Limerick	Past	Cow	Veg	Hard *waxed*	
Cahill's Cheese	Original Irish Porter Cheddar	Limerick	Past	Cow	Veg	Hard *waxed*	
Carlow Cheese	Carlow Edam (+ varieties)	Carlow	Raw	Cow	Trad	SH *waxed*	
Carrigaline Farmhouse Cheese Co.	Carrigaline (+ varieties)	Cork	Past	Cow	Veg	SH *waxed*	S
Carrigbyrne Farmhouse Cheese Co.	St Killian	Wexford	Past	Cow	Veg	Soft *white-mould*	
Carrigbyrne Farmhouse Cheese Co.	St Brendan Brie	Wexford	Past	Cow	Veg	Soft *white-mould*	
Carrigbyrne Farmhouse Cheese Co.	Emerald Irish Brie	Wexford	Past	Cow	Veg	Soft *white-mould*	
Carrowholly Cheese Co.	Carrowholly (+ varieties)	Mayo	Raw	Cow	Veg	Hard *waxed*	
Carrowholly Cheese Co.	Carrowholly Old Russet (+ varieties)	Mayo	Raw	Cow	Veg	Hard *waxed*	

Cheesemaker	Cheese	County	Raw / Past	MILK (Cow / Goat / Sheep)	RENNET (Veg / Trad)	Style	Blue / Smoked / Organic
Cashel Blue Cheese (J & L Grubb)	Cashel Blue	Tipperary	Past	Cow	Veg	SS	Blue
Cashel Blue Cheese (J & L Grubb)	Crozier Blue	Tipperary	Past	Sheep	Veg	SS	Blue
Castlefarm Cheese	Castlefarm Natural and Shamrock (fenugreek)	Kildare	Raw	Cow	Trad	Hard *waxed*	
Castlemary Farm	Castlemary Goat Cheddar	Cork	Raw	Goat	Trad	Hard	
Castlemary Farm	Castlemary Goat Gouda	Cork	Raw	Goat	Trad	SH	
Castlemary Farm	Castlemary Soft Goat Cheese (+ varieties)	Cork	Raw	Goat	Trad	Soft	
The Causeway Cheese Company	Ballybradden (Herbs & Garlic)	Antrim	Past	Cow	Veg	Hard	
The Causeway Cheese Company	Ballyknock (Black pepper)	Antrim	Past	Cow	Veg	Hard	
The Causeway Cheese Company	Castlequarter	Antrim	Past	Cow	Veg	Hard	
The Causeway Cheese Company	Coolkeeran (Dulse)	Antrim	Past	Cow	Veg	Hard	
Cléire Goats (Gabhair Chléire)	Cléire Goats Cottage Cheese (Garlic)	Cork	Raw	Goat	Veg	Fresh, soft	
Clonmore Cheese	Clonmore	Cork	Past and raw	Goat	Veg	Hard *waxed*	
Clonmore Cheese	Shandrum	Cork	Past	Cow	Veg	SH *waxed*	
Coolattin	Coolattin Cheddar	Wicklow	Raw	Cow	Trad	Hard *waxed*	
Coolea Farmhouse Cheese	Coolea (+ matured)	Cork	Past	Cow	Trad	SH to hard *waxed*	
Cooleeney	Chulchoill	Tipperary	Past	Goat	Veg	Soft *white-mould*	

Cheesemaker	Cheese	County	Raw / Past	MILK (Cow / Goat / Sheep)	RENNET (Veg / Trad)	Style	Blue / Smoked / Organic
Cooleeney	Cooleeney	Tipperary	Raw and past	Cow	Veg	Soft *white-mould*	
Cooleeney	Darú	Tipperary	Past	Cow	Veg	SH	
Cooleeney	Dúnbarra (+ varieties)	Tipperary	Past	Cow	Veg	Soft *white-mould*	
Cooleeney	Gleann Óir	Tipperary	Past	Goat	Veg	SH	
Cooleeney	Gortnamona	Tipperary	Past	Goat	Veg	Soft *white-mould*	
Cooleeney	Maighean	Tipperary	Raw	Cow	Veg	Soft *white-mould*	
Cooleeney	Tipperary Brie	Tipperary	Past	Cow	Veg	Soft *white-mould*	
Corleggy Cheese	Corleggy	Cavan	Raw	Goat	Veg	Hard	S
Corleggy Cheese	Creeny	Cavan	Raw	Sheep	Veg	Hard	S
Corleggy Cheese	Drumlin (+ varieties)	Cavan	Raw	Cow	Veg	Hard	S
Cratloe Hills Sheep's Cheese	Cratloe Hills Gold (+ mature)	Clare	Past	Sheep	Veg	SH	
Derreenaclaurig Farmhouse Cheese	Derreenaclaurig (+ varieties)	Kerry	Raw	Cow	Trad	Hard	
Desmond and Gabriel	Desmond	Cork	Raw	Cow	Veg	Hard *Thermophilic*	
Desmond and Gabriel	Gabriel	Cork	Raw	Cow	Veg	VH *Thermophilic*	
Dingle Farmhouse Cheese	Dingle Farmhouse Cheese	Kerry	Past	Goat / Cow	Veg	SH	
Dingle Peninsula Cheese	Beenoskee	Kerry	Raw	Cow	Veg	Hard *washed-rind*	

351

Cheesemaker	Cheese	County	Raw / Past	MILK (Cow / Goat / Sheep)	RENNET (Veg / Trad)	Style	Blue / Smoked / Organic
Dingle Peninsula Cheese	Dilliskus (Dulse)	Kerry	Raw	Cow	Veg	SH *washed-rind*	
Dingle Peninsula Cheese	Dingle Cream Cheese (+ varieties)	Kerry	Raw	Cow	Veg	Fresh, Soft	
Dingle Peninsula Cheese	Dingle Goat Cheese	Kerry	Raw	Goat	Trad	SH	
Dingle Peninsula Cheese	Dingle Truffle Cheese (Black Pepper & Garlic)	Kerry	Raw	Cow	Trad	Hard	
Dingle Peninsula Cheese	Kilcummin (+ varieties)	Kerry	Raw	Cow	Veg	SH	
Durrus Farmhouse Cheese	Durrus (+ Mini, Dunmanus)	Cork	Raw	Cow	Trad	SS *washed-rind*	
Durrus Farmhouse Cheese	Durrus Óg	Cork	Raw	Cow	Trad	SS	
Fermoy Natural Cheese Co.	St Gall	Cork	Raw	Cow	Trad	SH *Thermophilic*	
Fermoy Natural Cheese Co.	St Brigid (+ varieties)	Cork	Raw	Cow	Trad	SH *brine-washed*	
Fermoy Natural Cheese Co.	Cáis Dubh (+ varieties)	Cork	Raw	Cow	Trad	SH	
Fermoy Natural Cheese Co.	Cáis Rua (+ smoked)	Cork	Raw	Cow	Trad	Soft *washed-rind*	S
Fermoy Natural Cheese Co.	Hibernia	Cork	Raw	Cow	Trad	SH	
Fermoy Natural Cheese Co.	Emerald	Cork	Raw	Cow	Trad	SH	
Fermoy Natural Cheese Co.	Ballyhooly Blue	Cork	Raw	Cow	Trad	SH	Blue
Fermoy Natural Cheese Co.	Corkcotta	Cork	Raw	Cow	Trad	Soft *whey cheese*	
Fermoy Natural Cheese Co.	St Brigid Beag (+ varieties)	Cork	Raw	Cow	Trad	SS *smear-ripened*	

Cheesemaker	Cheese	County	Raw / Past	MILK (Cow / Goat / Sheep)	RENNET (Veg / Trad)	Style	Blue / Smoked / Organic
Fivemiletown Creamery	Ballyblue	Tyrone	Past	Cow	Veg	SS *white-mould*	Blue
Fivemiletown Creamery	Ballybrie	Tyrone	Past	Cow	Veg	SS *white-mould*	
Fivemiletown Creamery	Ballyoak	Tyrone	Past	Cow	Veg	SS *white-mould*	S
Fivemiletown Creamery	Boilíe	Tyrone	Past	Cow / Goat	Veg	Soft	
Fivemiletown Creamery	Cooneen	Tyrone	Past	Goat	Veg	SS *white-mould*	
Fivemiletown Creamery	O'Reilly's (+ varieties)	Tyrone	Past	Goat	Veg	Soft	
Fivemiletown Creamery	Oakwood	Tyrone	Past	Cow	Veg	SH	S
Gleann Gabhra	Tara Bán	Meath	Past	Goat	Veg	Hard	
Glebe Brethan (Tiernan Family Farm)	Glebe Brethan	Louth	Raw	Cow	Trad	Hard *Thermophilic*	
Glenilen Farm	Glenilen Cream Cheese / Quark	Cork	Past	Cow	Trad	Fresh, soft	
Gubbeen Farmhouse Products	Gubbeen (+ extra mature)	Cork	Past	Cow	Trad	SS *washed-rind*	
Gubbeen Farmhouse Products	Smoked Gubbeen	Cork	Past	Cow	Trad	SS *waxed*	S
Hegarty's Farmhouse Cheddar	Hegarty's Farmhouse Cheddar	Cork	Past	Cow	Veg	Hard	
JOD Old Irish Creamery	Old Irish Creamery Cheddar (+ varieties)	Limerick	Past	Cow	Veg	Hard	
Kellys' Organic Products Moon Shine Dairy Farm	Grace	Westmeath	Past	Cow	Veg	Soft	Org
Kellys' Organic Products Moon Shine Dairy Farm	Una (+ varieties)	Westmeath	Past	Cow	Veg	Soft	Org

Cheesemaker	Cheese	County	Raw / Past	MILK (Cow / Goat / Sheep)	RENNET (Veg / Trad)	Style	Blue / Smoked / Organic
Kellys' Organic Products Moon Shine Dairy Farm	Moon Shine Organic Emmental	Westmeath	Past	Cow	Veg	SH	Org
Kilbeg Dairy Delights	Kilbeg Quark and Fat-Free Quark	Meath	Past	Cow	Trad	Soft	
Kilbeg Dairy Delights	Kilbeg Cream Cheese	Meath	Past	Cow	Trad	Soft	
Kilbeg Dairy Delights	Kilbeg Mascarpone	Meath	Past	Cow	Trad	Soft	
Killeen Farmhouse Cheese	Killeen Gouda	Galway	Past	Goat, Cow	Trad	SH to hard	
Kilshanny Cheese	Kilshanny (+ varieties)	Clare	Raw	Cow	Trad	SH	
Knockalara Farmhouse Cheese	Knockalara	Waterford	Past	Sheep	Veg	Soft	
Knockalara Farmhouse Cheese	Knockalara Mature	Waterford	Past	Sheep	Veg	SH washed-rind	
Knockalara Farmhouse Cheese	Knockalara Hard	Waterford	Past	Sheep	Veg	Hard	
Knockalara Farmhouse Cheese	Comeragh	Waterford	Past	Cow	Veg	SH	
Knockalara Farmhouse Cheese	Dromana	Waterford	Past	Sheep	Veg	Soft	
Knockanore Cheese	Knockanore (+ varieties)	Waterford	Raw	Cow	Veg	SH	
Knockanore Cheese	Knockanore Oakwood Smoked	Waterford	Raw	Cow	Veg	SH	S
Knockatee Natural Dairy	Kerry Blue	Kerry	Raw	Cow	Trad	SH waxed	Blue
Knockatee Natural Dairy	Knockatee Cheddar	Kerry	Raw	Cow	Trad	Hard	
Knockatee Natural Dairy	Knockatee Gouda (+ varieties)	Kerry	Raw	Cow	Trad	Hard	
Knockatee Natural Dairy	Beara Blue	Kerry	Raw	Cow	Trad	SH	Blue

Cheesemaker	Cheese	County	Raw / Past	MILK (Cow / Goat / Sheep)	RENNET (Veg / Trad)	Style	Blue / Smoked / Organic
Knockdrinna	Knockdrinna Snow	Kilkenny	Past	Goat	Trad	Soft *white-mould*	
Knockdrinna	Knockdrinna Gold	Kilkenny	Past	Goat	Veg	SH *washed-rind*	
Knockdrinna	Knockdrinna Meadow	Kilkenny	Past	Sheep	Veg	SH *washed-rind*	
Knockdrinna	Lavistown	Kilkenny	Past	Cow	Veg	SH *washed-rind*	
Knockdrinna	Knockdrinna Brined Goat	Kilkenny	Past	Goat	Veg	Soft	
Milleens Cheese	Milleens	Cork	Past	Cow	Trad	SS *washed-rind*	
Millhouse Cheese	Millhouse Sheeps Cheese (+ varieties)	Offaly	Raw	Sheep	Veg	Hard	
Mossfield Organic Farm	Mossfield Organic Cheese (+ varieties)	Offaly	Past	Cow	Veg	SH to hard	Org
Mount Callan Farmhouse Cheese	Mount Callan	Clare	Raw	Cow	Trad	Hard	
Oisín Farmhouse Cheese	Oisín Farmhouse Cheese (+ varieties)	Limerick	Past	Various	GM free Veg	Various	Org
Old MacDonnell's Farm	Old MacDonnell's Soft Cheese (+ varieties)	Wicklow	Past	Goat, Cow	Veg	Fresh, soft	
Orchard Cottage Dairy	Cáis Cruinn (+ varieties)	Cork	Raw	Goat	Veg	Fresh	
St Tola (Inagh Farmhouse Cheese)	St Tola Log (Fresh and Mature) and St Tola Original	Clare	Raw	Goat	Trad	Fresh, soft *Geotrichum mould*	Org
St Tola (Inagh Farmhouse Cheese)	St Tola Crottin (+ ash-covered)	Clare	Raw	Goat	Trad	Soft	Org
St Tola (Inagh Farmhouse Cheese)	St Tola Divine	Clare	Raw	Goat	Trad	Soft	Org
St Tola (Inagh Farmhouse Cheese)	St Tola Hard	Clare	Raw	Goat	Trad	Hard	Org

Cheesemaker	Cheese	County	Raw / Past	MILK (Cow / Goat / Sheep)	RENNET (Veg / Trad)	Style	Blue / Smoked / Organic
St Tola (Inagh Farmhouse Cheese)	St Tola Greek Style	Clare	Raw	Goat	Trad	SH	Org
Sunview Goats	Kilmichael Soft Goats' Cheese (+ varieties)	Cork	Raw	Goat	Veg	Soft	
Toonsbridge Dairy	Buffalo mozzarella	Cork	Raw	Buffalo	Trad	Fresh, soft	
Triskel Cheese	Triskel Pyramid	Waterford	Raw	Goat	Trad	Soft to hard	
Triskel Cheese	Triskel Dew Drop	Waterford	Raw	Goat	Trad	Fresh, soft	
Triskel Cheese	Triskel Gwenned	Waterford	Raw	Cow	Trad	SH	
Tullynascreena Goats' Cheese	Tullynascreena Goats' Cheese (+ varieties)	Leitrim	Raw	Goat	Veg	Soft	
Wicklow Farmhouse Cheese	Wicklow Blue	Wicklow	Past	Cow	Veg	Soft *white-mould*	Blue
Wicklow Farmhouse Cheese	Wicklow Baun	Wicklow	Past	Cow	Veg	Soft *white-mould*	
Wicklow Farmhouse Cheese	Wicklow Gold (+ varieties)	Wicklow	Past	Cow	Veg	Hard	
Wicklow Farmhouse Cheese	Wicklow Goats Log	Wicklow	Past	Goat	Veg	Soft	
Wicklow Farmhouse Cheese	Wicklow Goats Gouda	Wicklow	Past	Goat	Veg	SH	
Wilma's Killorglin Farmhouse Cheese	Wilma's Killorglin Farmhouse Cheese (+ varieties)	Kerry	Past and raw	Cow	Trad	Hard	
Yeats Country Foods	Yeats Organic Soft Cheese (and Light in Fat)	Sligo / Donegal	Past	Cow	Veg	Soft	Org

Appendix 2: Farmhouse cheesemaker statistics

The table below represents the number of farmhouse cheesemakers per county and per province. These figures do not include quasi-industrial artisanal producers and repackers, those who are temporarily out of production or very small operations unknown to the authors.

Cheesemakers by county	No.	%
Cork	18	30.0
Clare	6	10.0
Kerry	5	8.3
Tipperary	3	5.0
Waterford	3	5.0
Meath	3	5.0
Wicklow	3	5.0
Limerick	2	3.3
Louth	2	3.3
Offaly	2	3.3
Carlow	1	1.7
Kildare	1	1.7
Kilkenny	1	1.7
Laois	1	1.7
Westmeath	1	1.7
Wexford	1	1.7
Galway	1	1.7
Leitrim	1	1.7
Mayo	1	1.7
Sligo	1	1.7
Antrim (NI)	1	1.7
Cavan	1	1.7
Tyrone (NI)	1	1.7
Total	60	

Cheesemakers by province	%
Munster	61.7
Leinster	26.7
Connaught	6.7
Ulster	5.0

Appendix 3: Distributors

Distribution is about how to get your product to market. Many Irish artisanal cheesemakers try to bring their product to market themselves. Some sell through farmers' markets, either directly to the public or via an associate. With the best will in the world, however, there is a limited volume that can be sold via a market. While there are some initiatives in at least partial self-distribution, an example being the arrangement between J & L Grubb (Cashel), Carrigbyrne and Knockanore, having to take care of distributing your cheese to multiples, on top of making it, can quickly become onerous. This is where middlemen distributors play a role.

Listed below are the major players in Irish cheese distribution. Some simply provide a route to market for the product, while others repackage the cheese under a brand.

Traditional Cheese Company

Established in 1984, the Traditional Cheese Company is based in Dublin and distributes both Irish and non-Irish cheeses around the country. The company now has a number of cheeses, mostly cheddar, branded under the Traditional Cheese Company label and has won a number of awards for the quality of its cheeses. A number of block, sliced and grated Irish cheddars are sold through retail.

Address: Unit 244 Holly Road, Western Industrial Estate, Dublin 12
Phone: +353 (0)1 450 9494
Web: www.traditionalcheese.ie
Email: info@traditionalcheese.ie

Horgan's Delicatessen

Horgan's are specialists in the sales, marketing and distribution of chilled food products, including Irish and Continental cheeses. Many of the cheeses distributed carry the Horgan's logo.

Address: Horgan's Delicatessen Ltd, Mitchelstown, Co. Cork
Phone: +353 (0)25 41200
Web: www.horgans.com
Email: enquiries@horgans.com

Pallas Foods

Pallas Foods is a family-owned company which was established in the 1980s. It is one of the leading food service distributors of fresh, frozen and ambient products in Ireland, including farmhouse cheese.

Address: Pallas Foods Ltd, Newcastle West, Co. Limerick
Phone: +353 (0)69 20200
Web: www.pallasfoods.eu
Email: info@pallasfoods.eu

La Rousse Foods

La Rousse is a leading Irish food supplier, run by a husband and wife team, that has been supplying top hotels, restaurants, gourmet retail outlets and fine food emporiums in Ireland since 1992. They source cheese from Irish artisanal cheesemakers and mature the cheeses on site in their own maturing room. They also sell cheese direct to the public via their website.

Address: 31 Park West, Nangor Road, Dublin 12
Phone: +353 (0)1 623 4111
Web: www.laroussefoods.ie
Email: sales@laroussefoods.ie

Sheridans Cheesemongers

As well as having several cheese shops, Sheridans distribute a range of Irish and international cheeses. See pp. 41–3 for a full description.

Appendix 4: Where to find Irish farmhouse cheese

A number of speciality cheese shops have established themselves around Ireland. Many of these started out as stalls in food markets and some still like to keep a market presence. Perhaps the largest and most influential cheesemonger in Ireland today is Sheridans. A short history of Sheridans can be found in pp. 41–3. Farmhouse cheese can often be found in delicatessens and other speciality food shops. Here's a selection of some of the top cheese outlets in Ireland.

- Avoca Handweavers: Kilmacanogue, Bray, Co. Wicklow; The Mill at Avoca Village, Co. Wicklow; Powerscourt House, Enniskerry, Co. Wicklow; Mount Usher Gardens, Ashford, Co. Wicklow; 11–13 Suffolk Street, Dublin 2; Rathcoole, off N7, Dublin; Letterfrack, Connemara, Co. Galway; Moll's Gap, Kenmare, Co. Kerry (www.avoca.ie)
- Ballymaloe Shop and Café, Ballymaloe, Shannagarry, Midleton, Co. Cork
- Burren Smokehouse, Kincora Road, Lisdoonvarna, Co. Clare
- Cavistons Seafood Restaurant & Food Emporium, 59 Glasthule Road, Glasthule, Co. Dublin
- The Cheese Pantry, 104 Upper Drumcondra Road, Drumcondra, Dublin 9 (www.thecheesepantry.com)
- Connemara Hamper, Lower Market Street, Clifden, Connemara, Co. Galway
- Country Choice, 25 Kenyon Street, Nenagh, Co. Tipperary (www.countrychoice.ie)
- Fallon & Byrne, 11–17 Exchequer Street, Dublin 2 (www.fallonandbyrne.com)
- Gleeson's Artisan Food & Wine Shop, The Manse, Market Square, Roscommon
- IAGO, English Market, Patrick's Street, Cork City
- Jacks, Lower Bridge Street, Killorglin, Co. Kerry
- Kate's Farm Shop, McQuillans Cross, Clonard, Co. Wexford
- Kate's Kitchen, 3 Castle Street, Sligo Town
- The Kitchen & Foodhall, Hynd's Square, Portlaoise, Co. Laois
- Liston's of Camden Street, Dublin (www.listonsfoodstore.ie)
- The Little Cheese Shop, Greys Lane, Dingle, Co. Kerry (run by Maja Binder of Dingle Peninsula Cheese)
- Mannings Emporium, Ballylickey, Bantry, Co. Cork

- Nude Food Café Restaurant & Deli, 86 O'Connell Street, Dungarvan, Co. Waterford
- The Organic Supermarket, 2c Main Street, Blackrock, Co. Dublin
- On the Pig's Back, English Market, Patrick's Street, Cork City; Douglas, Co. Cork
- Rua, Spencer Street, Castlebar, Co. Mayo
- Sheridans Cheesemongers: Dublin; Carnaross (HQ); Galway; Waterford (Ardkeen Quality Food Store) and several markets (www.sheridanscheesemongers.com)
- Urru Culinary Store, Bandon, Co. Cork (www.urru.ie)
- West Cork Gourmet Store, Staball Hill, Ballydehob, Co. Cork

Irish artisanal cheese outside Ireland

Many Irish cheeses from larger producers can be found outside Ireland. The biggest market is probably the UK. They can be found in bigger European countries and in the bigger cheesemongers on the east and west coasts of the US. In the UK, some can be found in the bigger supermarket chains, but the best places to look are speciality cheesemongers in big cities.

In the UK, most dedicated cheesemongers will have at least some Irish cheeses. In particular, try:

- Iain J. Mellis: 30A Victoria Street, Edinburgh EH1 2JW; 330 Morningside Road, Edinburgh EH10 4QJ; 6 Bakers Place, Edinburgh EH3 6SY; 492 Great Western Road, Glasgow G12 8EW; 149 South Street, St Andrews, Fife KY16 9UN; 201 Rosemount Place, Aberdeen AB25 2XP (www.mellischeese.co.uk)
- La Fromagerie: 2–6 Moxon Street, Marylebone, London W1U 4EW; 30 Highbury Park, Highbury, London N5 2AA (www.lafromagerie.co.uk)
- Neal's Yard: 6 Park Street, Borough Market, London SE1 9AB; 17 Shorts Gardens, Covent Garden, London WC2H 9AT (www.nealsyarddairy.co.uk)
- Paxton & Whitfield: 93 Jermyn Street, London SW1Y 6JE; 13 Wood Street, Stratford-upon-Avon CV37 6JF; 1 John Street, Bath BA1 2JL; in Gail's Artisan Bakery, Exmouth Market, London EC1R 4QL (www.paxtonandwhitfield.co.uk)
- The Teddington Cheese: 42 Station Road, Teddington, Middlesex TW11 9AA and online (www.teddingtoncheese.co.uk)

In the US, the best chance of encountering an Irish artisanal cheese is in the big cheese stores on the east and west coasts. Some large shops in other big cities do stock some Irish cheese. In particular, try:

- Bedford Cheese Shop: 229 Bedford Avenue, Brooklyn, NY 11211 (www.bedfordcheeseshop.com)
- Ideal Cheese: 942 First Avenue, New York, NY 10022 (www.idealcheese.com)
- Murray's: 254 Bleecker Street, New York, NY 10014; 43rd Street & Lexington, New York, NY 10017 (www.murrayscheese.com) www.igourmet.com (online)

Appendix 5: Non-farmhouse cheesemaking in Ireland

While this book is primarily about farmhouse and artisanal cheeses, Ireland does produce huge quantities of high-quality non-farmhouse cheeses. Moreover, the distinction between farmhouse and mass-produced cheeses can be blurred. If a farmhouse cheese is successful and the farm continues to expand, erecting extra buildings and taking on an expanding workforce, when does it cease to be a farmhouse cheese and become an industrial cheese? Many people have their own strongly held opinions on this subject and some countries have rules and regulations governing what constitutes farmhouse and artisanal cheese. As a rough rule, 'farmhouse' is a stricter term than 'artisanal'. Strictly speaking, farmhouse or farmstead cheeses must be made on a single farm and only from the milk of that farm's cows (or sheep, etc.). Some stipulate that the herd must not be mixed (a single breed). Others insist that the cheese must be handmade, but of course there are a number of interpretations of this term too. 'Artisanal' cheese is a broader term referring to cheese handcrafted by a small producer. The milk may come from several breeds and several farms, but generally must be traceable. Most farmhouse and artisanal cheeses are family owned and tend to have no artificial preservatives or flavours.

When cheese production is automated and large amounts are produced in a factory rather than on a farm, the cheese is referred to as industrial. In Ireland we have a very successful industrial cheese industry, making and exporting high-quality cheese. Of course there are some moderately sized Irish cheesemakers who get their milk or indeed pre-processed curd from other creameries and are neither strictly artisanal nor industrial. Other 'cheese farmers' ship their milk to a creamery, where the cheese is made and shipped back to the farm. This is sometimes done on a temporary basis to help the farmer/cheesemaker through a difficult patch or when the farmer has more milk than s/he can process him/herself. Other relationships are more permanent. Newmarket Co-op Creameries, in Cork, is good example of a creamery that makes some curd and cheese in this way. Newmarket has won several awards for its cheese on behalf of other cheesemakers and under its own brand, Killowen.

Most of the industrial cheesemakers produce what is called block cheese or perhaps the better-sounding natural cheese. Most of this is modern cheddar cheese. Some produce copies of other cheeses like Cheshire, edam, Emmental (Swiss), gouda, Red Leicester, Munster and Gloucester, though in some cases they are prevented from using these names under EU rules. Many are produced directly for the catering industry. Block cheddar is usually presented as a small block, a small round or typically pre-sliced or pre-grated. Industrial soft cheese is also produced, including cottage cheese, cream cheese, mascarpone, mozzarella and ricotta. Most block cheese is produced with a longer shelf life in mind than for farmhouse cheese.

One step further in cheese production perhaps is processed cheese. Processed cheese still has a huge following in Ireland and is produced in mass quantities. Processed cheese generally has cheese as a main ingredient. Other ingredients can include cream, butter, whey, 'cheese cuttings', water and preservatives, including emulsifiers, salt and colouring. Red annatto colouring is common in Irish block cheddar and processed cheese. Processed cheese is presented in several forms. It can look very much like block cheddar. It can be in the form of small blocks, triangular wedges, EasiSingles™, individually wrapped extruded slices or, more recently, as cheese strips or Cheese Strings™ (a major export success to France, of all places), or a myriad of other wrappings, packaging and dispensers. Many non-Irish brands of processed cheese can be seen on the shelves of supermarkets in Ireland. Regulations on what can legally be labelled as cheese vary from country to country. Both block cheese and processed cheese are always pasteurised. Block cheese tends to be cheaper than artisanal cheese because of economies of scale and perhaps cheaper ingredients used. Processed cheese is correspondingly cheaper.

While the authors of this book are very much in favour of promoting Irish farmhouse cheese, we know – having been brought up on them – that Irish industrial cheeses are of the highest quality in the world. Each cheese production style has its own merits and consumers should be aware of the type of cheese they are buying and read the label carefully.

Glossary

annatto

Annatto is a natural dye from the annatto seed. It is used as a colouring agent in butter, margarine, cheese and smoked fish, producing red, orange or yellow. Typically used to colour cheddar.

beestings

Milk from cows late in pregnancy, just about to give birth, or just after birth (also called colostrum). The milk is rich in nutrients for the new calf.

bloom

Name sometimes given to the brilliant white coating of mould that develops on the rind of cheeses where *Penicillium camemberti* or similar have been added.

booley/booleying (*bualie*)

The process of moving animals, particularly dairy animals, during the summer months to rich upland pasture unavailable during winter. Herders usually travel with the animals and live with them during the booleying period. Also known, outside Ireland, as transhumance and saeter-brucking.

bothy

A bothy was a small hut used, in the context of this book, during the summer months by cow-hands looking after cattle that have been moved to upland summer pasture (booleying).

boudin

A French word for a type of sausage.

Brevibacterium linens

This is a bacterium that is often applied, usually with a brush, to the rinds of smear-ripened washed-rind cheeses. The bacterium then grows, giving the cheese a rich, thick rind, strong flavour and distinctive 'smelly socks' aroma. This is an apt description of the aroma, as this is the very bacterium present on the human skin that makes our feet smell. The bacterium can also occur naturally.

butter

Butter is an emulsion of butterfat, milk and milk proteins, usually solid at room temperature. It is made through the agitation of unhomogenised whole milk, cream or whey, with buttermilk as a by-product. This agitation breaks down the membranes surrounding microscopic butterfat globules, allowing them to merge into contiguous grains of butter. Though usually made from cows' milk, it is also made from the milk of buffalo, camels, goats, sheep and yaks.

buttermilk

Buttermilk is the butter-flecked fluid left over from the production of butter from milk through churning. It can be imbibed as a drink in its own right but is mostly used in commercial baking and frozen desserts. Most modern buttermilk is cultured buttermilk made by adding bacterial cultures to skimmed milk.

Cáise Púca

The Pooka's Cheese. A round-shaped fungus, full of brown spores and found in Irish fields, probably the Common Puffball (*Lycoperdon perlatum*).

casein

Casein is a protein present in milk. Casein is split and precipitated, by rennet and other coagulants, in the production of cheese, forming curds and whey.

cheese

From the Latin *caseus*. A solid food made by man from the coagulated milk of a number of mammals, which are usually domesticated.

cream

Cream is a form of milk in which the fat globules are more concentrated than usual, collected after rising to the top in a bottle or from spinning off in a commercial centrifuge.

curd(s)

The semi-solid portion of coagulated or curdled milk. It later becomes cheese.

FDM

Fat content in dry matter. Usually expressed as a percentage. The percentage of fat in cheese, with normal moisture content, is smaller than the percentage of fat in the cheese if the moisture content was zero (dry matter).

firkin

A wooden container for carrying butter. Also a unit of weight used for various food products.

form

See mould.

Gjetost

Also known as brunost, this is a fudge-like cheese made from whey, mostly found in Norway. Similar whey cheese is also found in Sweden (mesost), in Iceland (mysuostur) and in Denmark (myseost). It is a heavy, brown-coloured, sweet-tasting cheese usually eaten at breakfast in these Nordic countries. Gjetost is produced by gently heating leftover whey, sometimes mixed with milk and cream, over many hours, until the lactose sugar caramelises, giving the sweet taste and brown colour.

homogenisation	The modern process whereby cream or butterfat in milk is distributed evenly through the milk. The process extends the life of milk. In the old days cream would separate and float to the top of the milk.
lactose	Natural sugar found in milk.
milch cow	A dairy cow.
mould	(1) (US 'mold') A container, typically made of plastic, metal or wood, in which a cheese may mature and from which it gets its shape. Some moulds are simple cylinders with no top or bottom. Many have holes through which excess whey escapes and many fit snugly into a pressing apparatus for extrusion of whey. The cheese usually spends only a brief period in the mould, but may be left to mature in the mould. Sometimes called a form, to differentiate it from the other type of mould. (2) (US 'mold') A fungal organism present in cheese (and other foods) in varying quantities. Some moulds are desirable and are deliberately added to the cheese, while some moulds (usually black or red) may be harmful.
pasteurisation	Pasteurisation is the heat treatment of milk (or other food) that destroys both the pathogenic and beneficial bacteria within. To be legally pasteurised, milk must be heated to required temperature x for required time period y, followed by immediate cooling (typically 71.7°C (161°F) for 15–20 seconds). Named after French chemist and microbiologist Louis Pasteur.
pate	A French word (strictly pâte), meaning 'paste', describing the interior 'meat' of a cheese, not including the rind.
Penicillium candidum	Aka *Penicillium camemberti*. A mould often added to soft-ripened cheeses that promotes the growth of a white, bloomy rind on the surface.

Penicillium roqueforti	A mould responsible for the tangy blue-green streaks in blue cheese, often occurring naturally in the maturing environment (a cave or cellar) or injected into the cheese directly by the cheesemaker.
pithiviers	A French word for a small pie. The pie filling, wrapped in some way, is placed in the centre of two rounds of pastry and the pie is baked.
pressing	The compression of curd (young cheese) to further expel whey.
probiotics	Probiotics are bacteria thought to have beneficial health properties, e.g. *Lactobacillus acidophilus*.
rennet	Rennet is an enzyme complex obtained from rennin in the stomach lining of a young milk-fed animal, typically a calf (or kid or lamb). It is used to curdle or coagulate milk, splitting it into semi-solid curds and liquidy whey. Alternative curdling agents from vegetable sources are now widely used, e.g. Cardoon thistle (*Cynara cardunculus*).
ricotta	Ricotta (meaning 're-cooked') is a fresh white cheese originating in Italy and originally made from sheep-milk whey.
rind	The external surface of a cheese.
smear-ripened	Smear-ripening refers to cheeses that have been smeared with a bacterial broth during their ripening period, usually giving them a distinctively pungent, albeit edible, rind with a soft pate.
starter	A starter is a microbial substance that, optionally, can be added in the early stages of cheese processing to speed up the curdling process and add flavour. A starter can sometimes be a cocktail of bacteria, moulds and a little cheese left over from previous production.
Streptococcus lactis	Bacteria present in souring milk and butter.
Streptococcus thermophilus	Bacteria used as a starter in thermophilic cheese production.
surface-ripened	A surface-ripened cheese matures from the surface inwards, through the action of bacteria and/or mould on the surface/rind that has occurred naturally or has been applied by the cheesemaker. Such cheeses, when young, are typically soft towards the outer edges and harder or chalky towards the interior, becoming entirely soft and creamy with age.

terroir	A French word describing the land on which food has been grown, raised or developed, often used in association with wine. For artisanal cheese, it describes the particular characteristics (vegetation, climate) of the land on which the milk-producing animals are grazed.
thermophilic	Dating back to the Bronze Age, this method of making cheese was once widespread in Ireland, but had largely been lost by the time of the Great Famine in the mid-nineteenth century. The cheese is made at a relatively high temperature (40–50°C/104–122°F typically) using *Streptococcus thermophilus* as a starter. It is used widely in the French/Swiss/Italian Alps in the production of cheeses such as Emmental, Gruyère and Comté. The bacteria used is resistant to, or indeed proliferates in, temperatures that would kill regular mesophilic bacteria.
truckle	A whole cheese in the shape of a cylinder or barrel; typically cheddar.
washed-rind	A washed-rind cheese has its rind bathed, washed or rubbed during maturation, usually with brine or sometimes alcohol such as marc, in order to mature the curd and hinder the development of unwanted bacteria and mould while encouraging the growth of others. Such cheeses usually have a terracotta-coloured rind, which is smelly and tacky to the touch from the presence of the bacteria *Brevibacterium linens* (*Geotrichum candidum* and others are sometimes used). A large subcategory of these cheeses is called smear-ripened when deliberately smeared with such bacteria by the cheesemaker.
whey	Whey is the curd-flecked liquid created, alongside curd, as a by-product of curdling milk. It is often fed to animals directly or added to animal feed, but in bygone days it was often drunk with various additives, including honey and alcohol. It is also reheated to produce whey cheeses like Italian ricotta and Norwegian Gjetost cheese.
whole milk	Whole milk is normal (cows') milk with about 4 per cent fat content.

References

1 INTRODUCTION

1 The measures 'small', 'medium' and 'large' are within the size limits of Irish farmhouse cheesemakers. Even the largest in Ireland is small by international standards. Few in Ireland produce more than 100 tonnes. 'Small' here means very small, some owning ten or fewer animals.
2 Source: Central Statistics Office (CSO).
3 Source: Teagasc, Moorepark.
4 Source: CSO.
5 A rennet-like substance can also be found in the gizzards of turkeys and other domestic fowl, which is said to produce a more tender and delicate curd.
6 *Galium verum* or Lady's Bedstraw (Irish *Rú Mhuire*) is a native Irish plant related to Cleavers. The pretty yellow flowers are used to curdle milk.
7 *Cynara cardunculus* or cardoon is a thistle-like member of the aster family and actually the same species as the cultivated globe artichoke. The blue flowers are used to curdle milk.
8 Christopher H. O'Brien Lynch, 'A Review of the Irish Farmhouse Cheese Industry 1980-1994', unpublished M Appl Sc (Food Sc) thesis, Faculty of Agriculture, University College Dublin, 1994, p. 9.
9 The EU Protected Designation of Origin name 'West Country Farmhouse Cheddar' may be given to cheddar made in the English counties of Somerset, Devon, Dorset and Cornwall.
10 From the tropical plant *Bixa orellana*.
11 Katie Thear, *Cheesemaking and Dairying* (Broad Leys Publishing, Saffron Waldon, Essex, 1978).
12 Rita Ash, *Self Sufficiency – Cheese Making* (New Holland Publishers, London, 2009).
13 G. R. Pesola, J. Iqbal and J. Damian, 'The Hygiene Hypothesis and the Primary Prevention of Allergic Diseases', *The Internet Journal of Asthma, Allergy and Immunology*, 3, 2 (2005).
14 Kevin Danaher, *Irish Customs and Beliefs* (Mercier Press, Cork, 2004).
15 Gaius Julius Solinus, *Collectanea Rerum Memorabilianum (Collection of Remarkable Facts)*, AD 200, translated in Philip Freeman, Ireland and the Classical World (University of Texas Press, Austin, Texas, 2000), p. 87.
16 'Its climate is hideous for ripening seeds, but the island is so luxuriant with grass – not only abundant but sweet – that sheep stuff themselves in a fraction of the day, and unless they are kept from the pasture, they burst from feeding too long.' Pomponius Mela, *De Chorographia*, translated in Frank E. Romer (ed.), *Pomponius Mela's Description of the World* (University of Michigan, Ann Arbor, Mich., 1998), p. 116.
17 Whitley Stokes, *The Destruction of Da Derga's Hostel, Revue Celtique*, 22 (Max Niemeyer, Halle/Saale, 1901), p. 56; full text at www.ucc.ie/celt/published/T301017A.html.
18 From the seventh century.
19 From P. W. Joyce, *A Smaller Social History of Ancient Ireland* (Longmans, Green & Co., London; M. H. Gill, Dublin, 1906).
20 Fergus Kelly, *Early Irish Farming: A Study Based Mainly on the Law-texts of the 7th and 8th Centuries AD* (School of Celtic Studies, Dublin Institute for Advanced Studies, 1997, reprinted 1998), p. 326.
21 Theodore William Moody, Francis X. Martin and Francis John Byrne (eds), *A New History of Ireland, vol. I: Prehistoric and Early Ireland*, ed. Dáibhí Ó Cróinín (Oxford University Press, 2005)
22 Padraic O'Farrell, *Superstitions of the Irish Country People* (Mercier Press, Cork, 2004), p. 37.
23 Kelly, *Early Irish Farming*, p. 328.
24 Regina Sexton, *A Little History of Irish Food* (Kyle Cathie, London, 1998), p. 98.
25 *A Tour in Connaught* (Dublin, 1839) ('by the author of "Sketches in Ireland"').
26 M. Malte-Brun, *Universal Geography* (Edinburgh, 1833), vol. IX.
27 J. P. Sheldon, *Dairy Farming* (Cassell, Petter, Galpin & Co., London, 1880).
28 Christopher H. O'Brien Lynch, 'A Review of the Irish Farmhouse Cheese Industry 1980-1994', unpublished M Appl Sc (Food Sc) thesis, Faculty of Agriculture, University College Dublin, 1994, p. 5.
29 G. W. Walker-Tisdale and Theodore R. Robinson, *The Practice of Soft Cheese Making* (London, 1903).
30 J. A. Phelan and A. O'Keefe, 'Number of Cheese Varieties in Ireland is Increasing', *Farm and Food Research*, 9 (1978), pp. 128-30.

31 K. Danaher, *Irish Customs and Beliefs* (Mercier Press, Cork, 2004).

32 Kelly, *Early Irish Farming*, p. 329.

33 *Ibid.*

34 www.irishmarketrights.org/history/index.htm.

35 www.specialistcheesemakers.co.uk/history.htm.

2 Cheesemakers and Their Cheeses

1 LEADER is the EU Community Initiative for Rural Development.

2 Marché International de Rungis – the principal wholesale food market of Paris, tracing its history back to the tenth century (www.rungismarket.com).

3 From Portuguese; a type of spicy capsicum or chilli pepper.

4 University College, Cork.

5 An Chomhairle Oiliúna (The Irish Training Council), now superseded by FÁS, the current Irish training and employment authority.

6 In association with the Traditional Cheese Company.

7 The Giant's Causeway is a UNESCO World Heritage site consisting of about 40,000 interlocking volcanic basalt columns on the northeast coast of Northern Ireland. Most of the columns are hexagonal, although some have four, five, seven or eight sides. The site is regarded as one of the natural wonders of the modern world.

8 Known as Dillisk in the west of Ireland, dulse (*Palmaria palmata*) is a native Irish purple/red-coloured seaweed. It has been traditionally used as food along the north Antrim causeway coast. Coolkeeran is one of only a handful of Irish artisanal cheeses made with seaweed, the others being Maja Binder's Dilliskus Cheese (Dingle Peninsula Cheese) and Wicklow Gold (Wicklow Farmhouse Cheese).

9 UK Department of Agriculture and Rural Development.

10 A constituent of the NI College of Agriculture, Food & Rural Enterprise (CAFRE).

11 From the World Wide Opportunities on Organic Farms movement, where volunteer work is traded for bed, food and learning (www.wwoof.org).

12 The *Goatman's Litany*, Claddagh Records.

13 As of the end of 2010.

14 See note 11.

15 See Note 8.

16 Fenugreek: *Trigonella foenum-graecum* is both a herb and a spice, often used in curries.

17 The Irish Agency for Personal Services Overseas (APSO) was the Irish government's overseas voluntary aid agency, since integrated into Irish Aid (www.irishaid.gov.ie).

18 Now found in other cheeses such as Livarot and Tilsit but still named after Gubbeen.

19 The Irish Moiled is a rare cattle breed, of medium size, used for both beef and dairy. The word 'moiled' is from the Irish *maol*, meaning broadly 'blunt', and refers to the distinctive domed head of the breed. The colour is generally a melange or red/brown and white, varying from white with red ears to all red.

20 Genetically modified food.

21 Most traditional German quark is made with souring agents without rennet.

22 Probiotics are live micro-organisms ('good bacteria') thought to be beneficial to their host organism.

23 Semi-hard cheese produced on farm or dairy with a total output not exceeding a weekly average of 2 tonnes.

24 Hard cheeses tend to be much larger and have a greater distance from the centre to the rind. Such cheeses ripen from the inside outwards.

25 *Geotrichum* is a genus of yeasts or yeast-like moulds. Some are present in the healthy human body. *G. candidum* is the strain usually used in ripening cheese.

26 The word 'crottin' comes from the French Crottin de Chavignol cheese from the Loire Valley, perhaps, rather unsavourily, from an old French word meaning 'dung'.

4 Irish Farmhouse Cheese Recipes

1 www.metro.ca/conseil-expert/fromager/fromages-menu/fromages-cuisson.en.html.

2 Romanesco broccoli, or Roman cauliflower, is the edible flower of one of the cultivated forms of *Brassica oleracea*, with the branched stems forming beautiful logarithmic fractal spirals.

Useful websites

British Cheese Awards (UK)   www.thecheeseweb.com/contentok.php?id=205

CÁIS (Ireland)   www.irishcheese.ie

Cellar Tours (Spain)   www.cellartours.com

cheese.com (US)   www.cheese.com

Curdnerds (US)   www.curdnerds.com

Food Ireland (US)   www.foodireland.com

Food Safety Authority of Ireland (Ireland)   www.fsai.ie

Fork & Bottle (US)   www.forkandbottle.com/cheese/irish_farmhouse_cheese.htm

Good Food Ireland (Ireland)   www.goodfoodireland.ie

Gourmet Food (US)   www.gourmet-food.com

Great Taste Awards (UK)   www.finefoodworld.co.uk/content/GreatTasteAwards/86.html

Ian Mellis (UK)   www.mellischeese.co.uk

igourmet.com (US)   www.igourmet.com

ilovecheese.co.uk (UK)   www.ilovecheese.co.uk

Irish Dairy Board (Ireland)   www.idb.ie

Irish Raw Milk Cheese Presidium (Ireland)   www.slowfoodireland.com/index.php/food/raw-milk-cheese

Murray's Cheese (US)   www.murrayscheese.com

Nantwich International Cheese Awards (UK)   www.internationalcheeseawards.co.uk/

National Organic Awards (Ireland)   www.bordbia.ie/aboutfood/organic food/pag es/nationalorganicawards2010.aspx

Organic Supermarket (Ireland)   www.organicsupermarket.ie

Sheridans Cheesemongers (Ireland)   www.sheridanscheesemongers.com

The Specialist Cheesemakers Association (UK)   www.specialistcheesemakers.co.uk

Teddington Cheese (UK)   www.teddingtoncheese.co.uk

World Cheese Awards (UK)   www.finefoodworld.co.uk/content/WorldCheeseAwards/100.html

Bibliography

A Tour in Connaught (Dublin, 1839) ('by the author of "Sketches in Ireland"')

Allen, Darina, *Irish Traditional Cooking* (Gill & Macmillan, Dublin, 1995)

Allen, Rachel, *Entertaining at Home* (Collins, London, 2010)

An Bord Bia, *Your Guide to Irish Farmhouse Cheeses* (Bord Bia, Dublin, 2011)
    Campbell, Georgina, *Ireland for Food Lovers* (Georgina Campbell's Guides, Dublin, 2010)

Anon., *The Vision of Mac Conglinne* (*Aislinge Meic Con Glinne*) (translation from the Celt Project http://www.ucc.ie/celt/published/T308002/index.html)

Asala, J., *Celtic Folklore Cooking* (Llewellyn, Woodbury, Maine, 2009)

Ash, Rita, *Self-Sufficiency – Cheese Making* (New Holland Publishers, London, 2009)

Bates, D. and E. Forge, *Great British Cheeses* (Dorling Kindersley, London, 2008)

Campbell, Georgina, *Ireland for Food Lovers* (Georgina Campbell's Guides, Dublin, 2010)

Carr, Sandy, *Pocket Cheese Book* (Mitchell Beazley, London, 1992)

Carroll, R., *Making Cheese, Butter & Yogurt* (Storey Books, North Adams, MA, 2003)

Cotter, Denis, *For the Love of Food: Vegetarian Recipes from the Heart* (Collins, London, 2011)

Dalby, Andrew, *Cheese: A Global History* (Reaktion Books, London, 2009)

Danaher, Kevin, *Irish Customs and Beliefs* (Mercier Press, Cork, 2004)

Dubach, J. and Bill Hogan, *Traditional Cheesemaking* (Intermediate Technology Publications, London, 1989)

Freeman, S., *The Real Cheese Companion* (Sphere, London, 2007)

Graham, Peter, *Classic Cheese Cookery* (Penguin, London, 2003)

Harbutt, Juliet, *The World Encyclopedia of Cheese* (Dorling Kindersley, London, 2009)

Harbutt, Juliet, *World Cheese Book* (Dorling Kindersley, London, 2009)

Herbst, S. and R. Herbst, *The Cheese Lover's Companion* (Morrow, New York, 2007)

Joyce, P. W., *A Smaller Social History of Ancient Ireland* (Longmans, Green & Co., London; M. H. Gill, Dublin, 1906)

Kelly, Fergus, *Early Irish Farming: A Study Based Mainly on the Law-texts of the 7th and 8th Centuries AD* (School of Celtic Studies, Dublin Institute for Advanced Studies, 1997, reprinted 1998)

Linford, Jenny, *Great British Cheeses* (Dorling Kindersley, London, 2008)

Malte-Brun, M., *Universal Geography*, Vol. IX (Edinburgh, 1833)

Masui, K. and T. Yamada, *French Cheeses* (Dorling Kindersley, London, 1996)

McKenna, Clodagh, *The Irish Farmers' Market Cookbook* (HarperCollins, London, 2006)

Mela, Pomponius, *De Chorographia*, translated by Frank E. Romer (ed.), *Pomponius Me la's Description of the World* (University of Michigan, Ann Arbor, MI, 1998)

Moody, Theodore William, Francis X. Martin and Francis John Byrne, *A New History of Ireland, Vol. I: Prehistoric and Early Ireland,* ed. Dáibhí Ó Cróinín (Oxford University Press, 2005)

Murphy, S. and K. Murphy, *Book of Sweet Things* (Mercier Press, Cork, 2008)

O'Brien Lynch, Christopher H., 'A Review of the Irish Farmhouse Cheese Industry 1980–1994', unpublished M Appl Sc (Food Sc) thesis, Faculty of Agriculture, University College Dublin, 1994

O'Farrell, Padraic, *Superstitions of the Irish Country People* (Mercier Press, Cork, 2004)

Pesola, G. R., J. Iqbal and J. Damian, 'The Hygiene Hypothesis and the Primary Prevention of Allergic Diseases', *The Internet Journal of Asthma, Allergy and Immunology*, 3, 2 (2005)

Phelan, J. A. and A. O'Keefe, 'Number of Cheese Varieties in Ireland Is Increasing', *Farm and Food Research*, 9 (1978), pp. 128–30

Rance, Patrick, *The Great British Cheese Book* (Macmillan, London, 1983)

Russell, Jane, *Irish Farmhouse Cheese Recipes* (Somerville Press, Cork, 2004)

Sexton, Regina, *A Little History of Irish Food* (Kyle Cathie, London, 1998)

Sheldon, J. P., *Dairy Farming* (Cassell, Petter, Galpin & Co., London, 1880)

Smith, R., *The Great Cheeses of Britain and Ireland* (Aurum, London, 1995)

Solinus, Gaius Julius, *Collectanea Rerum Memorabilianum (Collection of Remarkable Facts)*, AD 200, translated by Philip Freeman, *Ireland and the Classical World* (University of Texas Press, Austin, Texas, 2000)

Stokes, Whitley, *The Destruction of Da Derga's Hostel, Revue Celtique,* vol. 22 (Max Niemeyer, Halle/Saale, 1901); full text at www.ucc.ie/celt/published/T301017A.html

Thear, Katie, *Cheesemaking and Dairying* (Broad Leys Publishing, Saffron Waldon, Essex, 1978)

Walker-Tisdale, G. W. and Theodore R. Robinson, *The Practice of Soft Cheese Making* (London, 1903)

White Lennon, Biddy and Georgina Campbell, *Irish Food & Cooking* (Hermes House, London, 2008)

Index of Cheeses

(main entries are in **bold**, cheesemakers are in (brackets),
photos are <u>underlined</u>, non-Irish cheeses are in *italics*)

Abbey Blue, 22, 74, **304–<u>305</u>**, 348

Abbey Goats' Cheese, 304

Abbey Smoked Brie, 304–<u>305</u>, 348

Abbot (Knockdrinna), 254

Appenzeller, 57, 157

Ardagh Castle Gjetost, 52–<u>53</u>, 365

Ardagh Castle Goats Cheese, 52–53, 348

Ardagh Castle Ricotta, 52

Ardagh Wine Cheese (Cahills), 306–<u>307</u>, 308, 349

Ardrahan and Smoked Ardrahan, 7, 21, <u>39</u>, 55–56, **<u>57–58</u>**, 59, 254, 321, 348

Ardsallagh Cranberry Roulade, 62, **<u>64–65</u>**, 312

Ardsallagh Hard Goats Cheese, 62, **<u>66–67</u>**, 348

Ardsallagh Soft Goats Cheese, 21, <u>60–63</u>, **65**, 66, 327, 329, 335–336, 348

Ballintubber (Cahills), 306–<u>307</u>, 308, 349

Ballyblue (Fivemiletown), 22, 74, 191–**<u>193</u>**, 353

Ballybradden (Causeway), 116–**<u>119</u>**, 350

Ballybrie (Fivemiletown), 22, 191–193, **<u>194</u>**–195, 198, 353

Ballyhooly Blue (Fermoy), 180, **<u>189</u>**, 352

Ballyknock (Causeway), 116, <u>118</u>–**<u>119</u>**, 350

Ballyoak (Fivemiletown), 191–193, **<u>195</u>**, 353

Ballyporeen (Cahills), 306–<u>307</u>, 308, 349

Bandon Vale, 23, **<u>305</u>**

Bay Lough, 23, 68–**<u>69</u>**, 348

Béal (Pasteurised Handmade Mature Béal Organic Cheddar), 71–72, **<u>73</u>**, 348

Béal (Pasteurised Mild Béal Organic Cheddar), 71–**<u>73</u>**

Béal (Raw Milk Handmade Mature Béal Organic Cheese), 48, **<u>71–73</u>**, 348

Beara Blue (Knockatee), **249**–250, 354

Beaufort, 205

Beenoskee (Dingle), 162–**<u>163</u>**, **165**, 351

Bellingham Blue, 20, 22, 48, 74, **<u>75–77</u>**, 78, 319–320, 348

Bleu d'Auvergne, 110

Bleu de Bresse, 110, 294–295

Boilíe (Fivemiletown), 47, 133, 191–192, **<u>196–197</u>**, 199, 277, 291, **<u>312</u>**, 353

Boyne Valley Blue, 74–75, **<u>78</u>**, 348

brie, 6–7, 19, 22, 97, 99–100, 102–103, 133–134, 139, 141, 143, 191–195, 198, 293–295, 304–305, 314, 348–349, 351, 353

Burren Gold, 85, **<u>86–88</u>**, 349

Caerphilly, 34, 258

Cahills Porter Cheese, 306–<u>307</u>, 308, 349

Cahills Whiskey Cheese, 306–308, 349

Cáis Chléire, 120

Cáis Cruinn (Orchard Cottage), 277, 355

Cáis Cúil Aodha (see entry for Coolea)

Cáis Dubh (Fermoy), 180, **<u>184–185</u>**, 352

Cáis Rua (Fermoy), 180, **<u>186</u>**, 352

Cambozola, 294–295, 304

camembert, 6, 19, 22, 45, 97, 100, 102–103, 136, 142, 253, 255, 314, 364, 366

Cappagh (Knockalara), **<u>242</u>**

Carlow Edam, <u>89–91</u>, 249

Carrigaline, 7, <u>92–94</u>, **95**, 322, 349

Carrowholly, 104–**105**, 349

Cashel Blue, 7, 22, 74, 107–108, **<u>110</u>**, 111–112, 319, 332, 350

Castlefarm Natural, 113–**<u>114</u>**, 350

Castlemary Goat Cheddar and Goat Gouda, **115**, 350

Castlequarter (Causeway), 116, 118–**<u>119</u>**, 350

Charleville, 23

cheddar, 6–7, 11, 18, **22–23**, 34, 37, **45**, 48, 68–69, 71–73, 85, 96, 115–116, 119, 127–128–129, 138, 158, 191–192, 200–202, 215–216, 242, 244, 247–251, 260, 271, 274–275, 282–283, 293, 296, 305–311, 314–316, 348–350, 353–354, 358, 363–364, 368

Cheese Strings™, 363

Cheshire, 33, 363

chèvre, 135, 199, 276, 280, 333

Chevretta (Oisín), 310

Chulchoill (Cooleeney), 133–**<u>135</u>**, 350

Cléire Goats Cottage Cheese, 120, **<u>122</u>**, 350

Clonmore, **<u>124–125</u>**, 350

Coleraine cheddar, 23

Comeragh (Knockalara), 237–238, **<u>242–243</u>**, 354

comté, 22, 178, 182, 184, 205, 368

Coolattin, 23, 127–**<u>129</u>**, 350

Coolea and Matured Coolea, 7, 47, 130, **<u>131–132</u>**, 172, 330, 350

Cooleeney, 7, 22, 47–48, 133–134, **<u>136–137</u>**, 141, 351

Coolkeeran (Causeway), 116, 118–**<u>119</u>**, 350

Cooneen (Fivemiletown), 191–192, **<u>198</u>**, 353

Corkcotta (Fermoy), 180, **<u>189</u>**, 352

Corleggy, <u>16</u>, 48, 144–146, **<u>147–148</u>**, 351

cottage cheese, 18, 31, 120, <u>122</u>, 210, 306, 315, 350, 363

coulommiers, 22, 34, 120

Cratloe Hills Gold, 152–**<u>154</u>**, 351

cream cheese, 7, 14, 81, 85, 162–163, 166, 168–170, 191–192, 197, 208–209, 217, 219, 221–222, 224, 282, 285–286, 300–301, 314, 343, 352–354, 363

Creeny (Corleggy), 144, 146, **<u>149</u>**, 351

Crozier Blue (Cashel), 22, 74, 107–108, **<u>111–112</u>**, 237, 253, 257, 319, 350

Cygnus (Bluebell), 79, **81–82**, 344, 348

Danish Blue, 107

Darú (Cooleeney), 133–134, **<u>138</u>**, 351

Delphinus (Bluebell), 79

Derreenaclaurig, 155–**<u>156</u>**, 351

Desmond, 21–22, 47, 157–158, **159**, 160, 338, 351
Dilliskus (Dingle) 162–163, **165**, 352
Dingle Farmhouse Cheese, **161**, 351
Dingle Gold Cheddar, 311
Dingle Peninsula Cream Cheese, 162–163, **166**, 168–169, 352
Dingle Peninsula Goat Cheese, 163, **167**, 352
Dingle Peninsula Mozzarella, 162–163
Dingle Peninsula Truffle Cheese, 162–163, **170**, 352
Dromana (Knockalara), 238, **242**, 354
Dromona cheddar, 23
Drumlin (Corleggy), 144, 146, **150–151**, 351
Dubliner, 23
Duhallow (Ardrahan), 55–56, **59**, 348
Dúnbarra (Cooleeney), 133–134, **139**, 351
Dunmanus (Durrus), 173–174, 352
Durrus and Durrus Óg, 7, 21, 47–48, 172–173, **174–177**, 325, 352
Durrus Mini, 173–174, 352

EasiSingles™, 363
edam, 45, 89–91, 349, 363
Edam Holland, 45
Emerald (Fermoy), 180, **188**, 352
Emerald Irish Brie (Carrigbyrne), 99, **103**, 349
emmental, 34, 157, 188, 217, 220, 260, 271, 339, 354, 363, 368
Entrammes, 59
Esrom, 59

Feta, 45, 84, 100, 239, 254, 259, 269, 283, 310
fromage frais, 14, 300

Gabriel, 22, 47, 157–158, **160**, 317, 351
gjetost, 52–53, **365**, 368
Glandór (Bandon Vale), 305
Gleann Óir (Cooleeney), 133–134, **140**, 351
Glebe Brethan, 9, 22, 48, 160, 203 **204–206**, 324, 341, 353
Glenilen Low-Fat Cream Cheese, **208–209**, 343, 353
Gloucester, 33, 45, 191, 363
Gorgonzola, 45, 319
Gortnamona (Cooleeney), 133–134, **141**, 351
gouda, 7, 45, 66, 84–85, 88–90, 104–106, 113–115, 125–126,
    130, 132, 155–156, 185, **226**, 227–230, 234, 24, 249–250,
    252, 256, 269, 271, 274, 282–283, 293, 297–299, 309–311,
    314–315, 350, 354, 356, 363
Gouda Holland, 45
Grace (Kelly's Moon Shine), 217, **219**, 353
Grana Padano, 178, 286
graukäse, 180
gruyère, 22, 157, 160, 178, 184, 187, 203, 205–206, 271, 341, 368
Gubbeen & Smoked Gubbeen, xvi, xviii, 7, 21, 47, 210–211,
    212–214, 312, 331, 353

Havarti, 57, 59, 95
Hegarty's Cheddar, 23, 215–**216**, 353
Hibernia (Fermoy), 180, 182, **187**, 352

hobelkäse, 268

Imokilly Regatto, 45

JOD, 23, 308–**309**, 353

Kerry Blue (Knockatee), 22, 74, 249–**251**, 354
Kerrygold cheese, 23, 59
Kilbeg Cream Cheese, 221–222, **224**, 354
Kilbeg Mascarpone, 221–222, **224**, 354
Kilbeg Quark and Fat-free Quark, 221–**223**, 354
Kilcummin (Dingle), 162–163, **171**, 352
Killeen Gouda, 225–226, **227–229**, 354
Killorglin (Wilma's), **299**, 356
Killowen cheddar, 23, 363
Kilmeaden, 23
Kilmichael (Sunview), 284–**285**, 346, 356
Kilshanny, **230–234**, 354
Knockalara, 235, 237–238, **239**, 318, 354
Knockalara Hard, 238, **241**, 354
Knockalara Mature, 238, **240**, 354
Knockanore Oakwood Smoked, 245–**248**, 354
Knockanore Plain, 246–**247**, 354
Knockatee Cheddar, 23, 250–**251**, 354
Knockatee Gouda, 250, **252**, 354
Knockdrinna Brined Goat, 254, **259**, 355
Knockdrinna Gold, 253–254, **256**, 355
Knockdrinna Meadow, 253–255, **257**, 355
Knockdrinna Snow, 253–**255**, 355

Laguiole, 187
Lavistown (Knockdrinna), 253–254, **258**–259, 355
Leicester (Red), 191, 305, 363
Leerdammer, 34
Livarot, 57

Maighean (Cooleeney), 133–134, **142**, 351
Manchego, 149, 153, 267
mascarpone, 221–222, 224, 301, 315, 354, 363
Milleens, 7, 21, 47, 172, 244, 260–261, **262–263**, 325, 355
Milleens Dote, 261–262, 325
Milleens 'O', **260–263**
Millhouse, **264**, 266–**267**, 268, 355
Mitchelstown cheese, 23
Moon Shine Organic Emmental, 217, **220**, 354
Morbier, 287, 289–290
Mossfield, **269–273**, 355
Mount Callan, 23, 48, 274–**275**, 323, 355
mozzarella, 45, 162–163, 286, 315, 356, 363
Munster (cheese), 57, 162, 167, 174–175, 254, 262, 363
Murragh (Bandon Vale), 305

Oakwood (Fivemiletown), 191–192, **200**, 353
Oisín Blue, 22, 74, 309–**310**, 355

Oisín Gouda, 310, 355
Oisín Parmesan, 310, 355
Old Amsterdam, 106
Old MacDonnell's, **276**, 355
Old Russet (Carrowholly), 104, **106**, 349
O'Reillys (Fivemiletown), 191–193, **199**, 353
Orion (Bluebell), 79, **82**, 348
Ossau Iraty, 240

Paddy Jack (Abbey), 304
paneer, 16
Parmigiano-Reggiano/Parmesan, 45, 66, 73, 82, 106, 132, 157, 159–160, 178, 228, 271, 299, 310, 314–315, 317, 333, 338
Pastorello (Millhouse), 265
Pecorino, 45, 66, 84, 149, 159, 315
Pegasus (Bluebell), 79, **83**, 349
Pont-l'Évêque, 190
Port Salut, 59

quark, 7, 18, 32, **207**, 208–209, 221–223, 299, 342, 346, 353–354
Quivvy (Corleggy), 145–146

Reblochon, 83, 174–175, 186, 262, 315, 325
ricotta, 15, 52–53, 180, 189, 286, 315, 363, **367**–368
roquefort, 22, 45, 111
Round Tower, 23, **311**

St André, 315
St Brendan Brie (Carrigbyrne), 99, **103**, 349
St Brigid (Fermoy), 180, **183**, 190, 352
St Brigid Beag (Fermoy), **190**, 352
St Canice (Abbey), 304
St Gall,22, 48, 178, 180–**182**, 326, 339–340, 352
St Kevin (Wicklow), 293–294
St Killian, 7, 22, 96–**97**, 99, **100–101**, 102–103, 321, 349
St Paulin, 59
St Tola Crottin, 278, **281**, 355
St Tola Divine, 278–279, **282**, 355
St Tola Greek, 278, **283**, 356
St Tola Hard, 278–279, **282–283**, 355
St Tola Log, 278, **280**, 355
St Tola Original, 278–**280**, 355
Shamrock (Castlefarm), 113–**114**, 328, 350
Shandrum (Clonmore), 124–**126**, 350
Shropshire Blue, 250–251
Stilton, 33, 45, 75, 78, 85, 96, 189, 249, 319

Taleggio, 315
Tara Bán, 201–**202**, 353
Tilsiter, 183
Tipperary Brie (Cooleeney), 133–134, **143**, 351
Toma, 174–175
Tomme, 57, 165, 171, 174–175, 240–241, 256–258

Toonsbridge Buffalo Mozzarella, **286**, 356
Toto and Toto Blue (Boyne Pastures), **84**, 349
Triskel Dew Drop, **288**–289, 356
Triskel Gwenned, 288–**290**, 356
Triskel Pyramid, 288–**289**, 356
Tullynascreena, **291**, 356

Una (Kelly's Moon Shine), 217, **219**, 353

Vacherin, 98
Valençay, 289
Vintage (Bandon Vale), **305**

Wensleydale, 53, 71, 138, 140
West Country Farmhouse Cheddar, 45
Wexford Cheddar, 23, 96–97
Wicklow Baun, 22, 293–**295**, 356
Wicklow Blue, 22, 74, 292–293, **294–295**, 296, 337, 345, 356
Wicklow Goat, 293, **297–298**, 356
Wicklow Gold, 23, 293–294, **296**, 356
Wilma's Killorglin, 299, 356

Yeats Country Organic Soft Cheese, 14, 300–**301**, 356